Gender and Politics Series

Series editors: Johanna Kantola, Senior Lec
Helsinki, Finland and **Sarah Childs**, Profess
of Bristol, UK

This timely new series publishes leading monographs and edited collections from scholars working in the disciplinary areas of politics, international relations, and public policy with specific reference to questions of gender. The series showcases cutting-edge research in Gender and Politics, publishing topical and innovative approaches to gender politics. It will include exciting work from new authors and well-known academics and will also publish high-impact writings by practitioners working in issues relating to gender and politics.

The series covers politics, international relations, and public policy, including gendered engagement with mainstream political science issues, such as political systems and policymaking, representation and participation, citizenship and identity, equality, and women's movements; gender and international relations, including feminist approaches to international institutions, political economy, and global politics; and interdisciplinary and emergent areas of study, such as masculinities studies, gender and multiculturalism, and intersectionality.

Titles include:

Gabriele Abels and Joyce Marie Mushaben (*editors*)
GENDERING THE EUROPEAN UNION
New Approaches to Old Democratic Deficits

Phillip Ayoub and David Paternotte
LGBT ACTIVISM AND THE MAKING OF EUROPE
A Rainbow Europe?

Elin Bjarnegård
GENDER, INFORMAL INSTITUTIONS AND POLITICAL RECRUITMENT
Explaining Male Dominance in Parliamentary Representation

Elgin Brunner
FOREIGN SECURITY POLICY, GENDER, AND US MILITARY IDENTITY

Andrea Chandler
DEMOCRACY, GENDER, AND SOCIAL POLICY IN RUSSIA
A Wayward Society

Sarah Childs and Paul Webb
SEX, GENDER AND THE CONSERVATIVE PARTY
From Iron Lady to Kitten Heels

Jonathan Dean
RETHINKING CONTEMPORARY FEMINIST POLITICS

Elizabeth Evans
THE POLITICS OF THIRD WAVE FEMINISMS
Neoliberalism, Intersectionality, and the State in Britain and the US

Meryl Kenny
GENDER AND POLITICAL RECRUITMENT
Theorising Institutional Change

Andrea Krizsan, Hege Skjeie, and Judith Squires (*editors*)
INSTITUTIONALIZING INTERSECTIONALITY
The Changing Nature of European Equality Regimes

Mona Lena Krook and Fiona Mackay (*editors*)
GENDER, POLITICS AND INSTITUTIONS
Towards a Feminist Institutionalism

Emanuela Lombardo and Maxime Forest (*editors*)
THE EUROPEANIZATION OF GENDER EQUALITY POLICIES
A Discursive-Sociological Approach

Birte Siim and Monika Mokre (*editors*)
NEGOTIATING GENDER AND DIVERSITY IN AN EMERGENT EUROPEAN PUBLIC SPHERE

Anna van der Vleuten, Anouka van Eerdewijk, and Conny Roggeband (*editors*)
GENDER EQUALITY NORMS IN REGIONAL GOVERNANCE
Transnational Dynamics in Europe, South America and Southern Africa

Polly Wilding
NEGOTIATING BOUNDARIES
Gender, Violence and Transformation in Brazil

Gender and Politics Series
Series Standing Order ISBNs 978–0–230–23917–3 (hardback) and 978–0–230–23918–0 (paperback)
(*outside North America only*)

You can receive future titles in this series as they are published by placing a standing order. Please contact your bookseller or, in case of difficulty, write to us at the address below with your name and address, the title of the series and the ISBN quoted above.

Customer Services Department, Macmillan Distribution Ltd, Houndmills, Basingstoke, Hampshire RG21 6XS, England

---

The Politics of Third Wave Feminisms

Neoliberalism, Intersectionality, and the State in Britain and the US

Elizabeth Evans
Lecturer in Politics, University of Bristol, UK

palgrave
macmillan

Softcover reprint of the hardcover 1st edition 2015 978-1-137-29526-2

First published 2015 by
PALGRAVE MACMILLAN

Palgrave Macmillan in the UK is an imprint of Macmillan Publishers Limited, registered in England, company number 785998, of Houndmills, Basingstoke, Hampshire RG21 6XS.

Palgrave Macmillan in the US is a division of St Martin's Press LLC, 175 Fifth Avenue, New York, NY 10010.

Palgrave Macmillan is the global academic imprint of the above companies and has companies and representatives throughout the world.

Palgrave® and Macmillan® are registered trademarks in the United States, the United Kingdom, Europe and other countries.

ISBN 978-1-349-45181-4 ISBN 978-1-137-29527-9 (eBook)
DOI 10.1057/9781137295279

This book is printed on paper suitable for recycling and made from fully managed and sustained forest sources. Logging, pulping and manufacturing processes are expected to conform to the environmental regulations of the country of origin.

A catalogue record for this book is available from the British Library.

A catalog record for this book is available from the Library of Congress.

Contents

List of Tables

Acknowledgements

As with any endeavour, there are those without whom this book would not have been possible. I'd like to thank the British Academy (grant number SG121297) for funding that enabled me to travel to the US to undertake the fieldwork for this book. And I would particularly like to thank all of the feminist activists who gave up their time to talk to me. I was humbled by the inspiring work that they are engaged with and am extremely grateful for their candour and enthusiasm. I must also thank the numerous activists in New York and Portland who showed me round their cities, introduced me to their friends and took me to feminist events. Undertaking fieldwork is usually fun but special thanks go to those who made my summers in New York and Portland particularly special.

I started the research for this book whilst a newly appointed Lecturer in Politics at Kingston University, London, and I would like to thank my former colleagues and friends for their support and encouragement during the early stages of this project. I am also hugely grateful to my friends and colleagues at the University of Bristol whose enthusiasm and intellectual engagement has helped drive this research forward. Bristol is a fantastic university at which to undertake gender scholarship and I am grateful to be part of such a strong and vibrant feminist community which encompasses both students and staff.

I have presented various aspects of this work at workshops and conferences and at invited lectures. I would like to thank all of those who were part of the panel discussions that I participated in and those who have commented on my presentations, in particular at the European Conference on Politics and Gender (ECPG), European Consortium for Political Research (ECPR), Political Studies Association (PSA), Council for European Studies (CES), and International Political Studies Association (IPSA) conferences over the past four years. Several individuals have given of their time to read over various versions of this book, whether as an entire draft or as individual chapters or papers. In particular, I would like to thank Faith Armitage, Prue Chamberlain, Sarah Childs, and Francesca Gains. I would also like to thank the countless feminist activists I've met at various events and marches over the past few years who have chatted with me about this research.

Thanks must also go to my family and friends for listening to me go on about this research but also for distracting me from it; and to all those at Palgrave who have provided invaluable support. Finally, I'd like to express my thanks to Simon Choat: for forcing me to get on with this project; for his intellectual engagement and input; for bringing me pastries; and for believing that I could do it. For all these reasons, this book is dedicated to him with much love.

Introduction

The past 20 years has witnessed a renewal of interest in feminist activism on both sides of the Atlantic. In part this has been a response to neoliberal and neoconservative attacks, both implicit and explicit, on the gains made by feminists during the 1960s and 1970s (Walby, 2011; Reger, 2012). Such a backlash against women has occurred at both the legislative and societal level in Britain and the US, exacerbating, inter alia: sustained violence against women; an increasingly blatant sexual objectification of women and girls; persistent attacks on women's bodily autonomy; and continued economic inequality.[1] An increasing awareness of these and other multitudinous injustices helped spark and sustain a reinvigorated feminist activism in the US and Britain. And yet, despite the seeming commonalities between the two movements, it is not clear whether the blanket term 'Anglo-American feminism' has much empiric value. Drawing upon original qualitative data, this research identifies numerous differences between the two movements at the level of discourse and praxis, which are mediated both by the neoliberal political context and by the intellectual turn towards intersectionality. This book brings a comparative dimension to the ongoing analysis of feminism and feminist activism by mapping, analysing, and theorising third wave feminisms in the US and Britain.

The book explores third wave feminisms by situating them within a specific political context, neoliberalism, and in relation to feminist theories of intersectionality. Neoliberalism is here understood as an oppressive set of political, economic, and social policy regimes that promote a sense of atomisation and over-reliance on market forces. Governments, markets, and institutions of the state all, to varying degrees, create and recreate conditions which ultimately exacerbate and entrench patterns of inequality. Such inequality hits women particularly hard, although this is of course also mediated by class, race, sexuality, age, and disability. A framework for analysing the interactive effects of inequalities based upon group characteristics is advanced by the theory of intersectionality, which emerged from the writings of black feminists to explore the ways in which matrices of oppression effect power dynamics. Such an inhospitable political climate has necessarily had an impact on the challenges facing the third wave of feminism; moreover, the intellectual 'turn' towards intersectionality presents both radical opportunities and practical challenges for feminism and the feminist movement.

This introductory chapter provides the intellectual, contextual, and methodological framework for the book. The chapter begins by reflecting upon the resurgence of feminist activism in the US and Britain, before moving on to situate the third wave in relation to other waves. The chapter sets out the methodology employed in this book and considers the comparative dimension of the research by outlining the divergent political context within Britain and the US. The book is motivated by a feminism that both acknowledges and resists the existence of patriarchal structures that underpin political, economic, and societal gendered inequalities. Such inequalities are expressed through acts of violence against women; acts which are constituted physically, culturally, and materially.

Feminist resurgence

Since its renaissance, feminist activism has remained relatively high profile in both Britain and the US with a myriad of groups operating at local, state, regional, and national levels. Additional use of online technologies has created a space for virtual forums, introducing feminist debates and campaigns to a wider audience. Whilst in the US this renewal of feminist activism emerged in the 1990s, a similar return to a more visible and high-profile form of feminist resistance did not appear in Britain until around the early 2000s (Siegal, 2007; Dean, 2010). The renewed US and British feminist movements had to address many of the same challenges: expansion and awareness raising; combating an overwhelmingly anti-feminist media; promoting diversity and inclusivity within feminism; and dealing with ideological differences amongst and between feminists. For feminists active in the Women's Liberation Movement, these challenges were mostly familiar. However, a neoliberal context that advocates and rewards individualism has not always made it easy to promote collective identity and resistance. And at the same time, adequate recognition of the multiple inequalities facing women, who are not white, middle-class, heterosexual, and able-bodied, is yet to be fully realised. These challenges, and the ways and extent to which they are being, and can be, addressed, are of course also mediated by the different historical, political, and cultural specificities that exist within the US and Britain. Consequently, whilst the term 'Anglo-American feminism' can sometimes be helpfully deployed to refer to commonalities between US and British feminism, this book argues that there exist significant differences between feminist praxis and discourse across the two states.

The 1990s' resurgence of feminist activism in the US is referred to as the third wave (Henry, 2004) and although scholars have sought to explore the third wave in a British context, it has not had the same popular purchase as in the US (Gillis et al., 2004; Dean, 2009). Given that the 'third wave' label has not travelled particularly well from the US to Britain, added to the fact that some are keen to push for a fourth wave of British feminism (Cochrane, 2013), one might reasonably question the motivation for writing a book comparing third wave feminism in the US and Britain. The answer is fourfold. First, I was interested in exploring the concept of the 'long' wave narrative, a wave that ebbs and flows over a decade or two and contains within it various competing ideological strands (just as with the first and second waves); such a conceptualisation goes some way to allaying the fears of those who critique the wave narrative for its failure to address those who fall between waves (Reger, 2012: 11). Second, I wanted to build upon previous work to consider the extent to which the ideas and campaigns of the early US third wave feminists resonate with contemporary US and British activists (Dean, 2009). Third, I have paid attention to the interaction between the wave narrative and various ideological strands within third wave feminism, which has not been a prominent feature of much writing on third wave feminism. And lastly, if in Britain we are at the start of a fourth wave then it makes sense to have a clearer picture of what the third wave constitutes/d and the ways in which it has, and continues to differ from its better known US version.

The third wave has been conceptualised by scholars in multiple ways, including as a rejoinder to the second wave failure to address diversity (Archer Mann and Huffman, 2005); as a rejection of Academy-led theorising (Orr, 1997); as an empty signifier, undermined by an emphasis on generational framing (Dean, 2009); and as a movement lacking in an overarching philosophy (Renegar and Sowards, 2003). Indeed, anyone surveying the literature on third wave feminism in the US and

Britain will be struck by the divergent ways in which the term has been used, both as an ideological framework and in terms of its precise chronology. The highly contested nature of the third wave reflects its multiplicity of thought, action, and praxis. This book argues that the third wave incorporates a wide range of geographical, ideological, and historical specificities and that there are significant differences between US and British third wave feminisms. In short, there are a number of third waves. Indeed, as many third wave texts have argued, the messiness of the third wave is central to understanding its contribution to feminist thought and action (Dicker and Piepmeier, 2003). Its contradictions, multiple narratives, and moreover, the continued (and emerging) presence of both second and fourth wave feminism counter a priori assumptions regarding what we might consider to be the progressive notion of feminist history (Butler, 2004: 4).

Situating the third wave

Before we can get a better insight into third wave feminisms, it is important to provide a brief overview of what has gone before; namely, first and second wave feminisms and also what has been claimed to come after, namely, fourth wave and post-feminisms. Of course applying the wave narrative to feminism is neither a neutral nor an uncontested approach. Indeed, there are many who ultimately consider it to be an unhelpful and divisive metaphor: setting up false divisions where there are none and suggesting periods of inactivity that mask continuity (Gillis and Munford, 2004). Moreover, the wave narrative appears to be unique to the feminist movement: we don't for instance talk about 'socialist waves' (even though we may divide the intellectual history into classical Marxism, Euro-communism, post-Marxism, and so on); the one exception to this appears to be the environmental movement which has at times been structured by a wave narrative, although this has not had the same purchase as the feminist wave label (see Thiele, 1999). Certainly, the use of the wave metaphor can be seen as a way for some feminists to impose a teleology on feminism, one that subsumes the multiplicity of diverse (and sometimes competing) feminist goals and aims. These concerns, along with specific and legitimate criticisms regarding the focus on white western women (Springer, 2002; Henry, 2004), are important.[2]

Despite these critiques, a long wave narrative that accounts for both non-academic written accounts of feminism and empirical research undertaken with activists can offer a meaningful way in which to think through the development of specific moments and campaigns within feminism; an idea advanced by others who have sought to use the term to denote continuation of a movement (Whelehan, 1995: 3). Moreover, whilst some feminists reject the idea of belonging to a wave, and its use as a framing metaphor, all are (ultimately) compelled to engage with it, even if to repudiate its legitimacy (Evans and Chamberlain, 2014). Therefore, framing analysis of contemporary feminism within the wave narrative provides an opportunity for us to confront our understanding of feminist subjectivities and to better understand why and how some feminists choose to engage with it. The wave narrative allows us to think through how well feminist concepts and modes of activism 'travel' internationally (Goertz and Mazur, 2008). It also allows us to consider points of continuity and disruption from that which has gone before, whilst acting as an umbrella term under which different approaches and ideologies can be explored (Evans and Chamberlain, 2014). Therefore, in order to explore how and why a term such as the third wave differs between the US and Britain, we need to adopt a more reflexive and nuanced way of thinking about how the metaphor might be better applied. This will subsequently allow us to provide a more fulsome and politically relevant account of feminist praxis.

The first wave of feminism tends to refer to those movements that advocated for women's suffrage and for women's legal and constitutional rights across (primarily) North America and Europe in the nineteenth and twentieth centuries. Issues such as access to higher education and married women's property rights were central to this 'liberal' wave of feminism that sought to remove legal obstacles to women's equal opportunity (Rendell, 1985). The second wave is usually a reference to the activities associated with the Women's Liberation Movement that occurred between the 1960s and 1980s. Motivated by a desire to reawaken women and society to persistent sex inequalities, second wave feminists sought to highlight the importance of the personal and private sphere as a site of inequality, in addition to campaigning for legislative change around issues such as abortion rights and equal pay. Neither the first nor second waves were monolithic, with divergent tactics, multiple foci, and ideological differences guaranteeing a diverse movement. Thus, it is unsurprising that this third wave has not coalesced into an easily definable movement.

Of course, there are those who are already discussing a fourth wave of feminism, notably in media analysis rather than in academic scholarship (although see Munro, 2013): some have sought to portray fourth wave feminism as a post-9/11 response to global inequalities

(Baumgardner, 2012); others have conceived of it as an inevitable consequence of the perceived failures of third wave feminism (Schacht and Ewing, 2004); whilst in a British context, the term has been used to refer to post-2010 activity coinciding with the election of a Conservative-led government (Cochrane, 2013). It is in many respects unsurprising that there should be debates concerning a new wave of feminism at this very moment; after all, it has been nearly 20 years since the start of the US third wave but in a British context, the third wave only really emerged in the early 2000s and was not widely used as a term. Whilst the focus of this book is on exploring the various manifestations of third wave feminisms, it does not do so with the intention of denying that a fourth wave exists. The book uses a third wave framework as a means by which to provide a longitudinal comparative analysis of feminist discourse and praxis in the US and Britain. It considers how and in what ways the ideas of those early third wave feminists have shaped contemporary feminist discourse and activism.

Post-feminism, unlike the fourth wave, has already become an established part of the feminist scholarship, with several in-depth studies exploring the subject (see Coppock et al., 1995; Tasker and Negra, 2007). The term 'post-feminism' is used in two distinct and interrelated ways: firstly, to mark a period when the feminist movement is in abeyance and secondly, to signify a rejection of feminism (Henry, 2004). However, given the prefix 'post' rather than 'anti', it also suggests a period in which feminism is no longer needed, potentially because its aims have been achieved. Thus, the term 'post-feminism' at once implies success but also a repudiation of feminist goals. Self-identified US third wavers Leslie Heywood and Jennifer Drake explicitly rejected the conflation of third wave with post-feminism (1997: 1), whilst also naming several high-profile feminists whom they consider to be post-feminist rather than third wave (such as Naomi Wolf, Katie Roiphe, and Rene Denfeld). This clearly raises some confusion for those hoping to gain a better appreciation of who and what constitutes the third wave; it is for instance clear that Naomi Wolf would not herself identify as a post-feminist (1990). Clearly there is some overlap between post-feminism, as a cultural form that seeks to 'normalize' and 'empower' women and feminists as consumers (Tasker and Negra, 2007: 2), and some strands of third wave feminism that seek to empower women through consumer choices and professionalisation (Wolf, 1994; Armstrong and Wood Rudúlph, 2013). This overlap is important to note; however, it is also true that many other third wavers, and those whom we might consider third wave, would not recognise the tenets of post-feminism as reflecting their own feminism.

Methodology

This book provides a comparative analysis of British and US third wave feminist activism. The US and Britain were selected for a number of reasons: 1) in order to explore the utility of the Anglo-American label that is sometimes used to describe British and US feminism; 2) to question why the term 'third wave' was commonly known and understood in the US but not Britain; 3) to reflect upon the impact of different political systems in shaping feminist engagement with the state; 4) to evaluate how a neoliberal agenda effects feminist activism; and 5) to explore the responses of the movement to the challenges and opportunities of intersectionality. In order to provide a comparative analysis of the politics of third wave feminisms, original data was generated with feminist activists in the US and Britain. This section sets out the methods employed in this study before going on to outline the key points of differentiation between the US and British political and cultural systems. Although comparisons between the US and Britain are frequently made, it is worth remembering the different political structures within which feminists operate. Systems and structures effectively influence and shape modes of activism and the extent to which campaigners can and do seek to engage with the state.

Methods

This book maps, theorises, and analyses third wave feminisms in the US and Britain. As such, the research draws upon a range of different sources, including original interview data generated with feminists in the US and Britain; analysis of debates amongst and between feminists in the mainstream media, feminist magazines, and online spaces; and close reading of self-identified third wave texts and popular (non-academic) books on feminism. By making use of various data sources, the book also seeks to explore the important differences between the views advanced by popular feminist texts and the views of grassroots activists. During the period 2011–2014, I attended a number of feminist events and activist conferences in both the US and Britain where I observed panel discussions, roundtables, and debates; these observations do not constitute part of the formal data analysis that this book presents but it inevitably shaped my own understanding and approach towards contemporary debates within feminism.

Semi-structured interviews with feminist activists were undertaken in six cities in the US and Britain. Clearly, adopting a qualitative research methodology in order to undertake comparative research in a country as large as the US means that it is difficult to provide a representative sample. As the research is interested in the extent to which contemporary feminists in the US and Britain have been influenced by the agenda of the original third wave texts and the points of commonality and difference between activists in the US and Britain, I selected four cities which were well known 'hubs' of feminist activism, where there are a wide variety of feminist activists and campaign groups. For this reason, the US cities of New York and Portland, Oregon, were selected, whilst in Britain, London and Bristol (in the South West) were chosen. Interviews with activists in these four cities were supplemented by further sets of interviews with activists in Washington D.C. and Glasgow, Scotland. The interviews in D.C. and in Glasgow enabled me to interview activists who were involved with groups who had particular relationships with either the federal government in the US or the devolved government in Scotland.

In total, some 73 interviews were carried out between June 2012 and March 2014, with additional email 'interviews' with a few participants where a face-to-face meeting could not be arranged. The interviews are not intended to represent or stand for the 'feminist viewpoint' but are instead used as rich illustrative accounts of the ways in which activists approach political activism and campaigning. Participants were recruited via initial email contact with local feminist groups and organisations. The interviewees' activism manifested itself in a number of ways: the majority regularly participated in general feminist groups (local) and were members or supporters of large women's and feminist organisations (national) which covered a plethora of issues including longstanding feminist concerns regarding violence against women as well as new and emerging debates such as transfeminism and fat feminism; others spent most of their time focussing on specific themes such as reproductive justice or sexual objectification; whilst some attended events but were more active in online feminist forums and campaigning.

Due care was taken to ensure that the interviewees were not just white, middle-class, heterosexual, and able-bodied women and where an interview sample from a particular city looked too homogenous, a snowballing technique (whereby participants recommended other potential interviewees) was adopted in order to ensure that a range of activists were interviewed. The overwhelming majority of the interviews were undertaken with women – unsurprising, given that they are more likely to be active in feminist politics – with five interviews conducted with men. Interviews were undertaken with women of color (who were primarily based in New York and London), lesbian and bisexual women, trans women, women with disabilities, and a range of ages, including those specifically involved with older women's feminist groups. Interviewees were guaranteed anonymity, which means that quotations are referenced simply by the city that the activist was based in. For some trans women in particular, this was especially important, as certain comments and claims could have led to identification. See Appendix A for a full timeline of the interviews and Appendix B for a copy of the interview schedule. The interviews covered a wide range of topics; in some instances, this meant that there was occasional follow-up correspondence with interviewees in order to clarify points or to ask for additional information.

Popular texts written by US and British feminists were read and analysed, although there were undoubtedly more of these in the US than in Britain. I visited libraries, women's centres, and bookstores that had archives of feminist zines in both the US and Britain, although again there were more of these in the former than in the latter. In the US, there exist three nationwide feminist magazines, *Ms*, *Bitch*, and *Bust*; these magazines were collected during this period to keep track of the various issues that were being discussed. In Britain, there is no feminist magazine in print, as such, the *Feminist Times* website and *The Guardian* daily newspaper, which regularly hosts articles on feminism, were monitored.[3] A wide range of feminist blogs exist on both sides of the Atlantic, but no attempt was made to systematically monitor these sites, not least because blogs are susceptible to periods of inactivity or to disappearing altogether.

Finally, extensive use was made of the extant scholarship on third wave feminism and contemporary feminism in order to build upon previous understandings of some of the specific political narratives and debates within the third wave. Much of the work that has emerged on the third wave has undoubtedly been heavily influenced by postmodern and post-structuralist thinking; this is apt as it also reflects the deconstructivist element frequently identified within third wave feminism itself (Budgeon, 2011). Whilst this book certainly engages with the theories and ideas of such an approach, not least the impact of queer theory on feminist activism, it is largely driven by a commitment to a material examination of the political realities that regimes of gender inequality create and recreate for women. The book considers the discursive power of shifting paradigms within feminist activism with a critical eye on the potential challenges that they pose for those seeking to advance women's rights.

In exploring the various ways in which third wave feminisms negotiate the neoliberal political context and the conceptual challenges of intersectionality, the book seeks to answer a number of interrelated research questions:

- How can we theorise a third wave feminist framework?
- Is the term 'Anglo-American feminism' useful?
- What are the particular effects of neoliberalism on US and British feminism?
- How and when do activists adopt an intersectional feminism lens?
- What are the attitudes of feminists towards state representation of feminist issues?

These questions are intended to consider a wide range of issues within the movement, without being so broad as to lose the focus on both the political and conceptual context. Whilst intersectionality and neoliberalism are leitmotifs running throughout the book, they should not be read as explanans of third wave feminist praxis; rather they should be viewed as frames. As such, the material under study within the book engages with the frames to varying degrees. By addressing a series of case study analyses, such as views on women-only organising, women's political representation and abortion rights activism, the book draws together the multiple ways in which feminists view opportunities for change outside of, within, and in opposition to the state.

Comparing Britain and the US

The term 'Anglo-American feminism' has been used as a way of framing feminist histories and political narratives (Whelehan, 1995), and scholars have sometimes sought to contextualise the direction of British feminist campaigning by making links with the US. In many respects this is unsurprising; not only does the US play a dominant role in transnational debates but there are also points of commonality that exist between the two countries with regards language and culture. However, it is rare to find studies that provide a full and proper comparative analysis of US and British feminist activism (one notable exception is of course Shelia Rowbotham's rich and detailed history of the women's movement). Britain became increasingly aware of US news and debate in the 1990s (Rowbotham, 1997: 548); as such, the influence of the US women's movement on Britain is particularly salient when we consider the emergence of the third wave during this period. Such a growing awareness of developments within the US is important when exploring how well the ideas and campaigns often associated with the third wave have travelled across time and space.

It is perhaps inevitable that broader comparative analysis of US and British politics, culture, and public opinion are made, not just because of a shared language but also because, particularly recently, of closely tied geopolitical interests. However, it is important to remember, particularly when considering the focus and modes of mobilising amongst citizenry groups, that the different political structures makes it hard to simply read across the Atlantic when it comes to political struggles and windows of opportunity. There exist macro-, meso- and micro-level differences: the US operates under a federal system of government, whilst Britain, notwithstanding devolution, has a Parliamentary and centralised system of governance. There are also historic differences: the US has a specific racial legacy manifestly different to Britain's own colonial legacy, whilst class has been the traditional frame for analysing political cleavages in Britain. Ideologically, the key principles of liberty and individual choice underpin the US attitudes to welfare and public spending, whilst in Britain (despite increasing privatisation), defence of welfare spending is based upon a greater sense of social solidarity. The influence of the religious right in the US has a particular impact on the framing of so-called morality politics, whilst the presence of a more formalised and organised left wing in British politics allows for greater space for 'progressive' political debate. Beyond obvious differences such as geography and demography (which are not unimportant factors when we compare modes of feminist activism and engagement in the US and Britain), political systems, formal representative institutions, the various political parties, non-governmental organisations, and related actors who play a role in shaping the governance of a country are important to consider in relation to feminist engagement with the state.

Political systems rely upon norms and values, either expressed through a written constitution, as is the case in the US, or through a series of uncodified rules, as in Britain, (although of course the US also relies on uncodified norms). There has been a shift in the drafting and analysis of constitutions, from viewing them as a means by which to protect citizens and limit the power of the state to a document which can proactively integrate diverse social groups (Irving, 2008: 24); accordingly, written constitutions offer potential benefits for feminists. However, early campaigners for women's rights noted the constitution's 'silence' on the status of women, leading them to look to political and social opportunities for change (Kessler and Reid, 2013: 29). Whilst the US constitution has been used to advance women's rights (notably through its use in the passage of *Roe v. Wade*), the sex-neutral language and the failure to pass the Equal Rights Amendment demonstrates a determined attachment to the individual citizen as default male (Law, 1984).[4] Moreover, the equal protection clause which forms part of the Fourteenth Amendment has been criticised by feminist scholars who argue that it provides insufficient protection for women (MacKinnon, 1991: 1307).[5] Within Britain where there is no single codified constitution, laws governing gender equality are laid down in various statutes, pieces of legislation and in specific provisions; for instance within the 2010 Equality Act.

Both the US and Britain have traditionally been categorised as two-party systems; although this is still clearly true for the US, Britain has in recent years moved away from this model towards an overlapping multiparty system operating differently at each electoral level. A multiparty system is important for feminist activists as it has the potential to provide more opportunities for activists seeking to influence party policy and legislative behaviour. In such a system there are more windows of opportunity and such a set of conditions has the potential to increase competition amongst parties for the support of leading women's civil society organisations. Creating such a competition or marketplace for gendered representation (Kantola and Squires, 2012) could, in theory, encourage political parties to be innovators with regards women's policies. In the US where there is an extremely stable two-party system, there are fewer opportunities for feminists to influence the parties; where this is done tends to be at the individual politician rather than at the party level. In the US, the close associations between the large national women's organisations and the Democrats risk the party taking their support for granted; not least when one considers the continued evidence of the gender-voting gap, whereby women have been consistently more likely than men to vote Democrat. Whilst the contemporary GOP's 'war on women' has also meant that those Republicans who do articulate a more progressive agenda when it comes to women's issues are neither rewarded by the party nor by the voters (Swers, 2013).

As liberal democracies, both the US and Britain seek, at least in principle, to open up the democratic process in order to encourage a plurality of voices to contribute to the policy making process. Whilst in the abstract this is of course true, the role of money, lobbyists, and consultants, particularly within the US, means that those with the largest resources typically enjoy a greater degree of access and influence (Langbein and Lotwis, 1990). For feminist organisations, this necessarily creates a hierarchy; those with sufficient resources and access are the ones that benefit from greater consultation. In Britain, we also see a similar pattern whereby large leading women's civil society organisations tend to be at the forefront of any government consultation processes. This has implications for the wider movement, as the larger national organisations are apt to reflect a certain strain of liberal feminism, one that does not always accurately reflect wider concerns within the movement.

Whilst both the US and Britain are nominally secular states, the clear distinction between religious and public life is not straightforward. The impact of the Christian right has been a longstanding feature of US politics, with the emergence of conservative Protestants in the early 1970s (Bruce, 1988: 25). The effects and legacy of the early mobilisation and subsequent impact of the Moral Majority in the 1970s and 1980s have had a profound impact on US elections and on policy debate, particularly those relating to reproductive rights. A constituent element of the Moral Majority's evangelical platform relied upon the 'devaluation of women' (Pohli, 1983: 529) and the current neoconservative religious strain within the US continues to view women as secondary citizens in need of state, religious, and cultural control (Herzog, 2008).

Whilst there is no such obvious religious influence in political life in Britain, the upper house in the UK Parliament, the House of Lords, does contain within it reserved seats for bishops and archbishops in the Church of England (the established church); in total, there are 16 reserved seats. Whilst other faiths do have representation in the House of Lords, for instance the Chief Rabbi and Islamic leaders, these are not reserved seats. The presence of these religious figures within the second chamber is important, not least because legislation has to be approved by both houses before it passes into law, but also because of the influence their presence can have on other members of the House when matters of conscience are being debated. There are opportunities for religion to play different roles in the political life in the US and Britain, and this has specific ramifications for feminists particularly when issues such as abortion have the potential to act as 'deal breakers' for certain groups of voters. Whilst it plays out to a different extent across the two states, the impact of certain religious groups can, at times, be considered part of a wider anti-feminist lobby.

With the resurgence of feminist activism, it is perhaps inevitable that we can also identify a rise in those seeking actively to oppose the goals of the feminist movement. The anti-feminist lobby is a difficult term to define, not least because its membership is fluid. Moreover, just as the term 'feminism' is open to ideological interpretation, so too is anti-feminism. Anti-feminist groups are traditionally defined as those men's rights activists (MRAs) that explicitly articulate an opposition to feminism. This form of opposition was evident in both the first and second waves of feminism and in this third wave has been particularly active in online spaces. The MRAs' opposition to feminism manifests itself at the national, local, and individual level; in the US, the National Coalition for Men (NCM), a non-profit educational organisation, raises awareness about the ways sex discrimination affects men and boys; whilst in Britain, Fathers 4 Justice has long campaigned to end the 'anti-male' discrimination and reverse sexism that exists within the family court services.[6] There are various state chapters of the NCM whilst in Britain local groups of MRAs have sought to organise against feminist campaigns. MRAs are also very active online with individual blogs and websites set up to resist feminist agendas.

Beyond the obvious sites of anti-feminist activity, we can also identify anti-feminist sentiments and sympathies expressed by individual politicians and media commentators. Such individuals, and not always men, often thrive on the controversy that surrounds claims that they make about women and feminists. Evidence of sexist comments and behaviour is not hard to find in either country across all levels of society: for instance US Radio DJ Rush Limbaugh's public denunciation of Sandra Fluke as a slut for campaigning for access to contraceptives or British Labour MP Austin Mitchell claiming that women MPs are not interested in serious issues. Of course, anti-feminist sentiments are not always explicitly presented as obvious attacks on women. One could, for instance, identify economic policy decisions taken by governments as being anti-feminist given their detrimental impact on women and on feminist campaigns. Furthermore, the term 'anti-feminist' is not just used about those external to the movement; in the debates surrounding the issue of trans inclusion (discussed in chapters 4 and 5), the term is used by feminists against one another as groups and individuals seek to contest the aims and goals of the movement. That anti-feminism is a charge levelled at feminists by other feminists is indicative of the extent to which the term has been stretched to apply beyond the traditional MRAs.

Taken together, these differences in political and cultural contexts set the scene for the analysis of third wave feminisms. Moreover, awareness of the points of commonality and difference allows us to better appreciate how, why and in what specific ways feminist discourse and praxis shift between the US and Britain.

Structure of the book

As the book draws upon a range of literatures both scholarly and popular, alongside analysis of the empirical data generated for this project, specific texts and material are sometimes confined to individual chapters, although broader analysis ties the related themes together. Part I of the book establishes the intellectual context for the book: Chapter 1 outlines a typological framework for understanding third wave feminisms, before applying it to the empirical data; Chapter 2 provides a contextual framework for analysing some key and current debates within third wave feminisms, focussing specifically on the challenges that the neoliberal context and intersectionality present to advancing feminist interests; and Chapter 3 explores the extent to which third wave feminism constitutes a rebranding of the feminist movement. Part II addresses the importance of inclusivity, Chapter 4, and the extent to which there is any scope or justification for exclusion within feminist activism in the light of debates concerning intersectionality, Chapter 5. Part III considers where and how feminist and women's interests are represented through analysis of political representation, chapters 6 and 7, and the reproductive rights campaigns, Chapter 8. Finally, the conclusion draws the themes of the book together by addressing the research questions set out above. Often, early US third wave texts are somehow defined as the default third wave position, as if the wave somehow emerged and declined in one country over a span of a decade. This book is an attempt to provide a more complex analysis of how British third wave feminism differs from the well-documented US third wave.

Part I

1
Understanding Third Wave Feminisms

The term 'third wave feminism' has been interpreted in multiple and often contradictory ways. It has been viewed as both a neoliberal brand of feminism (Wlodarczyk, 2010) and as a more explicit feminist engagement with global social justice agendas (Heywood and Drake, 1997). Some note that third wave feminism seeks to reclaim and subvert traditional notions of femininity (Groeneveld, 2009) whilst others consider it a polemical defence of girlieness (McRobbie, 2009). It is frequently associated with women of color and intersectionality (Labaton and Lundy Martin, 2004) and yet the dominance of white, middle-class heterosexual voices has also been observed (Henry, 2004). The anti-academic nature of the third wave (Hernández and Rehman, 2002; Bobel, 2010) is at odds with the obvious anti-essentialist influence of post-structuralism and post-colonialism (Hines, 2005; Dean, 2010; Budgeon, 2011). Finally, it has been used generally to describe post-1970s, or second wave, feminist activism (Zack, 2005; Redfern and Aune, 2010) and as a way of signalling a specific generation of feminist activists who constitute Generation X (Baumgardner and Richards, 2000; Shugart, 2001). The confusion surrounding what constitutes third wave feminism is in some respects its defining feature (Walker, 1995; Siegal, 2007; Finley and Reynolds Stringer, 2010); hence, the need to avoid presenting the third wave of feminism as monolithic.

This chapter sets out a typological framework for interpreting the third wave; it then applies this framework to the interview data collected with feminists in Britain and the US in order to evaluate its 'fit' as an explanatory model. The central aim of this chapter is to explore the various interpretations of third wave feminisms and to consider the extent to which similar frames and discourses are used in the US and Britain. Whilst the wave narrative is the overarching frame for historical and contemporary analysis of feminism and feminist activism, competing ideologies and approaches have also been a staple part of the feminist story. Divergent views and tactics have meant that ideological strands within feminism have been central both to individual feminist subjectivities but also to the framing of issues. The importance and particular dominance of the liberal, radical, and socialist strands has been central to readings of the second wave; this chapter argues through empirical analysis that such categories still have purchase with activists. Third wave feminisms are diverse, and using it as shorthand to refer to one particular strain or theme is both inaccurate and misleading. As such, typological approaches to the third wave narrative should be read alongside ideological strands.

Typological approaches to the third wave

Identifying and fleshing out what constitutes the third wave is an important task, not least because so many feminists define themselves in relation to the second/third wave (even if this is simply to reject the wave narrative altogether). Those who identify as/with third wave feminism have themselves sought to provide various definitions:

> We define feminism's third wave as a movement that contains elements of second wave critique of beauty culture, sexual abuse, and power structures whilst it also acknowledges and makes use of the pleasure, danger and defining power of those structures.
>
> (Heywood and Drake, 1997: 3)

> For us 'third wave' feminism simply meant young women and men doing social justice work whilst using a gender lens.
>
> (Labaton and Lundy Martin, 2004: 13)

> Since the start of the millennium, a staggering number of feminist organisations and campaigning groups have formed in the UK. A name has even been coined for all this new activity: 'third wave feminism'.
>
> (Redfern and Aune, 2010: 10)

It is clear from the above quotations that there are a number of different themes and ideas expressed in connection to the third wave. Indeed the variety of ways of defining the third wave (explored in greater detail below) lends weight to the claims of Dicker and Piepmeier that the third wave has 'not coalesced into a larger, easily definable movement' (2003:

11). Thus, it is clear to see why scholars such as Jonathan Dean, drawing on Laclau, have considered the third wave to be an 'empty signifier' (Dean, 2009: 335). The polymorphic nature of the third wave is, in and of itself, something that many self-identified third wavers embrace, resisting attempts to provide concise definitions of the term. In short, there is no monolithic third wave feminism, something many consider to be a 'good thing' (Kaplan, 2003: 47).

Second wave feminism was ideologically diverse, and as with the second, so with the third. Given that there is any number of competing, overlapping, and complementary strands of feminist thought (Lorber, 2010), it would be incorrect to suggest that the third wave is driven by one political agenda or that it speaks to one homogenous set of ideas. The multiplicity of feminist approaches evidenced within the second wave (which went well beyond the social, liberal, and radical typology), shows that it is not always 'easy or desirable' to differentiate between different ideological strands of feminism (Whelehan, 1995: 2). The third wave has been charged with being synonymous with neoliberal individualism, with feminists defending porn, prostitution, and femininity on the grounds of individual choice (Wlodarczyk, 2010). It is true that all these positions can be identified within the third wave, however to suggest that those positions are the *only* positions within the third wave is to provide a rather narrow and unhelpful interpretation of what constitutes a 'wave'. As such, it is a mistake simply to dismiss the third wave as promoting a neoliberal agenda, even whilst it has to operate within such a context.

In order to think through how we might analyse feminist waves, it is useful to think about the various interpretive themes that tend to be associated with them. Table 1.1 below sets out a typology of the main ways in which the third wave narrative tends to be approached; to suggest, however, that academics and activists use *just one* of these approaches for understanding feminist history (and indeed for understanding their own feminist subjectivity) is too simplistic. Furthermore, each approach should necessarily also be understood in terms of specific geographical, historical, and cultural situatedness.

From a scholarly perspective, some of these approaches are more helpful than others are in thinking through the various ways in which we might characterise third wave feminism. Whilst academics may write about oppositional approaches, it is worth remembering that view is not always reflected in popular non-academic feminist texts. Thus, in addition to their scholarly value, it is also important to evaluate the heuristic value of the approaches to feminist activists in determining

Table 1.1 Approaches to third wave feminisms

Approach	Characteristics
Chronological	• Starting in the early 1990s in the US and the early 2000s in Britain; • Resurgence of feminism, attempts to reclaim the term from post second wave 'backlash'; • Such an approach stresses continuity.
Oppositional	• Attempts to resist the perceived 'dogmatism' of the second wave (more evident in US popular texts); • Heralds the 'newness' of the third wave; • Greater emphasis on inclusion and diversity.
Generational	• Appeal to younger feminists, especially those too young to have taken an active part in the second wave; • Association with Generation X, although cross-generational identification occurs.
Conceptual	• Intersectionality as a defining concept that recognises multiple and overlapping points of identity; • More evident in US feminist praxis than in Britain where it has only relatively recently gained traction; • Understanding and practising feminism through a lens of diversity and with a sharper focus on social justice issues.
Activist	• Emphasis on speaking to women of color, all self-identified women and inclusion of men; • Focus on inclusive discourse and praxis; • Greater use of online campaigning and networking.

their own feminist subjectivity. The approaches set out in the table above are intended to be broad enough to interact with one another. For instance, an African American woman identifies as third wave, she does not consider herself to be a young woman, nor was she born into the 'right' generation (i.e. between 1961 and 1981) but she does note the following: how her own feminism differs from what she understands to be second wave feminism; she engages predominantly with online-based activism; and she takes a specific interest in developing an intersectional feminist lens. All these different factors help shape her feminist subjectivity, although she does not necessarily 'fit' with some people's understanding of what constitutes a third waver. Likewise, a white lesbian British woman aged 25 who considers herself to be a socialist feminist, sympathetic to intersectionality and keen to engage with wider social justice issues, but who also rejects the idea of generational divides and an emphasis on individualism, might find herself seeking to identify on some issues and approaches with the second wave and on others with the third. The point is that it is neither easy nor obvious how feminists (particularly those who were not active in the second wave) situate themselves within the wave matrix (Graff, 2003; Reger, 2012). Before exploring feminist views on third wave feminisms, the chapter now briefly fleshes out the key ideas associated with each approach as set out in Table 1.1.

Chronological: Such an approach can be considered to be neutral, in that it indicates a moment in time when feminist activism is resurgent. As such, the emphasis tends to be on continuity rather than on opposition from that which has gone before. In other words, each new wave builds upon the previous one; this is a theme that can be identified in both US and British popular feminist texts (Heywood and Drake, 1997; Redfern and Aune, 2010). Although the third wave of feminism took off at different times in the US and Britain, they both emerged within a neoliberal context. This is important, as it provided both opportunities and challenges for collective resistance (discussed in further detail in Chapter 2).

Oppositional: As the name suggests, an oppositional approach seeks to highlight what is different about the new wave and how such a difference addresses the shortcomings of the previous wave(s). The oppositional framing is particularly popular amongst those US feminists who write as self-declared third wavers (Dicker and Piepmeier, 2003); whereas British popular feminist texts typically emphasise continuity over differentiation (Banyard, 2010; Redfern and Aune, 2010). There has been much written about the apparent tensions between the second and third wave generation, not least because of the 'temporal overlap' (Budgeon, 2011: 6), with some second wavers rejecting third wave characterisations of their politics as dogmatic and exclusive (Zack, 2005: 6; Bobel, 2010: 18). One of the key charges levelled at second wave feminism has been its apparent lack of attention to diversity; hence, the development of intersectionality has been central to third wave subjectivities and politics.

Generational: As with an oppositional approach, the emphasis on younger women has been a key feature of US feminist texts, with authors linking the third wave to Generation X (Baumgardner and Richards, 2000; Shugart, 2001; Dicker and Piepmeier, 2003). Although in some respects a focus on age chimes with a chronological approach (in that it addresses those who were too young to have been involved with the second wave), it also contradicts the focus on inclusivity that is central to an oppositional framework. Indeed, a focus on generation has for some created unnecessary divisions between activists which in many instances simply reinforces a perceived authority on the part of second wavers (Henry, 2004).

Conceptual: The rejection of essentialist and white heteronormative assumptions has been key to the development of the third wave, which has been conceptualised through the development of intersectional theory (Davis, 2008). For many, the theory and discourse of intersectionality has been central to establishing the need for a third wave of feminism. Although such framing could be used to pursue an oppositional approach, it can also be cited as an example of continuity, developing the work of second wave feminists such as Angela Davis. Although it has been argued that the US and Britain do share an approach to intersectionality, one that is grounded in a rejection of essentialist notions of identity (Prins, 2006: 278), as a conceptual approach, it is more advanced in the US than in Britain; this may, at least in part, be due to the greater provision and inclusion of women's studies programmes in US colleges and universities, now largely absent from Britain. Furthermore, intersectionality as feminist praxis has been a source of much tension within British feminist circles in recent years.[1]

Activist: We can break down the activist approach into two separate areas: who is included within feminist activism and how those forms of activism have changed. Many third wave texts and online sites have put inclusivity at the heart of the third wave of feminism (Hernández and Rehman, 2002; Redfern and Aune, 2010). Whilst there is broad agreement on the issue, the inclusion of specific groups (notably trans women and men) continues to be controversial amongst feminists, particularly in Britain. In part, a shift towards online activism has also changed the nature of those debates as virtual spaces have, for some, opened up feminist dialogue (Shaw, 2013). The use of and increasing power of online activism is also something associated with the emerging fourth wave feminism and it is perhaps this part of the typology where there is most scope for overlap between the third and fourth waves.

Activists on third wave feminisms

During the interviews, participants were asked to reflect upon the term 'third wave feminism'. Interviewees were not presented with a list of the approaches; subsequent analysis of the qualitative data was undertaken in order to explore the extent to which they engaged with the frames.

During the interviews, it became apparent that participants were more frequently referencing the chronological, conceptual, and generational approaches. Chronology was an important approach for feminists in the US and Britain, although the US participants had a much clearer sense of when the third wave emerged, with interviewees regularly citing Rebecca Walker's book (*To Be Real*, 1995). Whilst British interviewees also sought to frame the third wave in terms of chronology, there was some uncertainty regarding when it actually emerged, for instance one interviewee from Glasgow discussed how she associated it with 'contemporary feminism' whilst another from London referred to third wave feminism as 'emerging during the 2000s'. Such a difference is unsurprising given that the term 'third wave' is not as widely used in Britain as it is in the US.

The conceptual framing was also frequently cited as a way of defining third wave feminism; indeed, many interviewees named intersectionality specifically as a core element of the third wave. As one interviewee from New York put it: 'To me the third wave speaks to a specific agenda that prioritises intersectionality, it's about diversity and recognising how our multiple identities oppress us.' Participants also regularly linked third wave feminism to a younger generation of feminists and in particular, to those who were too young for the second wave; the reference to younger women was not perceived to be negative. Indeed, many highlighted how important it was that this third wave was engaging a younger generation. The interviewees engaged with those five approaches to varying degrees, with British and US feminists stressing slightly different aspects. The responses of the 73 interviewees to the question of third wave feminism were coded according to the categories in order to see which of the ways of defining third wave feminism were most useful. Table 1.2 below captures the extent to which interviewees referenced specific approaches in defining the third wave.

Table 1.2 Interviewees' definition of the third wave by category

Approach	US feminists	British feminists
Chronological	28	23
Oppositional	4	7
Generational	14	22
Conceptual	23	19
Activist	11	13

Many definitions crossed more than one category.

Table 1.2 above indicates that a chronological approach was the category most frequently used by US feminists in defining third wave feminism; interviewees regularly noted the media backlash against the second wave of feminism and specifically identified the early 1990s as the key starting point for the third wave. For US feminists it was a clear way of defining the third wave, even whilst some went on to explain it further through the use of different categories. British feminists also primarily used the chronological approach, but they were also more likely to note the generational characteristic of third wave feminism; in part, this is linked to chronology, but for many British feminists without a clear sense of when the third wave started, this meant that greater emphasis was placed instead on the role of younger women in the movement.

Contra to some claims about the newness of the third wave compared with the second, few chose to frame their definition through an oppositional framework. This highlights the divergence between popular feminist texts and the views of activists. For many interviewees, ideas of continuity were important and there was, from some interviewees, a notable reluctance to criticise the second wave:

> I think having a third wave shows strength and the power of the movement. The fact that our foremothers before us were also engaged in similar and sometimes identical struggles is really inspiring.
>
> (New York)

> The links with the past are really important; what they fought for during the second wave should be remembered and celebrated and should help us in our activism today.
>
> (Bristol)

For these feminists, discussions about the third wave necessarily precipitated reflections on the second wave of feminism. Understanding feminist history and the various struggles of the movement was seen as integral to developing and continuing forms of resistance against sexism and inequality.

There were, however, some British interviewees who associated third wave feminism with American feminism, which they saw as being antithetical to their own approach. Such a position was articulated by one London interviewee: 'I think of third wave as an American theoretical trend of feminism which I don't see as particularly feminist at all. If you take texts like *ManifestA* say which I think is a pretty good example of feminism being de-politicised.' For this interviewee and for others, the

Table 1.3 Interviewees' self-definition as third wave

Identify with 3W?[2]	US feminists	British feminists
Yes	15	9
Yes but...	7	7
No	9	10
Not sure	–	6
No wave	3	7

association with American feminism was the basis for their critique of what they perceived the third wave to represent. These feminists viewed American third wave feminism as being too 'individualistic' with too much attention paid to 'what you can wear'.

Interviewees were also asked during the interview whether or not they identified as or with third wave feminism. As Table 1.3 above indicates, US interviewees were more likely to identify as third wave than their British counterparts were.

Those who identified as third wave feminists typically stressed their age, the moment in time when they came to feminism and their focus on inclusivity. Many of these interviewees had discovered feminism at college or university, although not necessarily through women's studies classes. For these interviewees, self-identification as third wave was often articulated as a default response to the fact that they were too young to have been involved with second wave feminism. Where this was the case, there was less emphasis on intersectionality.

Such a question was not straightforward for all interviewees to answer, indeed although some initially responded positively, they then offered qualifications, whilst others, notably in Britain, were not sure whether or not they identified as third wave. The quotations below indicate the complexities with which the interviewees grappled in order to answer the question:

> Hmm, I don't know! I guess so but what does that mean? I wasn't around for the second wave so I probably am third wave...
>
> (London)

> Probably, I mean when I think about third wave and when I was in college reading those books and the ideas [...] but then some of the stuff that gets associated with third wave and the fact that it was still mainly white women makes me not so sure.
>
> (Portland)

In negotiating their 'waved' subjectivity, interviewees were forced to think through not only their position within the wider movement in terms of temporal and spatial location, but also to consider the attendant associations with the wave. For those interviewees who had previously stressed the importance of intersectionality, there was a more definite and confident identification with the third wave, whilst those who viewed it in terms of its opposition to the second wave were least likely to identify as third wave. British feminists were also more likely not to identify with a wave at all. For those interviewees, the idea of feminist waves was unhelpful, as one activist from London put it: 'I don't really get the whole wave thing, I think it suggests that feminist activism hasn't been constant over the years and it has.' Similarly, an interviewee from Washington DC who was involved with a large women's organisation noted that she avoided wave and ideological definitions because there was the need to appeal to all women: 'I don't really define my feminism in that way, we need to be careful that we don't exclude people and I think that the waves sometimes do that.' So for these interviewees, the idea of a waved identity created unnecessary barriers amongst and between feminists.

During the interviews, it became apparent that the more neutral chronological approach lessened the chances of critique of the third wave for those who might otherwise be hostile to, or at least sceptical of either the use of the wave narrative or what the third wave has come to symbolise in the minds of some feminists. Hence, the way in which third wave feminism is interpreted can have a significant influence on whether or not feminists may choose to self-define as such. This problem of interpretation becomes even more important when considering the rise in discussions concerning a fourth wave of feminism. Although the term appears from time to time on feminist blogs and also in some feminist writings (see Baumgardner, 2012; Cochrane, 2013), there is still little consensus concerning what it actually refers to and it was only raised by three of the interviewees.

Having explored the dominant interpretations of third wave feminism, the book will predominantly adopt a chronological approach to third wave feminisms. It does this in order to stress continuity between the waves but also in order to include feminist activism that has occurred post-1990s in the US and post-2000s in Britain; where reference is made to the views of third wave interviewees or writers, it will be solely used to denote those who explicitly identify as such. The chapter now turns to ideological frames, exploring the extent to which they remain a meaningful way for feminists to understand their own subjectivity. In so doing, the chapter seeks to highlight the compatibility of wave and ideological framing as a means by which to stress the plurality of feminist ideology within this third wave.

Ideological frames

Analysis of feminist ideology has tended to rely upon the three-part narrative of liberal, radical, and socialist feminism in order to explain the debates and strategies of the second wave (Tong, 1989). These three strands can be briefly defined as follows: liberal feminism tends to be characterised by its commitment to equality of opportunity and through its emphasis on a rational analysis of the public/private divide (Wendell, 1987); radical feminism has focused on women's oppression through an acceptance of the universality of the category of woman (Crow, 2000); and socialist feminism explores systems of power through a capitalist patriarchy (Eisenstein, 1977). However crude this distinction is, it does provide some heuristic value. These three ideological approaches have historically dominated interpretive accounts, even whilst there are other significant strands of feminist thought. It is clear, for instance, that black feminism in particular has paved the way for an intersectional approach to feminism through its commitment to tackling sexism, racism, and poverty (Taylor, 1998). Whilst psychoanalytic feminism, an approach that explores male dominance through emotion and primary relationships (Chodorow, 1989: 7), has not been obviously and popularly taken up by grassroots activists.

Feminist ideologies were not provided to the interviewees in terms of defining their feminism and nor were they asked explicitly about ideological strands (see Appendix B for the interview guide). That some 57 out of 73 interviewees explicitly identified specific ideological strands indicates the strength of such an approach in understanding feminist subjectivity. Moreover, it allows us to better appreciate points of continuity between the waves as well as shifting ideological patterns.

The data in Table 1.4 below illustrates a number of important points: 1) British interviewees were three times as likely as US feminists were to identify with radical feminism, which was the most commonly cited strand amongst the British participants; 2) in the US, a plurality (but not a majority) did not define their own feminism through an ideological frame; 3) identifying as a black feminist was more common in the US than in Britain; and 4) only a few identified as liberal feminists in either the US or Britain, although we should exercise some caution in over reading this and making wider claims about the death of liberal

Table 1.4 Interviewees' self-definition by ideology

Ideological strand	US feminists	British feminists
Liberal	2	3
Radical	4	13
Socialist	4	8
Black	6	2
Queer	2	1
Multiple	5	4
None	11	8

feminism, given its dominance within large national women's civil society organisations. These patterns of identification reinforce the need to avoid presenting feminism as monolithic (Humm, 1992) but also highlight the importance of eliding US and British feminism. The ideological identification offered by the interviewees when discussing their own definition of feminism was accompanied by the naming of specific feminist writers or activists or particular approaches. There was no attempt to categorise those who had not explicitly identified a particular strand. In order to further reflect on these identifications and to evaluate alongside third wave definitions, the chapter now turns to each of these ideologies in turn.

Liberal: A liberal feminist agenda can be readily identified in national organisations that work through existing channels in order to promote equal opportunity at the legislative level.[3] Whilst these organisations have significant support from their membership, not all of their members would necessarily identify as liberal feminist. The lack of self-defined liberal feminists in this (albeit small) sample does perhaps tell us something about the types of feminist who are active in grassroots organisations. Furthermore, many of those who did not identify an ideological strand could in some cases be classified as liberal feminists by dint of their approach and views (although such an interpretation was not included in the data in Table 1.4). For those few who did define themselves as liberal feminists, there was not always a strong sense of what this actually constituted, especially when compared with the responses of other interviewees:

> My own feminism? I guess most other feminists would call it liberal. I'm interested in equal pay and equal rights. I don't believe men are the enemy.
>
> (London)

> I'm pretty much a liberal. I believe in promoting women's leadership and working with other organisations to help realise that.
>
> (Washington DC)

For the five interviewees who did identify as liberal, there was a stronger emphasis on what they were not, rather than on explaining why liberal feminism best explained their own approach to feminism, for example several noted that they were not radical feminists. For the interviewee from London cited above, there was a sense that she was what others would define as liberal because of the fact that she did not agree with what she perceived to be a more radical approach adopted by other feminists. Those who were involved with national organisations either differentiated their own feminist identity from the agenda of the institution or sought to use their work as a means by which to illustrate their belief in the importance of equality and influencing policy.

Radical: During the end of the Women's Liberation Movement, many radical feminist groups disbanded, whilst at the same time the professionalisation of feminist groups enabled and facilitated the dominance of a more liberal approach (Whittier, 1995: 20). However, as Table 1.4 indicates, and in line with other scholarly research, it is also the case that radical feminism is alive and well (Whittier, 1995: 21; Mackay, 2015). Those participants who identified as radical feminists were perhaps the most articulate in their understanding both of the intellectual tradition and how that translated into feminist praxis. Some interviewees identified the influence of specific authors such as Shulamith Firestone or Kate Millett, whilst also situating their feminism as oppositional to post-modern or liberal feminism. As Table 1.4 above highlights, more of the British interviewees identified as radical than in the US. This is perhaps suggestive of wider differences between the movements and the fact that those who identified as radical in Britain were much more likely to be working with other likeminded feminists in specific radical feminist groups. Conversely, in the US, the radical feminists I interviewed tended to be a little more isolated within their feminist groups and communities, other than online of course. Those who identified as radical feminist were not typically involved with any other form of social justice activism and were amongst the most active of the interviewees:

> I identify with the strand of feminism that's most obviously linked to the radical element of second wave feminism.
>
> (Bristol)

> I'm a radical feminist. The ideas and writings of radfems have really inspired me. I'm anti-porn. I've campaigned in favour of targeting johns.[4] I'm willing to name and shame misogyny and patriarchy where I see it.
>
> (Portland)

Self-identified radical feminists highlighted the importance of the category of woman and were critical of attempts to shift discussion away from the central power dynamics of patriarchy and violence against women. Radical feminism was also the strand most likely to be cited by other interviewees as a means by which to define their own feminism in opposition to. Radical feminism was perceived by many of those who did not identify with it as being synonymous with an anti-trans perspective (an issue we will return to in chapters 4 and 5).

Socialist: Again, identification as a socialist feminist was more obviously apparent amongst the British rather than US interviewees, although it is certainly true that many US feminists spoke about the need to tackle poverty and economic inequality. That British feminists should be more likely to identify as a socialist feminist per se is not surprising, given the particularly close ties between second wave feminism and leftist politics in Britain (Lovenduski and Randall, 1993); moreover, the explicit articulation of socialism within British politics has not disappeared altogether. Conversely, within the US, the broad ideological polarisation between conservatives and liberals leaves little room for a clearly articulated socialist platform. Those who identified as socialist feminists were typically active in other leftist or anti-capitalist groups and campaigns and sought to stress the natural links between feminism and socialism:

> I'd say my feminism was socialist. I'm interested in exposing and resisting capitalism's exploitation of women both here and abroad.
>
> (Glasgow)

> You can't fight sexism and women's inequality without also looking at class and at structural economic inequality, so that's why I'm a socialist feminist.
>
> (Portland)

None of the interviewees who identified as socialist feminists discussed Marxism, whilst the use of the term 'socialist' ranged from its use to promote social democratic values through to class exploitation. Out of all of the interviewees, these participants were most likely to highlight the importance of international campaigns. Unlike with either radical or liberal feminists, there were very few attempts to define their own approach in opposition to other strands.

Black: Those identifying as black feminists were more likely to be found amongst the US interviewees rather than British. This is perhaps reflective of the number of groups that specifically advocate for women of color, in addition to the rich and diverse tradition of black feminist scholarship that is widely taught in US colleges on gender studies programs and African American studies programs, neither of which are a common feature of UK universities. For those who identified as black feminists, there was a strongly articulated sense of the need to practise their feminism in a more holistic way that centralised issues of racism and poverty:

> I call myself a black feminist because that's the approach that best reflects my work on the intersections of race and gender.
>
> (New York)

> I've been influenced by black feminism in particular; it's not possible for me to think about sexism without also thinking about racism or classism.
>
> (London)

Those who identified as black feminists tended to be involved with black or women of color groups and were also most likely to use the discourse of intersectionality when discussing their own feminist subjectivity. Specific authors such as bell hooks and Kimberlé Crenshaw were named by interviewees as having had a significant effect on their own approach to thinking through the interaction between gender and racial discrimination.

Queer: Historically, queer feminism has not been considered as a strand in and of itself (although see Marinucci, 2010) largely because of the post-modern influence on the term 'queer' with its celebrated 'amorphous' nature (Walters, 1996: 830). As such, providing a clear definition of queer feminism is not an easy task. We tend to think of queer as an approach to gender identity, one that seeks to subvert and disrupt, rather than as a coherent political platform. However, at least three of the interviewees self-defined as queer feminists. These interviewees could all broadly be described as articulating a post-modern feminism; in other words, there was no attempt to describe universal structural inequalities and gender, sex and sexuality were all presented as fluid concepts:

> My feminism is queer. By that I mean I don't accept fixed categories, I'm interested in transgender rights and getting away from the idea of putting everything in boxes.
>
> (New York)

> Queer theory has really influenced my feminism. I feel really uncomfortable now when I hear some pretty essentialist views being expressed by feminists.
>
> (Bristol)

For these feminists, transgender rights were central, as was a rejection of a woman-focused approach. Those who articulated such an identity tended to be amongst the youngest of the interviewees and were either in college or in university or had recently graduated.

Multiple: For some of the interviewees, defining their feminist identity in terms of just one ideological strand was not appropriate. In particular, many combined either black with radical or socialist, or radical with socialist. In addition, a couple mentioned other strands of feminism, specifically one mentioned eco-feminism whilst another referenced fat feminism. These interviewees sought to define their own sense of feminism through specific traditions or concepts that had influenced them.

> I consider myself to be a radical socialist feminist not a radical feminist; my focus is on women but women can't be freed from patriarchy until we also get rid of capitalism.
>
> (Bristol)

> I'd say I'm a radical black feminist. Those two strands of feminist thought have had the most important influence on my feminism and in particular the ways in which black women's bodies are viewed and controlled in a patriarchy.
>
> (New York)

Those who framed their feminism as being influenced by different ideological strands addressed multiple issues in terms of their interests. They were also less likely to be fully active in one particular feminist group.

None: When interviewees were asked about defining their own feminism, many chose not to frame it in terms of any ideological strand at all. Although they may have used terms such as 'patriarchy', 'poverty', and 'racism', there was no attempt to articulate this as part of a distinct traditional and ideological approach. For these interviewees, they discussed issues that they particularly cared about and what drew them to feminism in the first place. For some this was an individual incident, such as sexual harassment, whereas others had become involved through college or university groups. The focus of the answers that these feminists gave therefore relied less upon ideologies and more upon specific themes:

> I'm interested in issues like porn culture and the sexual objectification of women; the effect it has both on men and on women are really worrying.
>
> (Glasgow)

> I got into feminism when I was at college and a friend convinced me to go on a Take Back the Night march with her, I found it really inspiring and pretty much wanted to get more involved.
>
> (Portland)

Although analysis of the data would allow one to read into the responses of the interviewees themes or ideas that may be associated with specific strands, the fact that 19 of the participants chose not to identify an ideological strand is telling. Whilst the strands clearly continue to have value for feminists in defining their own feminism, there are either those who do not associate their feminism with them or those who do not fall neatly into one approach or another. This suggests that an over-reliance on ideological approaches as a means by which to understand feminist subjectivity would exclude those who do not define their own feminism through such an approach.

Looking at who had identified with the third wave by ideological strand, the data in Table 1.5 reveals some interesting patterns: 1) it is clear that those who identified as radical feminists were least likely to identify as third wave, 2) those who identified as queer feminist or those who had not articulated an ideological position were most likely to identify as third wave, and 3) that those who did identify as third wave include the full panoply of ideological strands as articulated by the interviewees. That radical feminists were least likely to identify with third wave feminism was driven in part by the extent to which they viewed the third wave as synonymous both with a rejection of the second wave but also with a US version of feminism that

Table 1.5 Third wave self-definition by ideological identification

Ideological strand	3W (incl. yes & yes but...)	No	Not sure	No wave
Liberal (5)	1	1	0	3
Radical (17)	4	10	0	3
Socialist (12)	5	3	2	2
Black (8)	5	2	1	0
Queer (3)	3	0	0	0
Multiple (9)	6	0	2	1
None (19)	14	3	1	1
Total (73)	**38**	**19**	**6**	**10**

was not sufficiently woman-centred. Those who had not framed their own feminism in terms of an ideological position were more comfortable identifying with the wave narrative, thus suggesting the importance of wave as a way of capturing feminist subjectivities that are not necessarily driven by ideology. Finally, the fact that interviewees from across the ideological spectrum identified as third wave clearly supports the claim that the third wave of feminism cannot be reduced to one strand of thought or praxis. Ideological approaches still have purchase with feminist activists and they are a useful way of understanding the different dynamics within the movement. To my mind, such an approach should be read alongside the wave narrative; this will avoid eliding say radical feminism with the second wave of feminism.

Ideological framing within a wave narrative

Continuity is vital to a successful and healthy feminist movement (Whelehan, 1995). Such a perspective does not preclude theoretical developments or new strategic and political goals, rather a focus on continuity allows for ongoing dialogue between the past and the present (Evans and Chamberlain, 2014). Although the third wave of feminism has been criticised for its attempt to establish a sense of newness and for its, at times, a-historicism (Snyder, 2008), there are those who have sought to stress that renewal does not mean disavowal (Heywood and Drake, 1997; Redfern and Aune, 2010). Of course, it is certainly true that the emergence of a new wave will elicit the question of why it is necessary. Although there are obvious temptations to stress newness, the use of the wave narrative need not necessarily be a means by which to break with the past (Evans and Chamberlain, 2014). The use of the wave narrative not only allows for but also provides a sense of continuity throughout the history of the movement, one that encapsulates within it the various ideological strands and campaigns that constitute any given wave.

Given that there is any number of competing, overlapping, and complementary strands of feminist thought (Lorber, 2010), it would be incorrect to suggest that the third wave is driven by one political agenda or that it speaks to one homogenous set of ideas. The multiplicity of feminist approaches evidenced within the second wave (which as has been well documented went well beyond the social, liberal, radical typology), shows that it is not always 'easy or desirable' to differentiate between different ideological strands of feminism (Whelehan, 1995: 2). As such, it is a mistake to simply dismiss the third wave as promoting a neoliberal individualist agenda and many have celebrated the ideological diversity of the third wave (Dicker and Piepmeier, 2003: 11; Finley and Reynolds Stringer, 2010). There are those within the third wave who espouse the full range of feminist positions. Third wave activism includes anti-porn campaigns *and* those who seek to promote and explore feminist porn; an emphasis on deconstructing gendered and sexual identity *and* a desire to embrace girlie culture, make-up and 1950s-style femininity; a focus on global campaigns concerning female sweatshop workers *and* the recognition that women purchasing designer labels with their own money is something to be celebrated; a commitment to sex workers' rights *and* campaigns to criminalise the men who pay for sex; and pole dancing and burlesque as forms of feminist empowerment and exercise *and* campaigns to close down lap-dancing clubs. In sum, to suggest a coherent ideological strain within the third wave would ultimately do a disservice to the multiplicity of feminist strands that co-exist within this third wave, even whilst recognising that at certain times and places some positions are more dominant than others are.

Conclusion

Scholars have long since argued that there need to be feminisms (plural) rather than feminism (singular) (Humm, 1992) and for this reason the temporal overlap of the waves of feminism is perhaps an inevitability. Furthermore, the continuing purchase of the ideological prefixes lends weight to the importance of continuity between feminist waves. Given that the 'wave' term can act as an umbrella under which multiple feminisms and feminist campaigns can coalesce, it is perhaps natural that new generations of feminists should seek to highlight the popularity of feminism by heralding a new wave.[5] Throughout this book, the idea of a 'long third wave' will be adopted, thus prioritising a chronological approach. This allows not only for comparative analysis between the early manifestations of the third wave in the US during the 1990s but also allows us to consider recent feminist activism in Britain. The advantages of adopting such an approach is that we are able to consider the extent to which those ideas expressed within the early manifestations of the third wave continue to have currency today. Moreover, it allows us to think through the extent to which such themes travel. What binds this long wave together is the resurgence of feminist activism and the wider political context within which such a wave occurs. The long third wave in this book therefore refers to the period from the early 1990s to the early teens of the twenty-first century. Such a span provides a useful temporal framework for considering the longevity of specific ideas, campaigns, and discourses. This chapter has sought to establish some initial foundations from which we can best explore what third wave feminisms mean in a comparative context. The chapter has set out a typology for defining feminist waves and has applied it to activist approaches to third wave feminism, arguing that a wave cannot be approached on one axis of definition alone. Given the importance of a conceptual turn towards intersectionality and the specific neoliberal context, the book now turns to explore the challenges that each presents to third wave feminisms.

2
Conceptual and Contextual Framework: Intersectionality and Neoliberalism

It is essential to assess the third wave of feminism through its specific intellectual and socio-historical milieu in order to identify points of continuity and departure with the second wave (Budgeon, 2011: 42). Accordingly, any critical analysis of third wave feminism is contingent upon a concomitant reading of intersectionality and the neoliberal context. There has been an increasing awareness of the need to recognise difference between women within the feminist movement. For some, this is a reaction to the perceived lack of diversity and more importantly, to the perceived lack of critical attention paid to diversity within both the second wave and academic feminism (Labaton and Lundy Martin, 2004; Archer Mann and Huffman, 2005). Prior to the emergence of a renewed feminist movement in the US, a call for an intersectional legal approach emerged, one that recognised multiple and overlapping points of oppression (Crenshaw, 1989; 1991). Such an approach proffers both possibilities – the chance to undertake radical and complex analysis of power – and limitations – the danger of reducing levels of analysis to an individual rather than collective level. The risk of a resultant turn not towards intersectionality, but instead towards individualism, is heightened within a neoliberal context. For feminists, the neoliberal hegemony also presents both opportunities and obstacles. On the one hand, it provides a set of discursive and political strategies against which feminists can mobilise; conversely, the normalisation of neoliberal values makes it difficult to identify and resist. Although this chapter is driven by a normative critique of neoliberal values, both economic and social, it is not also intended to serve as a wholly pessimistic reading of intersectionality; rather it considers the potential challenges for the feminist movement in adopting such an approach within a political context that rewards individualism. In short, it explores whether intersectionality can be incorporated within a feminist praxis that does not ultimately reduce analysis to the level of the individual. In order to consider these issues, the chapter firstly sets out a brief overview of neoliberalism and intersectionality, highlighting their specific challenges for feminism before moving on to consider how the two interact.

Neoliberalism

The post-1970s turn to neoliberalism has been almost universal, with the normalisation of deregulation, privatisation, and the withdrawal of the state from social provision. This turn has signified a 'new social order' that re-established the power and wealth of the ruling classes (Duménil and Levy, 2005: 9) and it is often identified as a conservative economic philosophy (Palley, 2005: 20). Given these claims, it is fair to assume that use of the term signifies a critique of the spread of global capitalism. Indeed, it is very difficult to find anyone writing sympathetically about neoliberalism, although the term was first used by neoliberals themselves (Mirowski, 2009: 418). And it is certainly true that the term is typically used pejoratively (Harvey, 2005), with its discursive use often characteristic of what some have interpreted to be the broader negative or 'anti' nature of leftist politics (Ferguson, 2009). Although neoliberalism and neoconservatism are sometimes used interchangeably, differentiating between the two is important, not least when considering the US. Neoconservatism tends to refer more specifically to the religious-political project of those in the US that seek to, inter alia, restrict access to abortion and oppose affirmative action (Brown, 2005: 37). Whilst it is rare that those who seek to espouse neoliberal values do so in its name, neoliberal policies and discourses can be identified in parties of the right and left in both Britain and the US (Chomsky, 1999; Harvey, 2005). Such a mainstream consensus can be identified through a reconfiguration of the state to implement, regulate, and sustain markets in place of direct state provision of services. Although neoliberalism has frequently been associated with policies that encourage both a limited role for the state and accompanying increased power for the markets (Saad-Filho and Johnston, 2005), a limited role for the state does not entirely capture the tenets of neoliberalism. Indeed, in order to achieve an increased role for markets, states often have to adopt a more interventionist approach (Mirowski, 2009).

It is a mistake to view neoliberalism as mere macro-economic doctrine (Ferguson, 2009: 170); it is a term typically used to describe the dominant economic, political, and cultural ideology of the late twentieth century and early twenty-first century (Saad-Filho and Johnston, 2005). Although widely used, neoliberalism is in many respects a difficult term to define, notwithstanding its proliferation within academic writing (Springer, 2012: 135). Saad-Filho and Johnston observe that is it 'impossible' to provide a purely theoretical account of neoliberalism (2005: 1), noting that the 'most basic feature of neoliberalism is the systematic use of state power to impose financial market imperatives, in a domestic process that is replicated internationally by globalisation' (2005: 3). That said scholars and critics of neoliberalism frequently talk about neoliberal values which underpin the behaviour of states at both the national and international level. David Harvey, one of the leading critics of neoliberalism, argues that it is 'a theory of political economic practices that proposes that human well-being can best be advanced by liberating individual entrepreneurial freedoms and skills within an institutional framework characterized by strong private property rights, free markets, and free trade' (2005: 2).

For Harvey, such an ideological neoliberal framework shapes state responses to political, social, and cultural problems; indeed, where there are no markets operating, the state provides an initial (and thereafter limited) intervention. Neoliberalism has a wide reach, influencing not only the economic and social positions adopted by parties, governments, and institutions but also the lives of individual citizens. A neoliberal agenda is pursued through economic and social policies, the delivery of which openly respond to market demands across the whole gamut of social issues (Brown, 2005: 41). The consequences of neoliberalism are such that we can identify increases in inequality, deterioration of public services and a drop in the quality of life for those most vulnerable members of society (Ferguson, 2009: 170).

Tellingly, those who advance what we might consider to be a neoliberal agenda do not defend neoliberalism qua neoliberalism. Part of its success has been the ability of those who espouse its values to present it as 'common sense', as conservative and even as social democratic. The claim that something is non-ideological usually alerts us to the fact that an ideological agenda is being pursued. Neoliberalism is in this respect rather like patriarchy: few openly speak in its name and the process of disavowal on the part of those accused of advocating such positions makes it harder to challenge and resist. For academics, the nebulous way in which neoliberalism as a term can be used is also part of the problem. As such, it is important to identify particular characteristics or values associated with neoliberalism. The following section sets out the specific neoliberal values and practices that are of particular relevance for feminists.

Neoliberal challenges for feminism

Not all feminists seek to critique or even challenge the prevailing neoliberal agenda, although it would be difficult to find anyone arguing for a 'neoliberal feminism' per se. We can, however, identify certain feminist sympathies with specific neoliberal values, in particular, individualism and the role of the markets (see for instance Wolf, 1994; and Cudd in Cudd and Holmstrom, 2011). The debate here is not whether those individuals and groups can claim a feminist identity, but rather the extent to which they represent typical feminist views. There are plenty of feminist scholars who are openly hostile to neoliberalism (Sidler, 1997; Fraser, 2007; Power, 2009); moreover, as the following chapter discusses, feminist campaigners have actively resisted neoliberal policies. This section sets out the effects of neoliberal principles for feminist campaigners. It does this by highlighting four key challenges: first, at a discursive level; second, through its amorality; third, by its focus on market-driven solutions; and fourth, in its inherent belief in the power of individualism and of individual agency. These four challenges represent plural and interrelated challenges facing feminist activists in Britain and the US.

Discourse: The discourse associated with neoliberalism has become increasingly commonplace: the promotion of values typically associated with individual growth and self-advancement are widespread in both the US and Britain, although the need to account for socio-spatial context is important (Springer, 2012). In the wake of the economic crash, the twin narratives of self-reliance and responsible decision-making prevailed; both considered key to the reduction of macro-economic deficits. Freedom for the state, through its removal from the depths of financial crisis, was closely aligned to the promotion of individual freedom, through personal responsibility and self-advancement. The circuitousness of the discourse ensured that macro and micro visions of freedom were inextricably bound. Within such framing, there remains little room for gender or group identity. Freedom, choice, and empowerment have been redefined: freedom to pursue individual ends free from the state is emphasised, choice is understood as consumerism within the marketplace, whilst empowerment manifests itself through entrepreneurialism and consumerism. Such a context makes it hard to create discursive possibilities for imagining collective freedoms or group advancement.

The co-option of terms such as 'empowerment', 'choice' and 'freedom' makes it difficult for any collective group seeking to articulate opposition to the hegemonic discourse of the day. The challenge lies in finding an alternative language that has resonance, particularly for feminist movements who necessarily have to speak to multiple audiences. The ideas of freedom and choice are of course very attractive and each imbues positive connotations; it is no surprise that the liberationist movements of the 1960s and 1970s should have taken them up. That societies pursuing neoliberal values have so successfully co-opted this discourse, presenting pole dancing as liberating for instance, is something that has been in part reflected in what we might consider to be a post-feminist popular culture (Gill, 2007a; 2007b). The subsequent re-integration of such terms (in the neoliberal rather than traditional meaning of the words) into popular culture targeted at women serves for some as a reflection of the extent to which young women have accepted and normalised such values; the hugely popular Sex and the City TV show is just one illustration of this (McRobbie, 2009).

Language, and its attendant power and potential effects, is of course something that feminists have long been aware of the need to challenge. The 'resignification' of the language of choice and freedom are particularly worrying for feminists when popular cultural texts seek to promote a vision of emancipated womanhood that frames choices as individual decisions divorced from their wider structural gender inequalities (Chen, 2013: 442). The a priori assumption of choice as a right runs through popular narratives for framing women's lives, whether that is the decision to start a family, to run for political office, or to have cosmetic surgery. There is typically no wider appeal to the structural and social constraints that are placed upon women in order to prevent, facilitate, or encourage women to make, or from making, any of these types of decisions. The acceptance with which the language permeates should perhaps come as no surprise. That younger women should want to believe that they are free to make whatever decisions they wish to is axiomatic and crowds out other values such as solidarity. Herein lies the strength of the value for neoliberalism in co-opting such terms; citizens are pre-disposed to believe that freedom, individual self-advancement, and the provision of choice are available to all.

Amorality: Neoliberalism is not of course morally neutral and terms such as 'individual choice' are morally loaded. The pretence at moral-value neutrality is part of constructing a binary, which posits rational free markets on the one hand and an ideologically driven and intervening state on the other (Brown, 2005: 40). However, such a framing does not account for the extent to which states frequently shift their positions, adopting at times a more paternalistic approach whilst at others claiming to 'roll back the state'. Governments, seeking to reassure citizens concerned about big government or the 'nanny state', adopt the language of morality in order to justify intervention; at the same time they may in other policy areas seek to emphasise individual responsibility with a more limited role for the state. Even when neoliberal institutions make attempts to pursue more interventionist strategies, these are typically driven by and in the interests of large corporations, for instance corporate social responsibility (Banjaree, 2008). Amorality is a particularly pernicious issue for feminists to deal with, as feminist campaigners often have to rely on some uncomfortable bedfellows when pursuing legislative change.

To illustrate this dilemma we might consider the UK government's approach to violence against women: it has recently promoted Internet filters to prevent accidental access to online hardcore pornography. For many feminists this would be a welcome move, given that research has highlighted that much hardcore pornography consists of illegal content constituted almost exclusively of depictions of violence against women (Long, 2012). However, it is not altogether clear that the UK government in its current iteration is explicitly committed to tackling sexual violence against women; rather there have been suspicions in some quarters that this filter system was merely a Trojan horse by which to increase state surveillance of individuals and to reinforce a paternalistic state.[1] Such interpretation gains traction when one considers that at the same time funding provided to services for victims of domestic and sexual abuse has been dramatically cut.[2] The challenge for feminists therefore lies in negotiating strategic alliances that do not act as a future wholesale compromise on subsequent campaigns and partnerships.

Market solutions: Neoliberalism, as a set of economic practices, has implications for all; however, women, as the poorest members of society, are most likely to be adversely affected by market-driven strategies to political and social problems. Many have highlighted how incompatible the aims of feminism are with a neoliberal agenda that seeks to promote unfettered market solutions to social and political problems (Walby, 2011). This raises questions for those self-identified feminist politicians who also seek to advance market-based solutions. The proliferation of privatisation (especially within Britain, where state-driven solutions were established as the post-war norm) clearly impacts women as the chief consumers of public services, whilst running services for profit, rather than for public good, has negative consequences in terms of levels of inequality and provision of adequate services. The adoption of market strategies as a means by which to address social issues facilitates a pretence of rational decision-making that belies the extent to which women in particular are negatively affected by market solutions and austerity regimes.

Where economic rationalisation is the chief determinant of whether or not any given service will be provided, women's services are invariably cut. Put simply, maternity leave and even women's healthcare provision are not profitable policies for states and markets to pursue. It is unsurprising that during times of economic crisis, marginalised and poorer members of society, most likely to be women, are hardest hit. When private companies take decisions that once rested with elected politicians, who are at least theoretically answerable at the ballot box, there ensues a subsequent lack of accountability for the delivery of public services. For instance, with much US medical care provided via private companies, and with a growing proclivity for outsourcing in Britain, there are limited opportunities for the women's movement and for feminist campaigners to try to effect change and improve provision. We might here consider the funding of abortion clinics, which are scarce in certain US states, or cuts to the funding of women's refuges.

Individualism: Perhaps the most prevalent and widely embraced value of neoliberalism is individualism. The individualist strain can often appear to monopolise discourse at both the level of state and citizenry, even when the latter would be better served by a more collectivist response (e.g. US debates over healthcare coverage). Of course the idea of individualism is inextricably linked to the narratives that states seek to promote about themselves, their histories, and their citizens; the apogee of which of course is the 'American Dream', whereby individual success is the just and inevitable reward of individual hard work. For states and markets, there is an obvious motivation to promote individualism. A belief in self-autonomy, self-reliance and self-discipline is the very means by which to pre-empt resistance to the state. During times of economic crisis, the rhetoric of individual responsibility, juxtaposed with increasing acceptance of competition across all spheres of public and private life, become heightened. A distinct process of 'othering' begins, whereby individuals are encouraged to compete against imagined others at local, national, and international levels. The chief relationship is not then between individuals and their neighbours, or those with whom they share group identities, but between individuals and the state and markets.

The normalisation of individualism as a default political ontology makes collective identity or action difficult to adopt, on either a theoretical or practical level. Take for instance the gender wage gap: it is well established in both the US and Britain that on average women earn less than men do for similar work. This is a mainstream topic for feminist and women's organisations and is usually an issue upon which feminists of all different political stripes can agree. Popular campaigns frequently highlight the inequality gap, through events such as Equal Pay Day, which marks the point in the calendar to which women would have to work to in order to earn as much as men had in the previous year (on average around three months extra per year).[3] However, strategies by which equal pay can be achieved are all too often individualised; individual women are encouraged to ask for a raise, an approach promoted by prominent women in business, such as Sheryl Sandberg.[4] With the slow decline of trade unionism across the west, and in particular the move away from national pay bargaining, responses to unequal pay are ultimately determined by individual women negotiating with their employers. For feminist activists the challenge lies in framing this not as a matter for individual working women, but rather as a wider structural and cultural discrimination that nearly all women will at some point in their lives experience (Fraser, 2013). And, more broadly, to address the fact that women often end up doing low-paid poorly regarded jobs.

The emphasis on individual responsibility also permeates national-level discussions surrounding rape and women's safety. All too frequently, governmental responses to sexual harassment and violence against women is to put the onus on the behaviour (and the dress) of individual women themselves. It therefore becomes a woman's responsibility to make sure she is getting into a licenced cab home late at night or it is a woman's responsibility not to drink too much on a night out. In short, it is a woman's responsibility not to put herself in dangerous situations that may result in her being raped. Focusing on women's individual responsibility deflects attention away from the need for either the state or wider society to re-evaluate rape culture or to increase funding to enhance security on public transport. And as a result, feminist campaigners have to spend considerable effort negating commonly held assumptions about rape and sexual assaults: that women are in some way asking for it. Rape crisis charities and coalitions of groups seeking to end violence against women therefore highlight the pervasive nature of rape and sexual assault, framing it as an issue for all women and not just for individuals or certain types of women.

Collectively, these challenges in no way represent all of the potential implications of neoliberalism for feminism. However, they do illustrate some key and interrelated ways in which a neoliberal agenda is pursued at a policy, rhetorical, and cultural level. Taken together they effect mobilisation, identity, and responses to structural inequalities. The chapter now turns to look at the specific responses of third wave feminism to the challenges of neoliberalism.

Neoliberalism and third wave feminisms

The chronology of the third wave dovetails with the peak of neoliberalism, which has dominated political agendas since the 1980s. Such a hegemonic economic and cultural condition has somewhat inevitably had an influence on the attitudes and activities of feminist campaigners, whether that is through resisting neoliberalism explicitly, co-opting some elements of the neoliberal discourse, or openly welcoming the associated values and ideals as a means by which to progress women's interests. For its critics, the third wave of feminism has gone too far in embracing the possibilities of a neoliberal world in achieving individual economic success (McRobbie, 2009; Wlodarczyk, 2010). This, however, is to conflate third wave feminism per se with a conservative brand of third wave feminism, a strand that is certainly not reflective of the whole wave. If one were solely to define third wave feminism by reading a small number of self-identified third wave texts, then it is easy to see why you might assume that this third wave of feminism has been too accepting of neoliberal values. Although it is true that the challenge of creating a collective movement is complicated by the acknowledged power of individualism, as Heywood and Drake note: 'The ideology of individualism is still a major motivating force in many third wave lives' (1997), other authors have sought to highlight and celebrate the links between women's empowerment and economic freedom (Armstrong and Wood Rudúlph, 2013). Conversely, a growing awareness of the limitations of neoliberalism, particularly post economic crash, has led many feminists to identify the failure of global economic systems to take account of the world's poorest citizens, typically women (Penny, 2014).

Pro/anti-capitalist debates within the third wave also speak to the place of feminism within the broader progressive movement. Traditionally, feminism has been associated with left wing movements. However, it has also been noted that women have been marginalised within the anti-globalisation movement (Eschle, 2005). This marginalisation has recently been compounded by accusations that the Occupy movement has covered up allegations of rape and sexual abuse at several of their sites.[5] Nonetheless, the links between the third wave of feminism and other transnational social justice campaigns has been important (Dicker and Piepmeier, 2003). Indeed, for some, the natural links between feminism and broader global social justice campaigns are axiomatic (Fry and Lousley, 2001).

Anti-globalisation has been a constituent part of this third wave of feminism (Lorber, 2010); even liberal third wave feminists have framed their understanding of women's exploitation in a global context, recognising the various ways in which financial systems can oppress and reinforce gender inequality (Kaplan, 2003: 53). Therefore, to suggest that third wave feminism in toto is a neoliberal brand of feminism is somewhat misleading; to re-state the point, the ideological plurality that could be identified in the second wave of feminism can also be found in the third. Accordingly, exploring third wave feminism through the prism of a neoliberal political context provides a useful way in which to highlight the various standpoints and positions articulated within a broader third wave umbrella. Whilst some articulate a discourse similar to those who seek to further neoliberal ends, there are many more within the feminist movement who actively seek to oppose it.

Anti-capitalist feminist groups exist and are flourishing; research undertaken for this project included a number of interviews with those involved with grassroots organisations that explicitly identified and critiqued the role of neoliberalism in further exacerbating women's oppression (for instance Radical Women in Portland, Feminist Resistance in New York and Women's Fightback in London). Whilst professionalised women's civil society organisations were less likely to be using the same language or making the same critiques, there was still a critique of the effects of particular economic policies on women, for instance the Fawcett Society's attempts to sue the UK government for failing to undertake a gender equality audit in its budget (although it is clear that those large liberal organisations were not seeking to advance an anti-capitalist agenda).

So far, this chapter has highlighted the significant impact of the neoliberal agenda and its implications, both economic and societal, for feminist activists. In distinguishing between second wave and third wave feminism, it is surely the emerging impact of neoliberalism that can help us understand the changing nature of the ways in which feminists can seek to bring about societal changes. Moreover, whilst we can consider the global impact of neoliberalism, it is also important to take into account the different national contexts within which neoliberalism operates. For instance, the nature of feminist campaigns for improved healthcare, whether that be sexual health services or greater provision of screening for breast cancer, differ between Britain, which operates a nationalised healthcare service (albeit one that is becoming increasingly privatised), and the US, which has largely been run for profit by healthcare medical organisations (HMOs). Thus, feminist debates on healthcare are contingent not only upon the prevailing neoliberal discourse which tells us that private is better, but also upon the specific historic political and cultural attitudes towards the relationship between the citizen and the state, and ultimately what the former can expect from the latter.

Having considered the implications of neoliberal values and practices for feminism, the chapter now moves on to explore the central idea often associated with the third wave, intersectionality. Before reflecting on the potential challenges that such a framework might provide for feminism, a brief overview of the key tenets and development of intersectionality is set out.

Intersectionality

Intersectionality has become the theoretical approach *de jour* for many gender scholars over the past two decades (Davis, 2008), considered by some to be a critical feminist research paradigm (McCall, 2005: 1771; Hancock, 2007). Although the themes and ideas of intersecting identities and structural social relations had been discussed during the early 1980s (Davis, 1982) and formed part of a wider anti-categorical critique within the Academy (McCall, 2005). Intersectionality denotes the multiple and overlapping layers of oppression that affect an individual's life (Crenshaw, 1989; 1991). As a concept, it chimed with work being done that sought to explore how certain identities, typically those most commonly associated with identity politics, could only be understood within the narratives of other identities (Yuval-Davis, 2006). Whilst Crenshaw was the first to give name to the ways in which multiple forms of oppression overlap, the approach itself can be traced back to various stages of the feminist movement (Lutz et al., 2011: 3). For instance, we can identify it in the early debates concerning women's suffrage both in the US and Britain, where divisions of race and class were hotly contested (hooks, 1981; Pugh, 2002). Furthermore, it became a central debate amongst US and British black feminists in the 1970s/1980s who felt that their interests as black women were marginalised; this critique, first articulated as the need for an 'integrated analysis and practice' by the Combahaee River Collective in 1977, led to the adoption of a double or 'triple jeopardy' approach to racism, sexism, and classism.

This three-pronged approach, however, was found wanting as it did not accurately reflect the 'dynamics of multiple forms of oppression' (King, 1988: 47); as such, the theory has evolved over time to explicitly include other points of discrimination, such as sexuality, age, religion, disability, and weight (Hernández and Rehman, 2002). Further development of the intersectional framework led Crenshaw to distinguish between political and structural intersectionality: the former referring to the responses of political institutions, whilst the latter captures the various ways in which intersectionality is experienced differently by those who face discrimination on the basis of more than one axis (1991). However, it is not clear how or whether the term can be operationalised or included as part of feminist praxis.

Intersectionality, as with most concepts, frames, and discourses, is contested (Marx Ferree, 2009: 86); the term emphasises the importance of analysing power relations through the intersections between multiple layers of oppression and identities. As a theory it is notoriously difficult to work with (Davis, 2008: 78) and the complexity of the concept makes it difficult to apply methodologically (McCall, 2005); moreover, as this book explores, it is also a particularly difficult approach for feminist activists to adopt, especially when trying to include intersecting identities (Redfern and Aune, 2010: 215). Whilst readily taken up by gender scholars over the past couple of decades as a way of resolving the post-structuralist critiques of identity politics, intersectional theory is both incomplete and rather vague (Davis, 2008). Indeed, it is important to note that the identity markers within intersectionality, gender, race, sexuality, and so on each have multiple meanings for individuals who construct and produce their own identity narrative (Marx Ferree, 2009: 87). And there is no model for living, experiencing, or performing different aspects of an identity (Dhamoon, 2011: 234).

Feminist scholars have differed in the ways in which they choose to interpret the concept both empirically and normatively (McCall, 2005: 1772; Dhamoon, 2011: 230). Whilst it has been claimed that both the US and Britain share an approach to intersectionality, one that is grounded in a rejection of essentialist notions of identity (Prins, 2006: 278), others have viewed the concept as too reliant upon dehistoricised and essentialised notions of identity (Brown, 1997: 94). This reinforces the need to account for both changeable macro systemic forms of oppression such as sexism and racism as well as individual experiences (Collins, 2000). Such an approach necessarily requires a commitment to engagement with contemporary social, political, and economic inequalities but it also requires an analysis of the ways in which those changeable structures affect different groups and individuals in a multitude of ways. Therein, from a theoretical and practical standpoint, lies the chief difficulty with applying an intersectional lens.

Of course, the nature of intersectionality as an abstract concept means that there is any number of intersecting points of identity; this makes exploring inclusivity via specific sub-groups a not unproblematic approach. In short, breaking feminists down into specific sub-groups renders impossible the project of considering how some of those points of identity also intersect, age with weight, sexuality with race, and so on. Taken in the round, it is not easy to see how such empirical analysis could in fact be undertaken, apart from undertaking 360-degree style analysis of individuals. Moreover, the dangers of emphasising a hierarchy of inequalities, through cataloguing multiple group identities, poses a challenge to those who wish to avoid framing marginalisation and discrimination as a points-based approach (Purdie-Vaughans and Eibach, 2008).

Early approaches to the study of multiple identities advanced an additive model, whereby a person with two or more intersecting identities experiences discrimination on two or more fronts, such as racism and sexism or racism, sexism, and homophobia (Yuval-Davis, 2006). More recently, scholars have conceived of it as an interactive model, whereby the distinctive intersecting identities result in a particular form of marginalisation and discrimination that are experienced as one, for example the specific forms of oppression facing black lesbian women (Crenshaw, 1991; Settles, 2006). Whilst others have sought to emphasise the interlocking nature of the systems that frame the interaction between individual identities and their relational dependency on others (Razack, 1998). Within this framework, individual and group subjectivities are relational, thus emphasising a more constructivist approach. By focusing on structural and systemic interdependency, scholars can account for forms of identity that are not divorced from the conditions within which they are formed. Moreover, it allows for a determined rejection of essentialised notions of identity.

Intersectional challenges for feminism

Unlike with the neoliberal context, the challenges highlighted in the following section cannot be, and indeed are not, viewed as wholly negative for feminism; although the challenges that they present are potentially significant to the coherency and effectiveness of the movement. There are three key issues that an intersectional framework presents for feminist activism: the practical difficulties with which such a lens is applied, the language of privilege, and the consequences for collective identity. Each of these three challenges presents difficulties for feminists. However, inclusivity, ensuring that the movement is non-discriminatory and addresses the concerns of those who are most vulnerable to the negative effects of patriarchy, must surely be of central concern for feminist activists. Moreover, the liberationist goals of the movement rest upon its willingness to engage with and resist the state in such a way that relies upon an advanced understanding of the fusion between the various forces that create and recreate patterns of inequalities within a society.

Application: Theoretical debates concerning the need to recognise multiple and overlapping points of identity are well established within the literature (Wilson, 2012). However, translating this into feminist praxis is not straightforward. One of the key problems of applying an intersectional lens lies in ensuring that a hierarchy of identities is not created and that certain groups are not rendered invisible. Furthermore, it is less clear, either from an academic analysis or from a policy standpoint, how such a concept can be operationalised. As Strid, Walby, and Armstrong point out in their analysis of intersectionality and violence against women policies, an explicit absence of a referral to different identities does not mean that no consideration has been given to them in preliminary discussions (2013: 559). Part of the ways in which intersectionality operates at a practical or organisational level is of course in the extent to which inclusivity is prioritised (an idea we will return to in Chapter 4). Inclusivity is not however a proxy for intersectionality; the limitations are such that it is typically gender plus another point of identity rather than considering the inclusion of those with multiple identities that interact, such as race, sexuality, and disability.

For feminist activists, using inclusive language is the first important step, as is ensuring that topics and campaigns under discussion are not solely limited to those affecting white, middle-class, educated professional women. Moreover, it is about recognising differences between women and acknowledging the various ways that an issue such as abortion or pornography might affect different groups, depending on age, sexuality, or class. However, in order for intersectionality to have a significant impact it must go beyond the level of the discursive. It is not yet clear what an intersectional feminism looks like, although as the previous chapter highlighted this is an approach that many of the US interviewees identified as a defining feature of third wave feminism. The challenge lies in how a movement that is fighting on many different fronts can adequately provide a coherent intersectional approach that is not simply tokenistic. On one level of course, presentation and symbolism are important, but in order for intersectionality to be a practical reality, we need a greater understanding of what intersectional policies and campaigns might look like. Although there is some analysis of the extent to which intersectionality features in specific pieces of legislation (Lombardo et al., 2009), the idea of intersectional mainstreaming has not yet taken off in the same way that gender mainstreaming has.[6]

Privilege: In accepting an intersectional approach, or at least in paying lip service to one, it has been very difficult for many feminists to grapple with the various issues that arise from adopting such a framework. Using an intersectional lens has seemingly resulted in the discourse of privilege. In order for an individual to fully adopt an intersectional approach, they must be first be aware of their own privileges; how they affect their opportunities and how they impact on others around them. Pease has defined privilege as 'the flipside of discrimination' (2010: 4); he also notes that people tend to get 'angry' or 'defensive' when they are accused of having privilege. As such, adopting the discourse of privilege into an intersectional framework requires not only a certain amount of self-awareness but also a willingness to confront the various ways in which your own gendered identity may be less politically relevant than other characteristics. This latter point has been particularly problematic for some who see this approach as too far removed from a woman-centred approach. As this book considers, of late some of the most politically charged discussions have revolved around the intersection between gender, sexuality, and the transgender community, with charges of cis-privilege[7] and transphobia often blurring debates about the need for female-only spaces.

The language of privilege though is perhaps most worrying when we consider the idea of 'owning' one's privilege. Not least because what constitutes privilege at a societal and individual level is clearly not fixed. Moreover, where an individual may own a class-based privilege they may at the same time be facing racial discrimination. Hence, one of the chief problems with the discourse of privilege is the extent to which it is considered to be a matter of individual ownership. Foregrounding much commentary, it has become typical to offer a disclaimer regarding one's own position and thus relative understanding of the issues and challenges facing women. In short, a return to a standpoint theory perspective.[8] Likewise it is problematic for groups of women to own privilege when one considers that within that group there exists a matrix of hierarchies and power dynamics. The enthusiastic take up of the discourse surrounding privilege speaks in part to the previous challenge of actually implementing an intersectional framework. By acknowledging individual or group privilege, there is a simultaneous recognition of difference. There are obvious limitations to such an approach, not least the idea that it can appear tokenistic. How then is this acknowledgement, and the public need for recognition, to be articulated if not through individual and collective ownership?

It is not clear if talking about opportunities is any better, although that at least acknowledges the structural and cultural context. The problem with such language is that it reinforces a binary of (positive) opportunities, being born white and able-bodied, whilst the default (negative) barriers or limitations become being born black and disabled. Extending opportunities is a phrase often used as a means by which to talk about how to tackle inequality. But how can the 'opportunity' of being heterosexual be extended, other than through legislative changes to say marriage or employment legislation? At heart, it does not acknowledge the entrenched power dynamics that exist in a heteronormative, racist, and classist society. Moreover, the language of opportunity takes us into dangerous essentialist terrain; one that reinforces a set of binaries and a hierarchy of individual experiences. This is not to suggest that accounting for individual experiences is not important; however, the use of the word 'privilege' can act as a silencer and can shut down any analysis based upon gender alone.

Collectivism: At the heart of the debate surrounding inclusion is of course the tension between both recognising and affirming individual identities as well as creating a sense of collective solidarity; in short, how the latter can be achieved without sacrificing the former (Weir, 1996). This speaks to both the practical realities of applying intersectionality as well as to theoretical considerations of the challenges posed to collectivism by such a framework. Umbrella terms or structural theories, such as 'woman' or 'patriarchy', provide the discursive tools by which to undertake a gendered analysis of oppression. However, in using such language there is the danger of reinforcing the notion that women are a homogenous group without accounting for difference amongst and between women. When discussions revolve around women's differences, there are the attendant problems of not only introspection but also of an unravelling of any sense of collective identity as more and more axes and life experiences are added to the list of those already acknowledged. Of course, this is not to suggest that to acknowledge different life experiences and multiple identities solely distracts attention, when clearly the need to address classism, racism, and homophobia within feminism is critical. At a linguistic and abstract level however, these debates have made the use of collective terms such as 'woman' problematic.

Within the Academy, feminist post-structuralist thinkers have largely argued that the very notion of identity is inherently problematic and should be considered rather as a socio-linguistic construction; for Butler, the gendered self is made real through practices and through the affirmation and reaffirmation of systems of power (1990). Despite the frequent misrepresentations of Butler's work as being wholly damaging for feminism and the women's movement by questioning the usefulness of the term 'woman', Butler makes it clear, as does Iris Marion Young, that despite its problems, the term 'woman' is politically important (Young, 1990; Butler, 1993). Whilst identity tends to be understood as a universal concept that represses the multiplicity of the self (Weir, 1996), the term 'woman', in and of itself, does not necessarily require the sacrifice of other aspects of identity. Rather it requires us to acknowledge that gendered identities are culturally, historically, and linguistically situated.

For feminist politics, the term 'woman', and the collective solidarity that goes along with that, is important because it refers to a real structural situation (Gunnarsson, 2011). In an attempt to reconcile the problems of difference within feminism, Spivak advocated 'strategic essentialism' as a temporary measure to advance a social movement (Spivak, 1996). The term was widely interpreted as a defence of essentialism. In fact Spivak suggested that the temporary nature of the identification, which in itself would be more indicative of a performance, did not require individuals to accept the essentialist identity of a group as a reality, but rather as a political mechanism for change. Although Spivak distanced herself from the term 'strategic essentialism', due in large part to frequent misinterpretations, she has not abandoned the concept.[9]

Intersectionality and third wave feminism

As the previous chapter identified, intersectionality is central to many feminists' understanding of what constitutes the third wave. Many of the self-identified popular third wave texts have highlighted the importance of intersectionality, implicitly if not explicitly. In part, this is because second wave feminism (and more latterly academic feminism) has frequently been criticised for marginalising the interests of non-white, non-western working-class women (Hernández and Rehman, 2002: xxii). Accordingly, some feminist writers, in accepting the characterisation of the second wave as a movement that privileged the voices of white, middle-class heterosexual women, have been keen to put inclusivity at the heart of the new feminist movement (Dicker and Piepmeier, 2003). This has manifested itself through a commitment to the discourse of intersectionality both in theory and in practice. Third wavers therefore largely accept the idea that identity politics has been frequently overlooked or has conflated intra-group differences (Crenshaw, 1991: 1242).

The scholarly literature on third wave feminism typically identifies intersectionality as one of the most obvious points of differentiation with the second wave. Despite the criticism that much of the third wave popular literature is anti-academic (Wlodarczyk, 2010), the plethora of personal and feminist confessional pieces contained within the numerous anthologies could also be considered as a form of 'lived theory' (Budgeon, 2011: 82). Regardless of the fact that younger feminists are typically part of a generation who have been exposed to feminism through the university curricula (Redfern and Aune, 2010), the popular texts of the third wave appear keen to avoid engaging in theoretical debates. There are several potential interrelated reasons for this: it suggests a desire to distance themselves from the second wave divisions between academics and activists; it may also reflect the fact that many feminist academics are still more likely to be drawn from the older generation of second wave feminists; and finally, it might be a deliberate strategy to appeal to the majority of women who do not identify as feminist and who therefore might feel alienated by academic theories. The exception to this though appears to be intersectionality. As Chapter 4 explores, inclusivity has been one of the key ways in which feminists have sought to put intersectionality into practice by being more inclusive and aware of the multitude of ways that sexism and misogyny can be experienced.

Despite its seeming dominance, not all feminist activists have embraced intersectionality and it has been particularly contentious in Britain. There have been those such as Louise Mensch, journalist and former Conservative Member of Parliament (MP) who have criticised its increasing prominence in Britain for being introspective; she contrasts it with what she describes as 'reality based feminism' in the US (this despite the fact that the US is where the term originated and is arguably more advanced in feminist theory and practice).[10] Intersectionality has also been critiqued from those on the left in Britain who were active within second wave feminism, and who consider the debate to be a repetition of that which has gone before, and moreover, as a way of alienating those who do not have a conceptual understanding of the term.[11] There is of course a danger of over-theorising; however, the extent to which intersectionality has taken off within feminist campaigns and groups demonstrates its purchase beyond academe.

The interaction of intersectionality and neoliberalism

The challenges presented to feminist activists both by intersectionality but also by the neoliberal context are significant; perhaps the area where they overlap, implicitly and explicitly, respectively, is in their tendency towards individualism. Crenshaw and others before her who sought to advance a more sophisticated analysis of the ways in which our heterogeneous identities interact were clearly not driven by the same desires as those who seek to promote an economic form of individualism that conflates 'citizen' with 'consumer'. However, the context within which intersectionality has flourished, both within and outside of the Academy, is not unimportant. The critiques made of collective political identity, and on a more abstract level, the absence of a fixed sexed or gendered ontology, are happening within a broader political context whereby individualism is prized above collectivism.

To suggest that intersectionality could *only* take off because of the neoliberal context is overstating the case. For sure, academics in their analyses of emerging theories and frameworks also help promote and reinforce dominant approaches and narratives. However, it could fairly be argued that the conditions were ripe for the popularisation of a framework that seeks to emphasise difference amongst and between women, at the same time that the prevailing political ideology seeks to promote a sense of atomisation. During a period when many western governments are pursuing an austerity agenda that does not recognise the needs of groups per se, to call into question the utility of presenting women as a homogenous group is a potential danger. Those who advocate for an intersectional approach do not couch their arguments in individualistic terms; however, a potential consequence of intersectionality is a potential return to standpoint feminism, whereby individuals can only advocate for themselves, rather than for the collective.

The language of privilege is clearly at odds with the discourse of neoliberalism. Neither the discussion of elites, nor hierarchies of power, feature prominently in much corporate discourse or in many policies advanced by states or political parties. In fact the very idea of acknowledging and articulating an awareness of privilege could be considered anathema to neoliberal values which presumes a level playing field from which all are free to compete and participate in the marketplace. Accordingly, the use of the term 'privilege' could act as a form of resistance to the neoliberal pretence of equality, even whilst it raises questions for feminist solidarity.

There are those who identify as intersectional feminists, although it is not always clear what such feminism would actually look like in practice.[12] Conversely, there are no explicitly self-identified neoliberal feminists. However, there are a number of conservative and right wing women who adopt a feminist label and seek to pursue a form of feminism that is grounded in a belief of the importance of market-based values (Kantola and Squires, 2012). Previous research has criticised the conservative nature of post-feminists such as Katie Roiphe and Rene Denfeld (Gill, 2007b); although there has long been a tension within feminism regarding whether one necessarily needs to adopt a leftist agenda in order to identify as feminist. These internal ideological disagreements amongst feminists do not stop those pursuing neoliberal values from doing so in the name of feminism. However, those who we might identify (or who self-identify) as conservative feminists oftentimes use the idea of acknowledging difference between women as a means by which to pursue a more individualistic approach to gender equality.

The co-option of diversity and difference by those who do not necessarily share a belief in the wider goals of the feminist movement is of course a potential challenge for intersectionality, especially when it is pursued at the policy level. If the goal is to ensure that intersectional policies are pursued at an institutional level, then the additive model would likely be more appropriate than interactive. This is of course problematic, not least the extent to which states and markets might choose to highlight the intersection between race and gender without any explicit engagement with debates concerning class or economic inequality. Thus, the ways in which those who seek to pursue a neoliberal agenda specifically choose to frame an 'intersectional' approach is something that feminists should be alive to.

Conclusion

This chapter has explored the implications of the specific political, economic and cultural context, neoliberalism, and the dominant theoretical intersectional framework that is currently evident in US and British feminist praxis. There are challenges and implications of both for feminism. The neoliberal context and intersectionality certainly, at least in theory, make it a propitious time for those advancing a more individualist brand of feminism to succeed at both a rhetorical and policy level. To be clear, I am not suggesting that intersectionality is, in and of itself, a conservative agenda. However, not to consider the ways in which such a framework could be used is problematic. Feminist responses to intersectionality are also instructive, and the extent to which they have resulted in a less collective sense of common purpose is a potential threat to the sustainability of this third wave. Chapters 4 and 5 take up the issue of inclusivity and explore the extent to which different groups are included within the third wave. Before that though, the following chapter assesses the idea that feminist activism and theory reflects and reinforces neoliberal values by considering the ways in which rebranding reclaiming feminism has shaped contemporary activism.

3
Reclaiming and Rebranding Feminist Activism

The third wave of feminism emerged in response to the prevailing anti-feminist backlash that occurred during the 1980s in the US and Britain (Faludi, 1992; Oakley and Mitchell, 1997). During this time, the Reagan and Thatcher administrations introduced cuts and increased privatisation, both of which negatively and disproportionately affected women (Eisenstein, 1984; Bashevkin, 1994). At the same time, larger feminist organisations underwent a process of professionalisation, whilst feminist activism and women's services moved off the streets and into town halls and university departments (Bashevkin, 1996). Part of the impetus for this new wave of feminism was the desire to reclaim feminism publicly, both as a means by which to reinvigorate feminist activism and as a necessary form of resistance to the anti-feminist backlash (Walker, 1995). Indeed, the reclamation project became, and has remained, a constituent part of feminist aims and objectives frequently articulated by feminist writers since the mid-1990s (Heywood and Drake, 1997; Baumgardner and Richards, 2000; Valenti, 2002; Redfern and Aune, 2010), whilst some, notably in the US, have also called for a rebranding of the movement in order to broaden its appeal (Wolf, 1994; Armstrong and Wood Rudúlph, 2013). The political, economic, and social circumstances within which this reclamation project was undertaken were not propitious. This chapter explores approaches to reclaiming feminism since the early third wave texts and considers the extent to which the term has been stretched or rebranded in order to respond to the neoliberal context. It argues that whilst neoliberalism has provided a difficult context for mobilising effective collective resistance, feminist movements have nonetheless managed it without needing to rebrand. The distinction between published feminist texts and activism is central to this analysis and this chapter allows us to appreciate the, at times, significant gap between popular feminist writing and grassroots activism.

Rebranding feminism in a neoliberal context?

Feminism's abeyance during the 1980s and much of the 1990s is an oft-cited feature of the wave narrative (Lorber, 2010). The political circumstances under which feminism largely retreated from the streets was a period in which individual aspiration was widely promoted, whilst at the same time women's agencies underwent a process of professionalisation that resulted in a form of gender managerialism that was more interested in elite, rather than grassroots-level politics (Bashevkin, 1996; Bagguley, 2002). The well-documented backlash against feminism and the various successes of the counter-movement (Faludi, 1992) illustrate the ease with which regressive policies can be introduced and cultures inculcated when a movement is not active, or at least is not *seen* to be as active as it once was. The absence of high-profile feminist activism was grist to the mill for many of those actors who constitute the anti-feminist lobby. Made up of individuals, civil society, and religious groups, online communities and actors within governments and the media, part of the anti-feminist agenda has been to shift discussion away from sex and gender identity towards a gender-free conception of the individual. This has been aided by a political period in which individualism and consumerism have each sought to deracinate any sense of collective identity; this meant that re-establishing political groupings that existed beyond the formal political sphere of parties and interest groups was not easy to achieve. And yet it is clear from even a cursory understanding of the range of feminist activities that exist today that reimagining and reclaiming a movement within such a context is not impossible.

As the previous chapter highlighted, individual identity and individual responsibility are prized above collective solidarity within a neoliberal framework. As such, opportunities (and barriers) are, at least rhetorically, targeted at individual citizens and are determined by market and (subsequently) state forces. With monetary and social policies firmly focused upon individual rationality, there is the implicit (if not explicit) assumption that group identity and group politics no longer have any significant purchase. The ramifications of this political and economic context for feminism are significant and wide ranging. A tendency towards individualism, and its reinforcement through state rhetoric and legislation, makes the job of promoting solidarity based upon group identity difficult. Somewhat counter-intuitively however, for those early third wave writers promoting a new wave of feminism pre-economic crash and in a world before the 'War on Terror', such an inhospitable climate offered its own advantages. Indeed, the resurgence of feminism has been significant. One could argue that it is not *in spite* of the economic and geopolitical context that feminism has witnessed such a resurgence but rather *because* of it. It is no coincidence that it is in the last decade or two that we have witnessed a renaissance of feminist activism. The conditions are such that the turn towards individualism promoted during the Reagan–Thatcher era has come under strain during a time of economic and democratic crisis when an otherwise compliant neoliberal citizenry might be least likely to resist. However, for feminism, such a condition serves to expose the multiple ways in which women often bear the brunt of economic and social policies adopted in the name of austerity.

That said, this does not mean that the recent resurgence of feminism, evident in terms of both the scope and range of publications and activism, has not had to respond to the pressures of the changing political context. In encouraging women (in particular) to identify as feminist, many of the authors and those running groups have sought to highlight perhaps a less 'radical' version of feminism (Dean, 2010). Although it is clear from the interview data generated with feminist activists and the extent and range of issues addressed by grassroots rather than national feminist groups, that the focus of organising, rather than writing, is suggestive of a more radical, collective, and resistant form of feminist politics. This distinction between third wave writing and activism is important. Early US third wave texts focused on individualism (Shugart, 2001); this was evident in the production of self-help style anthologies, which largely served to reinforce neoliberal values through self-improvement (Budgeon, 2011: 84). An attachment to individualism has largely remained constant in much popular feminist literature that continues to be produced, although this is noticeably more evident in US rather than British writings. This distinction could of course be linked to the idea that individualism has effectively 'trumped' collective action in the US over the past 30 years (Siegal, 2007: 5). But to suggest that Britain has been wholly impervious to the promotion and production of a more individualistic culture, both socially and politically, would be inaccurate.

The propagation of neoliberal values such as choice, freedom, and individualism, necessarily affects the ways in which women, and young women in particular, engage with feminism and their decision to adopt a feminist identity (McRobbie, 2009; Budgeon, 2011). The incorporation of feminism's ideals into neoliberal institutions has rendered feminist discourse safe and non-threatening (McRobbie, 2009). Additionally, the co-option of feminist discourse and ideals by neoliberal western governments in foreign policy rhetoric has been unsettling for feminists (Phillips, 2010). Such an overlap at the discursive level poses a threat to the radical and subversive act of identifying as feminist. Whilst these are very real concerns, and feminists should be alert to the idea that the goals of the movements are being used with other intentions in mind, the visible and increasingly high-profile awareness of the breadth and depth of sexism and misogyny within both the US and Britain ensures that there are those who still see feminism as a means by which to resist the neoliberal consensus.

On a symbolic level, some have argued that neoliberal societies seek to promote and invest in an acceptable form of femininity, to which the feminist is positioned as other (Scharff, 2012: 11), thereby inhibiting young women from identifying as feminist. In Britain, *Elle* magazine recently teamed feminist activists with advertising agencies to 'rebrand' feminism.[1] There is a strong emphasis in some recent popular feminist literature in the US on presenting feminism as something that is both politically important and fun. These discursive attempts to rebrand feminism in the face of the anti-feminist backlash tend to revolve around sex and consumption as a way of reassuring women (and it is largely women) that you can be straight, feminine, a consumer and be a feminist. In short, making feminism sexy and stylish; and thus making it an ideology based on individual choices (Groeneveld, 2009: 179). Making feminism 'fun' and appealing to young women is a key selling point for some texts. Consider the following titles of popular US feminist books: *A Little F'd Up: Why Feminism Is Not a Dirty Word* (Zeilenger, 2012); *Sexy Feminism* (Armstrong and Wood Rudúlph, 2013); and *Full Frontal Feminism* (Valenti, 2002).

Of course using sex and femininity as tropes plays into the patriarchal condition whereby a feminine image is rewarded socially and economically. Such a seemingly contradictory approach is designed to simultaneously celebrate and subvert femininity (Lorber, 2010). A knowing sense of irony is therefore required in order to square this circle. This allows young women to turn a blind eye to more blatant forms of sexual objectification by celebrating female sexuality, whilst at the same time allowing them to behave in ways previously considered degrading and in the interests of male sexual gratification (Renegar and Sowards, 2003). For instance, discourse surrounding pole dancing is split between the reality of female exploitation by male consumers and middle-class women taking pole-dancing classes as a form of exercise. Irony is paramount here for those feminists keen to reclaim the 'right' to enjoy female forms of exhibitionism. Opposition to such reclamation attempts are invariably labelled as 'anti-sex'.

Reclaiming femininity, in a 'knowing' and 'empowered' fashion, therefore becomes a critical part of reclaiming feminism and is illustrative of the ways in which feminists have sought to counter the fabricated image of feminists as man-hating lesbians (Scharff, 2012). Thus, discussions concerning how to reconcile being a feminist with a desire to shop, wear make-up, have sex, or go to burlesque clubs, all form part of a wider agenda to make a feminist identity safe and non-threatening. In these rebranding texts, the authors encourage readers to think about the individual choices that they make; adjectives such as 'empowering' and 'liberating' are frequently used to help the readers think through how to negotiate the competing demands of neoliberalism and individual fulfilment. More often than not, these books tend to reflect what some would refer to as a 'sex-positive' position – a standpoint that encourages and promotes sexual freedom and typically has a more liberal attitude to pornography in particular. For instance, as part of their 'Sexy Feminist Action Plan: Self-Help for Your Vagina', Armstrong and Wood Rudúlph advise readers, amongst other things, to 'watch some woman-friendly porn' (2013: 33).

Conversely, there are other popular texts that provide a more unflinching and critical analysis of structural gender inequalities and pervasive violence against women including *Female Chauvinist Pigs* (Levy, 2005); *The Equality Illusion* (Banyard, 2010); *Reclaiming the F Word* (Redfern and Aune, 2010); and *Meat Market, Female Flesh under Capitalism* (Penny, 2011). The authors in these books are not trying to make feminism 'fun' per se, nor are they willing to reconcile feminism with pervasive objectification of women's bodies, rather they serve as more of a sobering reminder of why feminist activism is still vital. Moreover, some are explicitly critical of those texts that do try to 'rebrand' feminism in order to make it less 'revolutionary' (Penny, 2014), reminding us that the very notion of branding is itself neoliberal. These texts tend to provide explicit criticisms of the books that seek to make feminism more palatable, arguing that too often these attempts at presenting pole dancing as liberating or buying expensive handbags as empowering presents a 'garbled attempt at continuing the work of the women's movement' (Levy, 2005: 75).

These critiques of the neoliberal context are certainly valid and it is not difficult to identify ways in which feminism has been 'packaged' so as to be more appealing to young women, particularly within the US. For instance in *Sexy Feminism,* Armstrong and Wood Rudúlph argue that a rebranding of feminism is important, but that this should be done at an individual rather than collective level: 'we've come up with our own sexy, fun, empowering brand of feminism [...] we encourage every woman out there to come up with her own as well' (2013: 12). For these authors therefore, the branding occurs at an *individual* rather than *collective* level, an approach that appears diametrically opposed to structural interpretations of gender inequality, and one that seems to encapsulate McRobbie's fears regarding the increasing overlap between neoliberal and feminist discourse. Indeed, exercise classes in pole dancing, which are now advertised as a form of female empowerment (Munford, 2010: 194), underline the extent to which feminist discourse has been adopted and adapted in a decidedly un-feminist fashion (McRobbie, 2009: 3).

This turn towards a more 'fun' form of feminism is something Ariel Levy puts down to 'a kind of generational rebellion' (2005: 74); it is certainly true that early third wave texts and recent popular feminist books are imbued with a liberal irony regarding raunch culture (Baumgardner and Richards, 2000; Moran, 2011). Feminists who 'get the joke' of pole dancing or strip clubs, seek to undercut the association with male power by subverting their meaning through active participation. The desire to express sexual liberty and freedom through participating in these activities is where the sense of oppositional third wave framing is at its strongest, although even this is misguided when we consider the strength of and disruptive influence of so-called sex-positive feminism during the fragmentation of the second wave (Loe, 1999: 710). Rather than framing it then as oppositional to second wave feminism, it is instead an opposition to the radical feminist tradition, where critiques of pornography and S&M have been most clearly and effectively articulated (Tong, 1989: 116–123). That said, it is worth repeating the point that a swing towards promoting a fun and sexy form of feminism is largely restricted to written feminist commentary rather than being an obvious or central element of feminist organising.

Countering these attempts on the part of some to assert a female sexuality which largely conforms to patriarchal expectations are the ongoing campaigns against the normalisation of porn or raunch culture in the US and Britain (Levy, 2005; Redfern and Aune, 2010; Bates, 2014). Indeed, it is often these very books and campaigns that appear to have re-energised the feminist movement, with younger women increasingly aware of the insidious ways in which technology makes the sexual objectification of women's bodies impossible to ignore. Whilst we can certainly find books and blogs extolling the virtues of rebranding feminism, analysis of grassroots feminist campaigns, groups, and the empirical research undertaken for this project reveals a more substantive commitment to the issues, with less attention paid to the image of feminism. Somewhat ironically, although there have been legitimate critiques of the loss of radicalism amongst the high-profile feminist groups and organisations (Dean, 2010), and there is a tendency within some feminist campaigns and groups to distance themselves from radical feminism as traditionally understood, the themes that are pursued by many feminists are undoubtedly influenced by second wave radical feminists such as Millett and Firestone. In documenting the multiple and various forms of violence against women and by continuing to name the problem that radical feminists first identified, feminists are centralising issues of violence against women. Thus, whilst there are those who are seeking to rebrand feminism, the majority of activism continues to focus on the very issues that radical feminists first theorised (Crow, 2000).

There were no participants interviewed for this research who argued that feminism ought to change its image. Indeed, some were very critical of discussions concerning the idea that feminism had an image problem, noting that it was playing into the hands of anti-feminists to accept the terms of the debate. Many were uncomfortable with the idea of rebranding; this was keenly felt by those women who had been involved with second wave activism. Whilst there was considered discussion about the ways in which feminism could reach out to more people and increase its diversity, the idea that making feminism fun or sexy was critical to the goals of the movement was not taken seriously:

> I get so annoyed when I read blogs or papers saying we need a new image. I mean what a way to distract us from the broader point: women's continued inequality.
>
> (London)

> I guess that some people think that making feminism into a lifestyle so people buy into it is the best way of selling the message, but really that compromises not only the message but the movement.
>
> (New York)

For these feminists, a rebranding exercise was not appropriate for a political movement and was more likely to be undertaken, as one interviewee noted, by corporations or political parties. Such a view only serves to reinforce the extent to which activists have been keen to resist neoliberalism. The antipathy towards rebranding was expressed across the board and, even during interviews with those who represented large national organisations, there was a definite hostility to trying to sell an image of feminism. Of course, feminist books and blogs do not always make representative claims about feminism, but they often serve as shorthand for the media and for scholars who want to explore trends and narratives in the movement. Moreover, the impact of a magazine such as *Elle UK* running a feature article on the need for a rebrand of feminism is particularly damaging given the reach of such a publication in the mainstream women's market with readers who may not know much about feminism.

Reclaiming a feminist identity and expanding the movement

The call for women to reclaim the label 'feminist' from the anti-feminist media initially manifested itself through the numerous 'confessional' style books which drew upon personal experiences in order to elucidate how and when individuals first embraced a feminist identity (Walker, 1995; Heywood and Drake, 1997; Baumgardner and Richards, 2000; Martin and Sullivan, 2010). The idea of reclamation resonated with British feminists who also published books and wrote articles extolling the importance of feminism as a political project and as a political identity (Banyard, 2010; Redfern and Aune, 2010). Conversely, and despite the tendency of some individual authors in Britain to draw upon personal experiences in order to explore gender inequality (Moran, 2011; Penny, 2014), British feminist texts have not typically consisted of multi-author confessional pieces (with the notable exception of Norris, 2011). This highlights an important difference in approach and style between the US and Britain, with greater attention paid to collective struggle and solidarity in the British texts.

Early feminist blogs such as *Feministing* (set up in 2004) and *The F Word* (set up in 2001) have been joined by a slew of popular feminist blogs such as *Vagenda, Feminist Times* and *Jezebel*, in addition to individual blogs and other sites that have come and gone. The importance of online space (discussed in further detail below) has also created a critical site for espousing reclamation rhetoric. In the pursuance of the reclamation project, the impact of Hollywood celebrities 'coming out' as feminist has attracted much attention; some feminist bloggers have welcomed this as a way in which to encourage others to identify as feminist.[2] Whilst others are concerned that those celebrities that reject feminism do so under a misapprehension of what feminism actually means and therefore simply serve to propagate anti-feminist discourse.[3] The presence of these sites both promotes the reclamation project whilst also problematising it, with critical analysis of the meanings and interpretations of the feminist label.

The discourse surrounding feminism and feminist identification contains within it inherent contradictions; on the one hand, women and those who believe in eradicating gender equality are encouraged to articulate a feminist identify, whilst for others, the act of identification should come with a commitment to activism – that is, not just to *say* you are a feminist but to *be* a feminist. The politics of feminist identification is of course contested, with endless speculation devoted to questioning whether individual behaviour is congruent with feminism.[4] Feminism is by its very nature a concept that is open to multiple, individual, and collective interpretations. Hence, for some, the reshaping or 'stretching' of the term and its attendant processes has become an ongoing part of feminist activism. Defining and redefining the term is an active iterative debate; at times feminists seek to open up the term to make it more inclusive, whilst at others, particularly in relation to more contested debates, it can be used as an exclusionary form of identification drawing lines between 'real' and 'faux' feminism. Thus, feminism is often positioned in general terms not only in opposition to patriarchy and anti-feminism, but also in contradictory ways by feminists who seek to advance competing aims.

To illustrate this point we might think about different kinds of feminist campaigns. Equal pay is a fairly uncontroversial campaign in both the US and Britain; in this instance a feminist stance is used to signify a common-sense approach and those beyond the usual suspects are encouraged to adopt the feminist label. Conversely, campaigns surrounding the legalisation of prostitution, an issue that divides feminists, means that the feminist label not only becomes a site of contestation but it also becomes much harder for those not already involved with feminism to understand the terms of the debate and the various positions. In short, both types of campaign are problematic for getting a proper understanding of what it means to be a feminist; this is because the term is constantly in a state of flux. It is a fluid subjectivity open to both individual and collective interpretation (and reinterpretation). Where one might seek to privilege the individual-level response to feminist identification, this may ultimately weaken the collective response (and responsibilities) to the wider movement. Whereas emphasising the views of the vocal majority (or minority) can serve to undermine individual agency and engagement. Hence, the terms 'feminism' and 'feminist identity' are often presented as a fixed form of identification and the articulation of that identity has become part of the process of 'being' a feminist, which for the most part feminist writers and campaigners have sought to promote.

At this point, it might be useful to think about the term discursively in order to consider the ways in which the term 'feminist' can be stretched to accommodate people or campaigns that were not previously associated with the term; this is particularly important for a third wave of feminism that prioritises intersectionality and occurs within (and in response to) a neoliberal framework. Thus, reclaiming the term 'feminism' (and for some, the additional prefix of 'third wave') provides an opportunity for people who had not previously identified as feminist or who had felt excluded from the previous wave of feminist activism. Being a 'third wave' feminist therefore signifies a process of differentiation; this, as we have seen, does not always mean an ideological break with what has gone before (see Chapter 1) but rather serves to highlight the means by which an individual political identity can be reinvigorated and closely aligned to a specific historical and political context. The symbolic value of new generations of feminists choosing to associate themselves with a pre-existing movement also reinforces the process of renewal. In order to explore this further, the chapter now turns to the empirical research undertaken with activists in order to explore attitudes towards reclaiming a feminist identity.

Feminist views on reclamation

As noted previously, for young women, the feminist label has both positive and negative connotations; on the one hand, feminism is seen as having had a positive impact, whilst for others, it constitutes an extreme political ideology (Scharff, 2012). In order to celebrate feminism's successes and to highlight the need for its continued influence, naming acts as feminist acts as well as identifying well-known feminists has proven an important strategy (Heywood and Drake, 1997; Baumgardner and Richards, 2000; Dicker and Piepmeier, 2003; Finley and Reynolds Stringer, 2010; Redfern and Aune, 2010). Indeed, identifying and naming others as feminist is cited by Baumgardner and Richards as the number one point in their *ManifestA*, 'To out unacknowledged feminists' (2000: 278). This also features in *Reclaiming the F Word* in which the authors note that most young people are feminist without realising it (Redfern and Aune, 2010: 5). The process of naming has significance for those who are seeking to reclaim and celebrate the feminist label. This push has been most obviously promoted by large national women's organisations with both the Feminist Majority Foundation (US) and Fawcett Society (Britain) selling T-shirts emblazoned with the slogan 'this is what a feminist looks like' as an attempt to normalise and popularise the term.

During the interviews undertaken for this research, the need to encourage others to think of themselves as feminist was considered critical. This was a view shared by interviewees in the US and Britain, as the quotations below highlight:

> I think it's really important that as many women as possible embrace feminism, we need to build the movement.
>
> (Portland)

> I love those Fawcett T-shirts, I think it's great to have all different types of people wearing them [...] it's about being proud to identify as a feminist.
>
> (Glasgow)

> Feminism is cool! We need to tell people that and encourage people to get on board.
>
> (New York)

Perhaps unsurprisingly, all of the feminists interviewed for this research supported calls for expanding the movement and more specifically for promoting a sense of pride at embracing a feminist identity. Interviewees spoke of the need to encourage those who do not currently identify as a feminist to think through the various ways in which patriarchy, sexism, and gender binaries affect their daily lives. Moreover, there was recognition that the label itself was important; it was an integral part of their identity, best summed up by one Portland feminist: 'I'm a feminist, that's who I am. Everything is directed through a feminist lens.' For the interviewees at least, it was assumed to be a natural part of being a feminist that you would seek to persuade others of the importance of the movement and of the label. Despite this, several interviewees, notably those who had identified as radical feminists, did raise a note of caution:

> I think it's great that feminist activism is on the rise. What we need to be a bit careful of though is that it doesn't become a kind of catchall

> label that gets so watered down in order to be made palatable that it really loses its radical edge and its focus on eradicating patriarchy.
> (London)

> We've got to grow the movement but we also have to acknowledge that not everything women do is feminist; actually in my opinion not everything that some feminists claim is feminist, is actually feminist.
> (Portland)

Echoing the concerns regarding calls for a rebranding exercise, these feminists sought to put qualifications on the process of identification and expansion. Namely that not all acts were feminist acts, even when undertaken by feminists. And that feminism must retain its critical analysis of existing power structures. The obvious problem with these qualifications of course is that there are a multitude of feminist strands and approaches; one person's feminist act is another's acquiescence to the patriarchy. To illustrate this, austerity has spawned a highly gendered construction of desirable feminine activities, including home baking, and in particular, making cupcakes: some consider this to be a harmless hobby, divorced from political activism; others view it as a *feminist* hobby which sees women producing their own cakes, rather than buying them; whilst yet others view it as part and parcel of gendered constructions of femininity, packaged up as retro-chic largely targeted at middle-class women.[5] That such an activity yields such a variety of contested interpretations underscores not only the difficulty with which agreement can be established regarding feminist activity, but also the plurality of opinion within the movement. The somewhat inevitable end result of such debates is of course that serious discussion about the collective aims of the feminist movement is reduced to contestations over individual acts. Of course reflecting upon trends in cultural activities is not unimportant for feminists, and yet such debates tend to deteriorate quickly into discussions concerning individual choice and the implications for feminist identity.

A frustration with a perceived inflexibility regarding the adoption of the feminist mantle has led some popular writers to expand the definition of feminism to encourage as many women (and men) as possible to identify as feminist. Naomi Wolf has argued for an open and inclusive definition of feminism that most people could subscribe to (1994), whilst Jessica Valenti, in a chapter entitled 'You're a Feminist. Deal', argues that whilst not all women are feminist, anyone who believes in equality and that women should not be beaten or raped is a feminist

(2007: 24). Arguably, a critical part of being a feminist is identifying as one (Lovenduski, 2005) and taking an active part in resisting gender stereotypes and inequality. For some, any feminist theory of subjectivity must provide an awareness and critical analysis of power in its multiple forms, recognising the 'asymmetries of power' that exist between individuals and groups of people (McLaren, 2002: 79). To that end feminism as a political ontology should account not only for power dynamics between men and women at both a collective and individual level, and between patriarchal institutions and female citizens, but also of the ever-shifting dynamics of power that are mediated by other intersecting identities.

So far, this chapter has highlighted a lack of support for a rebranding of feminism with greater emphasis placed on reclaiming the feminist label. The chapter now considers what this reclaimed feminism looks like in terms of activism and questions whether it has, in any case, been rebranded despite opposition. It does this in part by focusing on one of the most high-profile and controversial marches that has been organised in recent years: SlutWalk. Additionally, given the importance of online activism to the third wave, the chapter also considers the impact that this new mode of communication has had upon the movement.

Modes of activism

How, where and in what ways feminists choose to undertake their political activism are questions that help us understand points of continuity and change within the feminist movement. It is easy to link particular modes of activism with specific campaigns or moments in feminist history, for instance, the direct action undertaken by suffragettes which included smashing windows, the consciousness raising and street theatre of the second wave groups and the Women's Peace Camp such as Greenham established to protest against nuclear weaponry. But these straightforward links are misleading. Moreover, they suggest a homogeneity of approach and activism that misses the plethora of related activity undertaken by a wide range of actors all engaged with the same or similar campaigns. Indeed, the feminist movement has long utilised a wide repertoire of activism, for instance, whilst some militant suffragettes were happy to take direct action, other suffragists were keen to continue lobbying Parliament to bring about change (McGerr, 1990; Bartley, 2007). As with previous waves of feminism, we can identify a range of activist strategies adopted by feminist activists in the US and Britain; whilst these do increasingly include online campaigns, it is telling that much of the activism undertaken by feminists would also have been used by previous generations.

Much has been written about the decline in traditional forms of political participation and engagement, whether that is the declining number of people joining political parties, voting in elections or attending public meetings (Putnam, 2001). However, claims regarding a lack of citizen engagement have been considered by some to be misleading when we consider political engagement beyond the legislative sphere (Dalton, 2008). A wider definition of engagement is particularly important when we consider feminist activism: the legacy of the second wave slogan 'the personal is political' and a conceptual awareness of the extent to which power and politics frame our everyday lives means that any individual or group that identifies with a mode of political resistance is necessarily engaging in political participation, even if this remains purely at the discursive level. Indeed, feminist activists are seeking to engage with the state and influence the agenda in a range of traditional and non-traditional formats that speak to the increasing variety and modes of political activism.

The emergence of new groups is one of the key indicators that we are currently experiencing a third wave of feminism. Following the decline of second wave feminism, many noted the professionalisation of the feminist movement, with additional resources and specialisms dedicated towards ensuring that women and feminist voices were heard in the legislative arena. Such an emphasis required these organisations to adopt public affairs and policy strategies in order to compete for attention in political debates and in the media (Weldon, 2012). In both the US and Britain there exist leading women's civil society organisations that seek to promote a feminist agenda and provide a professional face of the feminist movement in its dealings with both legislators and business (Marx Ferree and Yancey Martin, 1995). Beyond the formal political sphere, feminists have reclaimed marching as a form of political protest (Mackay, 2015). Indeed, the plethora of marches and visible public protests that now constitute part of the feminist resistance is testament to the symbolic power of such forms of protest but also to the limited opportunities afforded by the Internet.

Online

Widespread use of the Internet in the US and Britain, and its particular appeal to both the young and politically engaged, has ensured that online spaces have become a key site for feminist discussion, but also for feminist activism. There are well-known and highly read feminist sites, such as Feministing, Jezebel, Vagenda, and The F Word, but there are also thousands of individual blogs, Facebook pages, Tumblr sites, and Twitter discussions which create a diffuse set of spaces in which feminist dialogue is occurring. Such sites are neither fixed nor continuous as new spaces emerge whilst others fall into abeyance. This section does not map the existence of all of these sites and spaces, such an endeavour would require its own book-length project, rather it considers the opportunities and limitations of online spaces.

The Internet has been credited with opening up forms of transnational campaigning, allowing a range of voices to engage in political debate. As Tilly and Tarrow observe, this has been particularly important for the US, as the Internet has brought once 'parochial American activists' into greater contact with counterparts abroad (2007: 20). Moreover, it has been important for cross-national dialogue in the US where spatial and temporal differences have in the past prevented 'real-time' discussions of emerging issues. One of the central benefits of online activism for feminism in particular is the extent to which it provides opportunities for those who cannot physically attend meetings, whether because they have caring responsibilities, have disabilities, or are simply too far away to remain engaged and included in the movement. Although online activism has been the subject of study and scrutiny for well over two decades now, there is still a residual sense that it does not constitute a 'legitimate' form of activism. However, charges of 'slacktivism' or 'clicktivism', intended to denigrate the impact and value of online campaign strategies, have been found wanting, with scholars identifying online modes of activism as offering very real and tangible means of engaging with the political (Karpf, 2010). Moreover, the emergence of and increased reliance upon new technologies necessarily requires a shift in our understanding of what constitutes political resistance (Koerber, 2001). The potential for disruption and destabilisation meant that in the early days of new technological advancement, the possibilities of online spaces for advancing feminist goals and agendas was widely anticipated (Spender, 1995; Van Zoonen, 2001).

Much early analysis of the discursive and ontological possibilities of the Internet for feminism was concentrated within post-modern discussions of cyberfeminism, a term used to foreground the significance of new media technologies as an approach to challenging power dynamics between men and women (Hawthorne and Klein, 1999: 2). Scholars identified the potential of new technologies to bring about a paradigm shift in our conceptualisation of gendered identities. An identity reliant upon technology, rather than sex or gender, was theorised;

such an identity was crystallised in the image of the cyborg (a fusion of machine and organism) as the central being within this post-gender world (Haraway, 1985). The Internet was viewed as a means by which to free users from fixed embodied realities (Braidotti, 1996) and women and feminists were encouraged to become 'active agents' in using, developing and analysing new technologies in order to 'reinvent the world' (Arizpe, 1999: xiii). Scholars also recognised the power of the Internet as a site where pre-existing spaces could be opened up for women, but in such a way as to undermine the 'material reality' of patriarchy (Plant, 2000: 325).

Analysis of how far the Internet has provided a useful space for feminists to contest gender norms reveals a mixed picture. And it certainly is true that the Internet has not always been liberating for feminists and women; beyond the proliferation of online pornography, the Internet has been an important site for anti-feminist rhetoric and abuse. Additionally, we might think about the ways in which men have used the relative anonymity of the Internet in such a way as to damage the credibility of causes; recall the case of the Edinburgh student who pretended to be a Syrian lesbian teenager or the male editor of US lesbian and gay site LezGetReal who posed as a lesbian blogger.[6] Whilst these examples certainly illustrate the extent to which sex, gender, and sexuality can be performed and disrupted on the Internet, they have also damaged the integrity of those marginalised voices and campaigns. Conversely, scholars have highlighted the various ways in which online forums have opened up safe spaces for feminist dialogue (Preece, 2000) and support groups for women, including feminist mothering (Koerber, 2001), breast cancer support groups (Orgad, 2002) and radical feminist sites (Jeffreys, 2014). And yet despite the opportunities that the Internet presents for online discussion forums and genuine transnational and cross-ideological discussion, feminists have experienced particular problems with online forms of abuse and trolling.

The objective of trolling is to entice others into meaningless and endless discussions, the point being to frustrate and annoy others (Herring et al., 2002: 372). The power dynamic that underpins the activities of the trolls is such that only the troll understands the rules of the game, making it a particularly distressing experience for their victims (Donath, 1999: 45). Trolling has now taken off to such an extent that scholars have also sought to distinguish between those 'career trollers', whose sole goal is to disrupt, and those who merely want to attract attention (Herring et al., 2002: 374). Scholars have noted that feminist forums are particularly susceptible to online trolling; this is partly because of the nature of the topics being discussed but also because the forums attract some very marginalised and vulnerable people (Herring et al., 2002). The subject of trolling is a popular discussion both online and in feminist texts (see Bates, 2014; Penny, 2014) and for those high-profile feminists who are active on new social media, the attacks from anti-feminist trolls are an almost constant presence.

The frequency with which feminist sites and forums are attacked by trolls is also compounded by the very public, anonymous violent threats that are made against feminist campaigners. In Britain, activist Caroline Criado Perez, who successfully campaigned against the removal of the sole woman, Elizabeth Fry, from Bank of England notes, was subject to explicit and violent threats;[7] whilst founder and editor of the US-based blog *Onward and F-Word* has also been the victim of online threats.[8] The intensity and frequency with which feminists in particular have become targets for anti-feminist hostility and violence somewhat undermines the earlier feminist hope that the Internet would prove to be a safe and revolutionary space for campaigners. The ease by which trolls and those seeking to threaten women can use the anonymity of the Internet is particularly worrying, although it is worth reflecting upon the fact that this high-profile manifestation of misogyny is in itself just a more public manifestation of pre-existing misogyny.

Despite the often-inhospitable climate online within which feminists undertake their campaigning, the impact of the Internet has also facilitated awareness raising, highlighting issues that might otherwise not have received much attention. Take for instance the highly successful Everyday Sexism project which allows women to post their experiences of sexism from gender stereotyping to sexual assault. The project has a website, Twitter hashtag and Facebook wall, whilst the founder Laura Bates has recently written a book collating some of the posts (2014). It has attracted widespread media attention and has also effectively illustrated the pervasive nature of sexism. This is particularly true for those issues that have a particular effect on women and girls outside of the west. Whilst the use of online petitions, blogs, and Twitter have facilitated and sustained specific campaigns, for instance Britain's No More Page 3 campaign calling on daily tabloid newspaper *The Sun* to scrap its page 3 which features topless female models. Such use of online space also means that many do not have to rely on professional organisations to promote their cause, indeed the No More Page 3 campaign has a virtual office for those involved with coordinating the campaign. A shift to online organising and coordinating also provides an alternative to the professionalised and often elite-level focus of national women's civil society organisations. In theory at least, online activism should signify a shift towards a more democratic form of civil society resistance, one that is less reliant on a 'chequebook model' of participation (Tilly and Tarrow, 2007).

The potential democratising and equalising effects of the Internet are made somewhat problematic by two charges: that online activism does not require much active engagement and that it has a potentially atomising effect. It is certainly true that 'liking' a campaign against a form of sexual objectification is not quite the same as giving up an afternoon to attend a protest march or rally. Nevertheless, resisting online forms of patriarchy through feminist engagement is central to a cyberfeminist approach (Hawthorne and Klein, 1999: 2); indeed, naming, challenging, and resisting patriarchy whether it is found offline or online is common practice for feminists. Furthermore, given that the Internet provides, to some degree, a reflection of society, then it is important for feminists to make use of and challenge the patriarchal values found online. Of course, engendering a sense of community is central for any social movement and, as has previously been addressed, the need for collectivism is particularly strong for identity-based political movements. The dangers of online activism lie in its apparent ability to create individual activists with no sense of community or purpose. Although there are a range of online communities and forums that provide spaces for collectivism, it would be difficult to argue that activism through the *sole* use of the Internet does much to enhance group identity and solidarity.

The advent of the Internet has fostered a different approach to campaigning. The modes of communication may have changed, with new instantaneous spaces for engagement and dialogue across different geographical locations, and greater collaboration between marginalised groups of women and feminists who might otherwise have struggled to make personal connections. Here we might also think of the extent to which it has been a space in which advancing an awareness of intersectionality can be realised, for instance the Twitter hashtag #Solidarityisforwhitewomen highlighted the extent to which women of color continued to be marginalised within feminist debates (Holm and Ojeda Castro, 2014). Although the Internet has undoubtedly facilitated a different type of feminist dialogue and campaign, this does not mean that the current iteration of feminist activism is so far removed as to be unrecognisable by those who were active in the second wave. Juxtaposed with the growth in online activism there has also been a resurgence of more familiar forms of feminist activism, specifically marching (Mackay,

2015). The two forms of activism work symbiotically, with new social media providing an effective platform from which to promote feminist marches and to host a virtual archive of such events. In order to explore this further, the chapter now turns to consider feminist marching by focusing specifically on SlutWalk.

SlutWalk

Marching has been a staple mode of feminist activism for well over a century. Feminists have marched for suffrage, against various wars and to demand reproductive justice. However, the recent SlutWalks garnered a significant amount of media attention, partly because of the controversy they caused amongst and between feminists but also because of their provocative name (Mackay, 2015). The march was arranged in response to a Canadian police officer who advised women to 'avoid dressing like sluts to avoid victimisation'.[9] Outrage amongst feminists was widespread and to date more than 200 SlutWalks have been held in cities across North America, South America, Australasia, Asia, and Europe. The SlutWalks were intended to encourage women to challenge established conventions regarding the monitoring of female sexuality. Whilst they have been important symbols of feminist activism in societies where the media had largely heralded the advent of a post-feminist age, they have divided opinion amongst feminists and have also been used by anti-feminists to deride the aims of the movement. Ostensibly, there were two aims of SlutWalk: the first was to argue that women should be free to wear what they want without fear of attack, which is a protest against victim blaming; and the second more controversial aim was to re-appropriate the term 'slut'. The controversy and division amongst feminists came not from the first aim but from the second.

Feminists have long argued that words matter: they frame our thoughts and the world around us and specifically suggest hierarchical structures (Kleinman et al., 2009). The process of naming is important, often revealing who has the power to name and who can be named. Therefore, reclaiming words that have traditionally been used to denigrate or oppress specific groups is fraught with difficulties. Whilst reclaiming words and self-naming can result in self-determination, this can be hampered both by the historicity of the term and also by a lack of power over the term's trajectory (Butler, 1993: 173). Whilst it has been successful at times, note the transformation of the term 'queer', certain words, such as 'bitch' or 'nigger', merely reinforce sexism and racism (Butler, 1993: 169; Kleinman et al., 2009). Whilst it is important for feminists to name things as they are, for instance identifying patriarchy and sexism where they exist, adopting and subverting terms previously used against women is politically dangerous.

'Slut' has a long association with dirt and pollution (Attwood, 2007), making it a specific way of framing (and therefore governing) female sexuality. Moreover, it has also typically been a term of abuse for working-class women. The word 'slut' has had a particular role in the iconography of third wave feminism. Specifically, Riot Grrrl bands (early 1990s, mainly all-female punk bands) used to write 'slut' on their bodies at concerts as a way of demonstrating sexual empowerment and liberation (Attwood, 2007: 236). It was a way of illustrating the complexities of the term with women drawing attention to the word in order to reclaim and pre-empt perceptions about their sexuality (Attwood, 2007). This was also the tactic and intention adopted by some of those who participated in the SlutWalk. Much of the advertising surrounding the SlutWalks encouraged women to feel empowered by their own sexuality. For some the suggestion of empowerment as a means by which to encourage women to participate in the SlutWalks represented a critical misinterpretation of the core feminist critique of power. Power resides in patriarchal structures and is reinforced discursively in order to, in part, maintain and police female sexuality. Hence, ongoing feminist campaigns against gendered language that demeans women, such as the word 'slut'. The term was traditionally used to refer to slatternly or working-class women and subsequently as a way of labelling women perceived to be sexually promiscuous. Whilst the precise meaning of the word may have shifted with history, culture, and context, it has yet to be imbued with a positive connotation.

The media sought to portray the divisions between feminists over SlutWalk as being generational. However, both older and younger women politicians opposed the SlutWalk[10] whilst high-profile second wavers such as Germaine Greer spoke out in favour.[11] Whilst some activists have been willing to defend the re-appropriation of the term 'slut', there was evident division. Many of those who participated in the SlutWalks were either encouraged or chose to dress 'like a slut'; that is, in clothing deemed by society at large to be sexually provocative (Mackay, 2015). Such a move meant that, in marked contrast to previous feminist marches, a worldwide media were keen to provide coverage with accompanying photographs of scantily clad women protesting against victim blaming. The backlash against SlutWalks came predominantly from within the feminist community, many of whom were horrified at the naiveté that feminists displayed in gratifying a male audience. This is a charge that has also been levelled at Femen, who regularly undertake topless feminist protests.[12]

SlutWalks occurred in London, Bristol, Glasgow, New York, Washington DC, and Portland, and interviews were undertaken with activists involved in organising them. Many, although not all, of those who had been involved with the organising were in their 20s at the time and had indicated during the interviews that being involved with such a large-scale and high-profile event had been their first experience of feminist activism. For some interviewees, they were less convinced now by the appropriateness of the march, not as a means by which to protest violence against women, but rather its name and the attempts to reclaim the word 'slut'. Whilst some admitted that they had not been fully prepared for the fallout within the feminist community, others thought it had been wilfully misinterpreted in order to draw attention away from the key issue of women's safety and their right to occupy public spaces:

> It was a great experience and I learnt a lot from it. Would I do it again? Probably not if it was going to be called SlutWalk. But I still think the wider message is important.
>
> (New York)

> I thought it was a great march and didn't think it was really about the word slut, it was about ending violence against women. There were loads of people there, first time that many had been on a march, which was just really energising.
>
> (Bristol)

As the above quotations indicate, for the interviewee from New York the internal conflict within the feminist community that came about as a result of SlutWalk was something that she regretted. Indeed, an open letter was sent to the organisers of the New York SlutWalk by a black feminist group, accusing the organisers of failing to think about the racial implications of re-appropriating a term such as 'slut'; the critique rested upon the fact that the organisers had failed to appreciate the term's specific racial connotations and that no thought had been given to the fact that not everyone was privileged enough to claim such an identity. Conversely, there was some anger on the part of those who had helped organise the marches who felt that the idea of reclamation had hijacked the original intent of the march. For some, the idea of embracing and reclaiming the word 'slut' had not been the point, and the name was merely a useful way in which to engage younger women in feminist activism. Moreover, there was a sense of frustration that those who sought to criticise the march were creating divisions where none existed.

Those who identified as radical feminist or as black feminists were more likely to be critical of the SlutWalks, whilst those who had not identified with a particular ideological strand and had identified as third wave were most likely to have been involved with organising them. The interviewees who had not taken part in the SlutWalks were either openly hostile or torn between wanting to support feminist activism whilst not condoning the accompanying message regarding 'slut'. Indeed, the Bristol SlutWalk organisers took a conscious decision to have a banner with the word 'slut' crossed out in order to distance themselves from other SlutWalks where there had been attempts to reclaim the word. Many of the images of the SlutWalks published online and in national newspapers featured photographs of scantily clad women or women wearing tight T-shirts emblazoned with 'proud to be a Slut'. These were the very messages and images that many within the feminist community had feared would make the movement look not only ridiculous, but also compliant in terms of male expectations of female sexuality:

> I was devastated when I found out about SlutWalk. I mean to have all this energy and anger against male violence and objectification turned into this media circus. I just don't know what they were thinking.
>
> (London)

> I guess for many younger women it was a way of energising feminism? I felt really conflicted about it all. I didn't go in the end although I have friends who did and they wore normal clothes. I can't help feeling that the message got lost though.
>
> (Washington DC)

The sense of subversion that underpinned the SlutWalks was in many respects typical of the ways in which some forms of contemporary feminism have sought to disrupt staple acts of protest within the feminist repertoire. The deliberately provocative images that emerged from the SlutWalks certainly challenged traditional images of feminist activism. Something that a few interviewees considered to be a good thing, particularly with regards to engaging younger women.

So, can SlutWalk be considered an attempt at rebranding feminist marching? Certainly, the language and clothing worn by some marchers was not typical of feminist marches; additionally, the significant amount of attention it attracted from the media and from those who had not previously been involved with feminist activism made it a different type of march. That said, whilst it was high profile for a few years, it has not had the longevity or the consistency of more traditional feminist marches such as Reclaim the Night or Take Back the Night, both of which protest against violence against women (Mackay, 2015).

Instead, SlutWalks might be better viewed as being a specific temporal moment that galvanised and attracted younger women to feminism. It is not clear whether or not those who participated in the marches with no prior experience of feminist activism are still engaged with the movement. There have not been any SlutWalks in either the US or Britain in the past couple of years, which suggests that they did not have sufficient purchase within the feminist community to ensure they became a regular occurrence. Despite the controversies surrounding attempts to reclaim the word 'slut', a US campaign entitled 'Rock the Slut Vote' has sought to use the word in order to rally opposition to the GOP's War on Women,[13] whilst British feminist Laurie Penny has sought to champion the idea of 'slut power': 'Slut power means speaking up. It means standing your ground when those around you are attacked for wanting too much, demanding fair treatment, for taking up too much space' (2014: 105). It is not clear what purchase the 'slut vote' or 'slut power' could have within a movement that has reflected critically on the use of the term both during and after the SlutWalks. Moreover, it is not obvious what 'slut' offers the movement either discursively or practically.

Conclusion

This chapter has sought to highlight the extent to which feminist activism has been reclaimed and rebranded and the views of activists towards expanding the movement. Feminist activism is thriving in new and traditional spaces, despite, and perhaps because of the neoliberal context. Whilst the anti-feminist lobby continue to denigrate both the image and aims of the movement, feminists on both sides of the Atlantic have sought to reclaim the label. Despite calls from feminist writers to rebrand the feminist identity, this is not something that has been embraced by activists, nor is it self-evident when we consider the types of feminist activism that have occurred in recent times. Whilst the SlutWalk certainly constitutes an attempt at encouraging, particularly younger, women to engage, the variety of SlutWalks demonstrates the different approaches taken by those organising the marches, not all of whom were keen to see it as a way in which to re-appropriate 'slut' as a feminist term. The Internet provides a space for campaigning and for feminist forums; whilst it has successfully raised awareness of specific issues, it is clear that the Internet has not always provided a safe space for feminists. Points of continuity can be found between third wave feminist activism and previous waves, indeed many of the debates and issues remain remarkably similar. Whilst the modes of communication may have changed, this has not led to a loss of a feminist community. Nor has the pressure of individualism eradicated a sense of collective identity. The following chapter considers the extent to which this third wave has sought to prioritise inclusivity and whether modes of activism have proven to be more or less conducive for the voices of traditionally marginalised women within the movement.

Part II

4
Feminist Inclusivity

Intersectionality and the promotion of inclusivity have been considered a cornerstone of this third wave of feminism (Zack, 2005). And yet the exclusion and marginalisation of specific groups of women remains a salient problem for feminist activists. Although both early and later third wave texts typically demonstrate a commitment to diversity (Walker, 1995; Redfern and Aune, 2010), certain groups and identities are more prominent than others are. Indeed some issues that affect specific groups of women continue to be addressed at a rather superficial level. Analysing feminist debates and modes of activism allows us to explore the extent to which inclusive discourse has been translated from theory to praxis. The dominance of white, middle-class able-bodied women continues to be an issue for feminism and feminists on both sides of the Atlantic (Zack, 2005; Penny, 2014). Whilst online spaces have 'opened up' potential sites for greater inclusivity, it is not always clear that those voices have real influence within the wider movement, specifically in terms of shaping campaign agendas. There is of course any number of specific group identities that could be explored in relation to feminist inclusivity. However, this chapter focuses on the most salient and contentious identity categories within feminist debate: race, trans, sexuality, age, class, and disability. I readily acknowledge that breaking up identities into discrete categories runs counter to the very idea of intersectionality; in fact, this only serves to reinforce the difficulty with which activists might seek to consider issues of inclusion and interconnectedness. That said, it is important to consider the inclusion of specific groups in order to evaluate how all-embracing this third wave of feminism is in practice. Each section will address the ways in which third wave texts have sought to address the need for including specific groups of women and the views of the activists; framing that will also be a brief overview of the role of associated ideological strands within feminism and their impact on the movement.

Race[1]

Black feminists have long documented racism within the women's and feminist movement, illustrating the various formal and informal ways in which women of color have been excluded, marginalised, or discriminated against by white women (hooks, 1981; Davis, 1982; Lorde, 1984). Despite the continued dominance of white women within academic feminism, a legacy of the 'intellectual content' of second wave feminism that preserved white middle-class exclusivity (Zack, 2005: 3), black feminist thought has had a particularly strong influence on feminist theory and practice. Pioneering black feminist scholars developed theories of identity and power (hooks, 1981; Lorde, 1984; Collins, 2000) and of course conceptualised intersectionality (Crenshaw, 1989). Black feminist theorists have argued that eliminating intersecting oppressions is the *only* means by which women of color can be fully empowered (Collins, 2000: 36). In order to achieve this, the work of black feminist scholars includes analysis of the intersection between sex and race across the full panoply of issues that affect women's lives including, inter alia, family, work, sexuality, and reproductive rights (hooks, 1981; Collins, 2000).

Some of the early US self-declared third wave texts sought to use the idea of a new wave to challenge the dominance of white feminism, making it all the more ironic when the initial association of the third wave of feminism with women of color had declined by the end of the 1990s (Henry, 2004). Whilst high-profile third wave feminists have specifically identified the influence of black feminism on the development of the third wave (see for instance Jennifer Baumgardner on bell hooks, 2012). Collections of essays written by women of color (see Moraga and Anzaldúa, 1984) were in evidence long before the publishing trend of edited confessional-style accounts in the US. From Rebecca Walker's edited collection onwards, all of the subsequent edited US feminist texts had at least one chapter dedicated to women of color.

Whilst women of color were certainly included within popular US third wave books, many of the texts lacked adequate examination of the distinction between the issues facing, say, African American women and Hispanic women. Hernández and Rehman's 2002 edited collection *Colonize This!* addressed this gap by providing a wide ranging and more nuanced reflection upon the specific power dynamics present within both society and the feminist movement. For instance, Lisa Weiner-Mahfouz considers the problems facing mixed-race feminists when calls are made at feminist gatherings to separate out into a white caucus and women of color caucus (2002: 34). Whilst Susan Muaddi Darraj critiques the 'universality of white feminism' (2002: 301), arguing that sufficient space is not afforded to other feminist visions especially within the confines of a women's studies programme that prioritises the 'canon' of feminist literature. Such a popular text stands out as a critical site for a less tokenistic approach to race and one that provides a platform for multivocality.

Whilst there is a strong history of black feminism within Britain, the popular feminist books that have been published in recent years have not included any written by or specifically directed at black or ethnic minority women. Although books that have garnered media attention have sought to highlight the specific problems facing non-white women in British society (Bates, 2014), the absence of black and minority ethnic women's voices is telling. Whilst some authors have tried to include sections that address women from outside of the west, this again has shades of tokenism (Banyard, 2010; Redfern and Aune, 2010). Thus, whilst issues concerning women of color have, to a variable degree, been mainstreamed within US popular texts on feminism, they tend to be absent from British popular books.

Of course, one could argue that race and the specific historical legacy of slavery is such that US feminists would be more aware of the need to address the issue; however, Britain also has its own particular history when it comes to race, immigration, and the legacy of empire. It would be incorrect to suggest that there were no active black women's groups in Britain; therefore, the high-profile feminist campaigners that typically produce popular books are self-evidently a narrow demographic that is unreflective of the feminist movement in Britain. The relative absence of black feminist women in the British media and as producers of popular texts on feminism is underscored by the proclivity of broadcasters to invite black and ethnic minority (BME) women to comment only on issues that specifically affect black women, such as the wearing of the veil or female genital mutilation (FGM).

At feminist conferences it is typical to find breakout sessions for black feminists, moreover the current prominence of FGM as a feminist issue has meant that a more ethnically diverse set of voices are being heard on the main platforms. Within the US there exist a number of women's organisations and groups set up specifically to lobby, organise, and advocate for women of color, for instance the Black Women's

Health Imperative, National Asian-Pacific American Women's Organization, and National Congress of Black Women (although note that not all of these identify as feminist). Likewise, in Britain there are a number of women's groups dedicated to BME women (see for instance the Iranian and Kurdish Women's Rights Organisation, Muslim Women's Network UK, and Southall Black Sisters).

National and local feminist organisations are aware of the need to, as one interviewee put it, 'look less white'. Interviews undertaken with those working for or heading up major national feminist organisations revealed the importance of thinking about race and ethnicity when considering future projects or campaigns:

> We think carefully about ensuring we aren't just campaigning for white middle-class women. We want to think about how particular groups of women are affected and a focus on the rights of ethnic minority women is really important to us.
>
> (London)

> Of course, feminism has to be inclusive of all women and we really pride ourselves on being committed to ensuring that women of color are at the forefront of our work and are in key leadership roles.
>
> (Washington DC)

Indeed, the 2014 US National Organization for Women (NOW) annual conference, entitled 'Faces of Feminism: Strength in Diversity', hosted sessions devoted to 'marriage equality within and beyond communities of color' and 'women of color in academia'.[2] However, there are still those who perceive the leading feminist and women's organisations to be too white. In particular, black feminists I interviewed in the US were dubious of how successful the 'mainstreaming' of their concerns into wider feminist groups had been, as one interviewee noted: 'well those major groups based in Washington, I'm not sure they really speak to a properly diverse agenda. They're interested in advancing equality for rich white women as far as I can tell.' So, for this interviewee at least, there was a need to maintain women of color caucuses and campaign groups in order to champion specific issues but also to provide opportunities for women of color to determine the agenda.

Interviews with feminists involved with local groups across the US and Britain, save for those specifically established to advocate for black women or women of color, nearly all identified the need to do more to encourage greater racial diversity:

> You go to a feminist book group and it's all white. It's a bit embarrassing considering how diverse the city is.
>
> (London)

> Sometimes you can be at a meeting and you look up on the stage and there are all these white women talking and no women of color on the platform. It's not always clear that they've actually tried to get a woman of color to speak.
>
> (Portland)

For some, the lack of racial diversity was due to the types of activities being pursued, whilst others were not confident that much had been done to improve inclusivity. The 'public face' of feminism in the US and Britain remains overwhelmingly white, indeed the hostility directed towards Beyoncé, from other feminists, when she identified as feminist made many women of color suspect racial bias (see the feature that *Ms. Magazine* ran on Beyoncé's 'Fierce Feminism', Spring 2013). Writing on her blog, one black woman wrote about how she in fact no longer identified as a feminist because of latent racism within the movement.[3]

Of course, cultural and religious sensitivities often complicate discussions regarding gender and race; not least when read through a multicultural lens that champions cultural diversity. Whilst feminists have been critical of multiculturalism, seeing it as a means by which to overlook or tolerate discrimination against women within religious frameworks (Okin, 1999), the principles at the heart of multiculturalism are concerned with the protection of identity rights, something that is also of importance to feminism (Young, 1990). In charting the development of multiculturalism as a public discourse, Anne Phillips has argued that issues of gender (e.g. FGM, forced marriages, and the wearing of the veil) have come to dominate critiques of multiculturalism, but that these critiques are not often deployed by feminists themselves but rather by western institutions who have used the idea of the oppressed non-western woman as a means by which to advance a slew of unrelated policy goals (Phillips, 2010). And it is certainly the case that the emphasis on gender equality in the foreign policies of western states is not reflected in actual levels of support given to minority women (Phillips, 2010: 3).

For feminists, many of whom are keen to avoid 'othering' non-western women, this has led to ideological uncertainty with regards to specific issues, the wearing of the veil being chief amongst those. Whilst women who wear the veil have argued passionately that they themselves have freely made that choice, there are others who see it as symbolic of the various ways in which religion dictates how a woman should be seen and behave in public (Read and Bartkowski, 2000). This tension means that, as an issue, it rarely features at feminist conferences or in feminist magazines.[4] It is not obvious where or how feminists should position themselves on matters such as the wearing of the veil, with discourses of choice and religious freedom competing with claims of oppression and subjugation. Indeed, feminists critiquing the veil or the hijab run the risk of being accused of cultural insensitivity or of neo-colonial tendencies. Martha Nussbaum has argued that feminists should not allow the fear of being charged with 'do-gooder colonialism' prevent them from seeking to analyse critically the structural and cultural ways in which women face oppression (1998: 32). However, there are legitimate concerns for feminists when gender equality and women's rights are used as a Trojan horse by which to pursue specific foreign policy objectives or to attack Islam (Phillips, 2010: 42).

Feminist consensus can perhaps be found on the issue of FGM, which is illegal in most countries. FGM as a feminist issue has gained significant traction in recent years in Britain and the US, with leading campaigners such as Nimko Ali and Jaha Dukureh taking on leadership roles within the movement and gaining significant media attention. Indeed, the issue of FGM has risen in the collective western feminist consciousness over the past few years, with several high-profile campaigners and campaigns seeking to ban the practice. Moreover, the campaigns around the issue of FGM are operating at a transnational level.[5] Despite the legal clarity on the issue, there are still those who accuse western feminists of hypocrisy, given that cosmetic surgery is not (widely) seen as mutilation (Boddy, 1998: 105–106). This returns us to the difficulties for feminists in negotiating not only racial but also ethnic and religious inclusion.

Awareness of the ideological and symbolic need for the feminist movement to look less white is in evidence on both sides of the Atlantic; however, the extent to which this translates into significant change is less clear. Given the political importance ascribed to intersectionality, one would assume a greater racial diversity in feminist activism. Whilst there are undeniably strong and influential feminist groups dedicated to advocating on behalf of women of color, this has not necessarily led to high-profile leadership positions or to the full inclusion of black women within the feminist movement. As one young black woman I interviewed in London put it: 'I go to things and look around me and if all the women are white, it just feels like nothing's moved on and we talk about intersectionality in theory but not in practice.'

Trans

Whilst there is a long and established history of the role of black women in feminist activism and the failure of the wider movement to address its own racism adequately, trans issues are a comparatively recent part of the inclusion debate. The extent to which trans issues should play a more central role in feminist activism is contested, specifically in online fora. Whilst the following chapter explores the debates surrounding women-born-women-only organising, this section evaluates the role of trans issues within feminist writing and activism. Books written during the second wave of feminism warned of the 'dangers' posed by the trans agenda to feminism (most notably Raymond, 1979), whilst leading second wave feminists were on the record disputing the very idea of transgenderism. However, it was not until relatively recently that feminist attention returned to the issue. Despite the 'T' in LGBT (lesbian, gay, bisexual, and transgender) coming into common usage in the 1990s, it took a while for the trans agenda to permeate the collective feminist consciousness.

The rise of interest in trans issues can clearly be linked with the turn towards queer politics, which has sought to complicate the assumed a priori links between sex, gender, and sexuality (Marinucci, 2010). Within the Academy, significant contributions from post-structuralist theorists, who identified both sex and gender as a fluid artifice (Butler, 1993), influenced many feminist activists to reject the idea that sex is a fixed identity any more than gender is (Dicker and Piepmeier, 2003). Even so, whilst transfeminism has long been a preoccupation of gender scholars (Hines, 2005: 57), it is only relatively recently that transgender issues have figured prominently in feminist debates. The widespread acceptance of sex and gender as unstable categories led some to argue that trans issues were a constituent part of the feminist project; namely, the eventual breakdown of fixed gendered identities. Indeed queer politics provides an opportunity for individuals to imagine their lives beyond the 'paradigmatic markers of life experience' such as marriage, parenthood, and so on (Halberstam, 2005: 2). However, transfeminists themselves have sought to distance themselves from their perceived role as the vanguard of revolutionary gender pioneers (Serano, 2007), even whilst acknowledging that pre-determined categories of sex and gender are clearly inadequate.

For sure, not all those who are trans activists identify as feminist and the advancement of queer politics as both an intellectual discipline and as a recognisable political movement has helped to confirm the importance of transgender politics to the wider queer, if not feminist, movement (Marinucci, 2010). Concomitantly there are those who note the negative implications for lesbians who, already marginalised within a movement that celebrates gay masculinity, find their own particular interests sidelined (Jeffreys, 2003: 17). Moreover, the fear of perceived 'entryism' on the part of trans activists into the feminist movement compounds a sense of frustration that feminist issues, such as ending violence against women, become overlooked through the need for introspective debates on inclusivity. Both the in-fighting that comes about as a result of debates concerning inclusion and the idea that trans women's concerns are diametrically opposed to those of feminists have led some scholars to decry the emphasis placed upon trans issues by the feminist community (Jeffreys, 2014).

The ideological opposition to trans inclusion is based upon three interrelated arguments: first, that sex is a fixed category, one based upon biological reality and situated within a culture where female bodies are subjected to continual forms of violence (Jeffreys, 2014); second, trans men are seen as acquiring male privilege at the expense of embracing a lesbian identity (Hines, 2005: 58); and third, trans women are seen as reinforcing traditional notions of femininity (Raymond, 1979). Countering these claims, trans activists and their allies seek to stress the extent to which sex is a spectrum based on chromosomal and hormonal makeup, oftentimes citing the existence of intersex individuals as proof that not everyone is born into the male/female binary (Serano, 2007; Penny, 2014). There is typically less attention paid to the role of trans men within feminism, and indeed research has shown that they are less likely to adopt traditional notions of masculinity post-transition and continue to identify as feminist (Hines, 2005: 69). The final charge, of course, returns us to whether or not femininity and feminism are incompatible; in short, whether what one looks like precludes one from embracing a political identity. Research has noted the extent to which the medical profession typically requires those wishing to transition to perform an exaggerated version of femininity in order to be approved for surgery (Butler, 2004: 71), thereby making the negotiations between a feminine and feminist identity particularly problematic.

The third wave of feminism has been more welcoming for trans activists than the second wave has (Hines, 2005: 73), although many of the early US third wave collections published from the mid-1990s onwards did not include any reference to or analysis of trans issues (Findlen, 1995; Walker, 1995; Heywood and Drake, 1997). Jennifer Baumgardner blames the absence of transgender issues from *ManifestA*

(2000) on her own privilege and entitlement: 'After years of working in feminism, I've had to rethink all of the assumptions I entered the movement believing. I'm ashamed I was once so bigoted with regard to transpeople, but I'm proud that I evolved – as feminists and feminism must – when faced with new information and new times' (2012 195–196). Whilst Jessica Valenti, in her foreword to the latest edition of *Full Frontal Feminism* (first published in 2002), acknowledges the 'glaring gap' of trans issues, arguing that when she wrote the book they were 'not seen as an integral part of feminism' (2007: 4). Both authors offer up a post hoc mea culpa of the exclusion of trans issues, reflecting on both privilege but also upon the changing dynamics of feminist priorities.

There were, however, a few US feminist books published from the mid-2000s onwards that addressed trans issues. For instance Dicker and Piepmeier's edited collection of essays included Emi Koyama's 'Transfeminist Manifesto', which called for more trans women to align themselves to transfeminism, an ideology which argues that both gender and sex are socially constructed and the distinctions remain because they are a 'matter of convenience' (2003: 249). Whilst Labaton and Lundy Martin's book included a chapter exploring how the US legal system negotiates the transgender label (Kirkland, 2004). These examples notwithstanding, trans issues have remained largely absent from popular feminist books on sex and gender, even whilst they have recently dominated online feminist discussions. It is not just the absence that is noteworthy; trans feminists have observed how 'antagonistic' some feminists have been to the experiences of transsexual women (Serano, 2007: 4).

There has also been relatively little attention paid to trans issues in British popular texts until recently (Bates, 2014; Penny, 2014). Indeed, scholars have noted that trans activists found a more welcoming home in the US than in Britain (Hines, 2005). Again perhaps the lack of attention paid to the issue by British writers and campaigners can be attributed to the comparatively later emergence and awareness of intersectionality. Moreover, it is certainly true that prior to the re-emergence of feminist activism in Britain from the 2000s onwards, the dominant approaches tended to be those of liberal feminists seeking to advance women's rights within public institutions and radical feminists who were, perhaps, less likely to be interested in taking up the cause of trans issues. It is largely due to the explosion of online feminism as a space for dialogue and campaigning that greater awareness of trans issues and the various attendant discourses have received wider attention in British feminist circles.

The fieldwork undertaken for this research included a number of interviews with transfeminists, all of whom identified as women. In discussing the extent to which they felt included within the movement, it was clear that it was partly contingent upon the forms of activism that they were keen to get involved in:

> I would say that most of my feminism comes about through online discussions where there are other transfeminists to engage with. It was hard at first going to actual meetings and events and worrying about whether or not I would be accepted.
>
> (Portland)

> My experiences have been almost totally positive; the other feminists I've met and been involved in campaigns with have all been totally welcoming and it's just been brilliant. I was scared at first because I'd heard from some in the trans community that certain feminists were transphobic but I haven't personally experienced any prejudice at all but maybe that's just the things I choose to go to.
>
> (London)

For both of these feminists there was an initial fear of rejection and whilst this had not affected the second interviewee, the first felt 'more comfortable' (her words) online rather than through physically meeting and attending events. Some had discussed with others in the trans community, the 'problem', as one interviewee put it, of radical feminists who were thought to be openly hostile to trans activists. This reflects the predominantly online framing of the debate between those within the trans community and what they call TERFs, an issue we will return to in the following chapter. In fact, none of the transfeminists I interviewed had experienced individual-level hostility from other feminists, although they were aware that there were certain groups who they thought would not necessarily welcome them. Many thought that transphobia was limited to a small but vocal minority within the feminist community and was made more evident through events that sought explicitly to exclude trans women and through online discussions.

Attitudes amongst those interviewees who were not transgender were broadly positive regarding trans inclusion, with only a few expressing some reservation. Many made analogies with racial exclusion within the early feminist movement and highlighted that trans women were often particularly vulnerable to violence:

> I think it's vital that we're an inclusive movement and that we, in particular, make all women who identify as women welcome.
>
> (Bristol)

> It makes me feel really uncomfortable when I hear about transphobic comments from feminists, or outing women as trans women. That's really dangerous.
>
> (New York)

> I don't like the idea of excluding women; it smacks of the racism that women of color faced.
>
> (Washington DC)

For these interviewees, trans inclusivity should be a central part of a movement that seeks to fight on behalf of marginalised women. There was anger directed towards those feminists who sought openly to exclude trans women from engaging in feminism, which was considered not only counter-productive but also discriminatory. Conversely, there were a few that raised concerns about the extent to which issues of trans inclusion sat comfortably with feminist beliefs:

> Feminism is about overthrowing the patriarchy and resisting gender stereotyping – it's not always clear that those in the trans community agree with that position as they're invested in reinforcing gender.
>
> (London)

> You can't go to a meeting now or an event without someone asking about trans issues. It's like it's the new hot topic and no one wants to talk about rape or porn or prostitution anymore.
>
> (Portland)

Hence, for some feminists, notably those who identified as radical feminists, the very issue of trans inclusion is both politically problematic and acts as a distraction from the central issues that feminists 'should' be discussing.

In interviews undertaken with those involved with national organisations, they admitted that there was still room for improvement in terms of how they addressed trans issues. As one feminist from London indicated: 'we're really aware of the need for us to get up to speed with specific issues facing trans women'. Whilst in the US, an interviewee based in New York conceded that they had 'some way to go' to make sure that they were advocating for trans women. Recent popular books have sought to highlight the specific forms of discrimination and sexism faced by trans women (see for instance Bates, 2014: Chapter 9), although it is certainly true that at times, the inclusion of, or reference to, transgender issues can appear tokenistic at best. For instance, Armstrong and Rudúlph Wood in claiming make-up as feminist, argue that it has long worked for trans women as a form of self-expression (2013: 61). It is in homemade zines and on feminist websites where issues of trans inclusion have been most evident. There exists a wealth of zines exploring transfeminism, where individuals discuss everything from realising they did not identify with the sex or gender assigned at birth to the process of dating as a transgender woman who identifies as lesbian.[6] In the US, zines proved an early way in which trans voices could be heard, replicating the means by which young women were able to discuss their lives, political views, and feminism. Whilst websites such as *The F Word, Jezebel, Bitch, and Feminist Times* have regularly explored trans inclusion and promoted the idea of transfeminism.[7]

The debates surrounding trans inclusion speak to the much deeper question of who or what constitutes a woman. How a feminist might choose to answer this is contingent upon their own ideological strain within feminism and the extent to which they are convinced by post-structuralist and queer critiques of fixed sex and gender identities. The debate has led to several high-profile feminists who have long been active within the feminist movement being publicly denounced and attacked for critical comments made in the past, even when some, but not all, have sought to distance themselves from those remarks.[8] The protests and counter-protests that now regularly occur both online and offline are indicative of the extent to which those involved feel that the issue of trans inclusion has become a watershed issue for feminism.

Sexuality

The role that lesbians have played in both the creation and sustenance of the feminist movement on both sides of the Atlantic has been documented (Whittier, 1995; Jackson and Scott, 1996) even if not always widely acknowledged. Indeed, the history and attendant debates within the Women's Liberation Movement demonstrate the significance of lesbian feminists both to the production of feminist theory and also to the day-to-day organising and co-ordination of activities. Betty Friedan's infamous description of lesbians as the 'lavender menace' was widely rubbished by lesbian feminists who sought to highlight the limited and superficial level of Friedan's feminist politics and understanding of solidarity. At the same time, lesbian scholars sought to highlight the dangers of heterosexuality for women, arguing that lesbianism (or women-identified-women) offered the only true means by which to resist a patriarchy which sought to control female bodies and sexuality through the promotion of compulsory heterosexuality (Rich, 1980; Poirot, 2009). Such a claim has led conservative commentators to argue that lesbian feminism, and in particular the theory of compulsory heterosexuality, is anti-heterosexual, anti-sex, and ultimately responsible for the fact that young women feel alienated from feminism (Denfeld, 1996).

The fears raised by Friedan are reflected in anti-feminist rhetoric which presents feminist identity as both lesbian and man-hating. For some young women, the association of feminism with lesbianism has led them to reject feminism (Scharff, 2012). At the same time, and certainly not in response to the depiction of all feminists as lesbians, contemporary lesbian feminists are less likely to portray their lesbianism as a means by which to reject male–female power dynamics (Allen, 1990; Calhoun, 1994). Debates and discourses concerning sexuality have moved on. The role played by lesbians within the contemporary feminist movement is critical, although the move towards queer politics in the 1990s has not been wholly embraced by lesbian theorists who see it as an attempt to celebrate specific male gay cultural forms, such as camp and drag (Jeffreys, 1994). For such writers and activists there is a fear that the acceptance of queer politics by feminists will undermine the woman-focused nature of feminism. Thus, despite the fact that lesbian feminist theory and organising have played a pivotal role in shaping feminist praxis, there have long been disagreements within the movement about strategy and agenda.

The links between queer politics and third wave feminisms lie in a shared understanding of sexuality as a means by which to subvert traditional expectations of conventional gendered behaviour. Indeed, queer identities are not just restricted to sexuality (homosexuality, bisexuality, pansexuality, and so on) but instead are open to all who choose to embrace a queer vision of gender, sex, and sexuality (Lorber, 2010). It is certainly true that a more open and fluid interpretation of sexual identity is espoused in many third wave texts, with sexual freedom often trumpeted by self-identified third wavers as a fundamental right (Baumgardner and Richards, 2000). However, the celebration of femininity and accompanying female heterosexuality has been interpreted as a rejection of the perceived 'mandated lesbianism' of the second wave (Henry, 2004: 104). Projects to reclaim a specific 'girlie' form of feminism, one that is both stylish and sexy, ultimately reflects heteronormative neoliberal expectations (Groeneveld, 2009: 179; Munford, 2010: 195). Examples of third wave role models are provided in some popular texts, all of whom are deemed to embody a confident representation of heterosexuality, such as Madonna, Jennifer Lopez, and Courtney Love (Heywood and Drake, 1997; Finley and Reynolds Stringer, 2010). For writers such as Jeannine Delombard, the term 'femmenism' provides the conceptual link between third wave feminism and American lesbianism; something she defines as 'looking like a straight girl and living like a dyke' (1995: 21). This emphasis on femininity that crosses sexual identities will be nothing new for many active within the second wave. Indeed the lesbian debates over the butch/femme binary and the question of whether you can be a feminist and wear lipstick have been ongoing.

Whilst popular British feminist texts have placed less emphasis upon celebrating a traditional version of heterosexual femininity, the 'fashionability' of burlesque, pole dancing, and erotic performance has taken off in mainstream culture (Holland and Attwood, 2010; Moran, 2011). The majority of popular British feminist books have not necessarily sought to reclaim a specific girlie (and heteronormative) form of feminism and femininity, indeed, quite the opposite, as authors have demonstrated the damaging impact of the normalisation of the objectification of women (Banyard, 2010; Redfern and Aune, 2010; Walter, 2011). That said, they have not always addressed the intersection between sexism and homophobia. This is something picked up by Redfern and Aune who argue that failing to address heterosexism is 'worse than short-sighted' (2010: 65).

Within Britain and the US, there are several lesbian groups such as the Astrea National Lesbian Action Foundation and African Ancestral Lesbians United for Social Change in addition to groups that exist virtually. Whilst there is a tendency to associate lesbian feminism with radical feminism, it is clear that not all those prominent lesbian feminist scholars are considered radical in the traditional feminist sense. At feminist conferences there have tended to be sessions on sexuality, whilst the annual Dyke Marches have, at least, the potential to offer specific spaces for lesbian feminists. During the interviews undertaken for this fieldwork there was a sense on the part of some (British-based) feminists that popular feminism (or at least those feminists who regularly appeared in the pages of *The Guardian* or *The Huffington Post*) were more likely to be those who had no critical understanding of heteronormativity. That said, there was also a recognition of the fact that many prominent feminist scholars and journalists were openly out as lesbian.

None of the interviewees reported any incidences of homophobia within the feminist community and perhaps that is not so surprising. Whilst we may find evidence of some early and some later third wave US texts looking to promote a heteronormative model of femininity, this was not apparent in either the interviews, feminist discussions at events or within local or national feminist groups. However, as discussed in the previous section on trans inclusion, there are those who see the pursuance of the trans agenda as being anathema to the interests of lesbian feminists.

Class

Socialist feminist thought has, in its various guises, had a significant impact on feminist activism, most notably during the Women's Liberation Movement (Gimenez, 2000). Economic inequality has been and continues to be an entrenched condition in both Britain and the US. And a socialist feminist ideology that sought to demonstrate the inextricable link between patriarchy and capitalism had and continues to have widespread critical purchase (Hartmann, 1979). There were of course those who criticised socialism for its failure to adequately address issues of sex inequality, for instance Shulamith Firestone's influential *Dialectic of Sex* which sought to replace a classic materialist view of power and inequality with one based upon sex is perhaps the best known critique (1979). It is certainly true that there has traditionally been a greater attachment to socialist feminism in Britain than in the US (Rowbotham, 1997); whilst specific historic and cultural legacies have made British debates of social class more prominent and explicit, it would be inaccurate to suggest that US feminists have failed to name and subsequently address class as a feminist issue (Davis, 1982). Within academe, there have long been critical contributions made by socialist feminists and moreover, the neoliberal context has perhaps presaged a return to a more materialist feminism (Fraser, 2013).

The changing nature of employment patterns and the decline of industrial labour in the west have made offering a satisfactory definition of social class difficult. For the purposes of this analysis and within the context of a chapter exploring feminist inclusion, I am looking specifically at the inclusion of those who either identify, or can be labelled, as working class or as economically poor. The term 'class' is politically important when we consider issues of collective identity and of structural and cultural inequality. Adequately addressing issues of class within a broader feminist framework is not an easy feat to achieve, as Donna Haraway notes: 'It has seemed very rare for feminist theory to hold race, sex/gender, and class analytically together – all the best intentions, hues of the authors and remarks in prefaces notwithstanding' (1991: 129). Of these issues, class in particular appears to be a difficult element for feminists to grapple with, due at least in part to the difficulties of operationalising the term.

Whilst third wave texts have sought to identify diversity and inclusivity as a core part of the movement, scholars have argued that US third wavers are most closely related to an image of a white middle-class woman (Shugart, 2001: 155). Moreover, those who hold leadership positions within the movement tend to be university and college educated, something which, in the US in particular, those from poorer economic backgrounds struggle to finance (Herrnstein and Murray, 2010). The influence of such an education not only brings about individual benefits but can also play an important role in developing feminist consciousness. This is a point tacitly acknowledged by many writers who either note their privileged education (Penny, 2014) or discuss their time at college (Levy, 2005). Moreover, the provision of women's studies courses across US colleges and the vibrancy of campus feminist groups in both the US and Britain provide additional 'entry' points into the movement. If university and college do offer a way into feminism, then the class inequality in terms of attendance is important.

Third wave texts have varied in their willingness to address class inequality. Some have argued that the portrayal of the feminist movement as exclusively middle-class is part of the anti-feminist backlash (Finley and Reynolds Stringer, 2010). Others have discussed the ways in which class is inextricably linked to negative sexual stereotyping of women (Penny, 2011: 7). Whilst edited collections have included chapters from those seeking to highlight the specific challenges facing women working in low-paid jobs (Sidler, 1997) or the specific intersection between low-paid work and migration (Poo and Tang, 2004). The emphasis on class has not been as obvious as that on either race or on sexuality, although issues of class are frequently addressed in the writings of black feminists.

When it comes to including women from poorer economic backgrounds, many feminist groups that use a subscription-based model offer either free or reduced membership. Despite this, it is still very difficult to ensure that events, meetings, and conferences are made accessible for those who may struggle to attend for financial reasons.

One interviewee told me how their local group ensures that women who might not be able to afford childcare are encouraged to bring their children along and that they tried to meet in people's houses. Additionally, feminist conferences also offer reduced registration fees for those on low or no income. Whilst the shift towards online activism has opened up social movements and arguably made them more inclusive, there still remain issues of access, particularly for those living in poverty in the US and Britain. More broadly, there is also the concern that working-class women do not see feminism as being 'for them', but rather as a movement dominated by, and in the interests of, middle-class women.[9]

Feminist campaigning organisations specifically aimed at advocating on behalf of poorer women tended to die out during the 1970s and 1980s, such as the National Welfare Rights Organization, Wages for Housework, and Women against Pit Closures, the latter being a rare example of working-class women participating in high-profile political action (Lovenduski and Randall, 1993: 122). And whilst there still exist women's networks within trade unions, see for instance the Coalition of Labor Union Women in the US or Britain's Trade Union Congress (TUC) Women's Committee,[10] there are no groups whose sole focus is on issues affecting the poorest women in society, specifically low wages, poor working conditions, patchy childcare assistance, and a lack of access to healthcare and benefits; such an absence matters (Kornbluh, 1998). When the US government scrapped the Aid to Families with Dependent Children, there was a notable lack of protest from within the feminist community, which led some to suggest that welfare was not considered a 'feminist issue' despite the fact that many women rely on it (Nadasen, 2002: 270).

During this recent economic crisis, women have been disproportionately affected in the US and Britain; cuts in social expenditure and welfare reforms have a detrimental impact on the extent to which women can rely on the public sector for either stable employment or for sufficient welfare provision (Karamessini and Rubery, 2013: 4). The response to the cuts has mobilised grassroots groups to protest against such measures, whether through formal marches or through the organisation of specific national coalitions of women's groups resisting austerity.[11] At the national level, not all feminist groups have economic inequality listed as part of their aims, projects or work, although some do cite economic justice as part of their agenda:

> NOW advocates for wide range of economic justice issues affecting women, from the glass ceiling to the sticky floor of poverty. These

include welfare reform, livable wages, job discrimination, pay equity, housing, social security and pension reform.[12]

The specificity of NOW's approach to economic justice is telling, although they are in truth fairly liberal reforms. Likewise, the British Fawcett Society also cites the economy as a core issue. Indeed, following the 2010 budget cuts announced by the newly formed coalition government, which saw significant welfare cuts, Fawcett took to the courts to seek a judicial review of the government's seeming failure to account for gender in its proposals.[13]

During my interviews with activists, class was not always mentioned. In discussing issues of inclusivity or intersectionality, analyses of race, trans issues, and sexuality were more prominent than those concerning class specifically. This is not to suggest that the interviewees were not aware of the particular challenges facing poorer women but rather they chose to address those in other sections of the interview rather than in a discussion of inclusion. Issues of class came up for instance in discussions of women's political representation (Chapter 6) or in the various campaigns surrounding reproductive justice (Chapter 8). Where issues of economic inequality also came through very strongly was when interviewees discussed transnational campaigns. It is widely established that there are problems with the global exploitation of women workers (Groeneveld, 2009: 183) and this has been recognised by the activism of feminists through protests against western corporations such as UK Feminista's protest against Nike's exploitation of women workers.[14]

Whilst explicit discussions of class per se did not really feature in the interviews with feminists, there were references to austerity and to women's economic inequality. As Chapter 7 discusses, for many interviewees economic justice did not constitute one of their main priorities. Whilst there were those whom I interviewed who identified as socialist feminist, this did not mean that their feminism was necessarily focused on economic justice at the national level. Rather the effects of globalisation and a growing awareness of the poverty experienced by women in the developing world led some to pursue their interests in economic inequality through activism in international feminist campaigns.

Age

As noted in Chapter 1, the third wave of feminism is frequently associated with a younger generation of feminists and such a framing does have some purchase, even if the boundaries of what constitutes a young feminist are not altogether clear. It is clear that those who were not born or who were too young to have been active within the second wave of feminism have made significant contributions to this third wave, both in providing written accounts of feminism but also in terms of leadership roles within the movement. The influx of new activists somewhat inevitably creates a sense of tension with those still active feminists who were involved with the Women's Liberation Movement. Whilst many of the issues remain the same, violence against women, objectification, reproductive rights, and so on, the shift towards online activism has, at least partially, changed the dynamics of the movement. There has been some criticism of the younger generations' absorption of the neoliberal agenda, which has produced some fairly incoherent feminist interpretations of choice and empowerment (McRobbie, 2009: 66). However, it is clear from the analysis presented in chapters 1 and 3 that to reduce the movement to an individualistic strand within feminism is too simplistic. Moreover, debates amongst and between feminists show that that the acceptance of neoliberal values and pursuance of individual pleasure at the expense of collective solidarity is not simply a case of younger versus older feminists.

Some scholars have criticised the ways in which the early third wave texts sought to divide generations of feminist activists by a rather arbitrary age distinction (Henry, 2004). Indeed, influential US third wave anthologies repeatedly and explicitly make reference to who they understand the third wave to be: young and educated (Heywood and Drake, 1997; Baumgardner and Richards, 2000; Dicker and Piepmeier, 2003). For a movement and wave of feminism that purportedly had inclusivity at its core, the obvious attempt on the part of a younger generation of feminists to distinguish themselves from older feminists made little sense. Indeed, it is clear reading through the various popular feminist texts produced since the 1990s that there is virtually no space given to older women to discuss specific issues that affect them. There is no discussion, for instance, of bodily concerns such as the menopause, or of sexuality in older age, of widowhood, or of a western media that refuses to take older women seriously. Even when authors are not trying to explicitly appeal to younger women, little is done to include older women.

Nevertheless, the idea of making feminism appeal to young women is clearly a project worth pursuing if young women are reluctant to identify as feminist (Scharff, 2012). Additionally, there have been claims from some feminists that younger women's voices are often ignored

(Redfern and Aune, 2010). At the same time, there has been a visible increase in the number of active young feminists on both sides of the Atlantic in recent years. In the early third wave texts, there was a perceptible need to create roles for younger women within a movement that continued to be dominated, both intellectually and organisationally, by those who had been involved with the Women's Liberation Movement. In part, the drive towards promoting the voices of younger women came at the expense of older voices; this in a western culture that already marginalises older women. In the 2000s when much feminist campaigning and discussion moved online, older women's inclusion became a more pertinent issue.

Groups exist in Britain and the US specifically focused at older women including the Older Feminist Network (OFN) and the Veteran Feminists of America (VFA), respectively. Formed in 1982, the OFN meets in order to 'give voice to the concerns of older women which we felt were being ignored in feminist circles and in society generally'.[15] For those involved with the OFN, the need for separate spaces was important in order to ensure that issues that are of specific concern to older women are discussed. With a slightly different remit, the VFA seeks to preserve the legacy of the second wave feminist movement, with the intention of both celebrating its successes and in order to encourage younger generations of feminists.[16] Interviews with those who had been active within the Women's Liberation Movement highlighted that there was a feeling that the concerns of older feminists were often overlooked:

> I've been to a few of these recent feminist conferences and nowhere is there any discussion of aging; it's the one thing that will happen to us all and yet it's conspicuous by its absence.
>
> (Bristol)

> I'm not sure that there is much there in terms of analysis of older women, but you know I can't remember talking that much about it in the '70s when I was young!
>
> (New York)

There was agreement amongst the interviewees who had been active in the second wave about the lack of visibility for older women's concerns within the movement, and this was true in both the US and Britain. However, as the second quotation illustrates, this was perhaps nothing new. During the research for this project, I attended feminist events and conferences in Britain and the US and saw the diversity in terms of the ages of those present. Although there are plenty of younger women occupying leadership positions within the movement, there is still a significant amount of respect for those older feminists who had been involved in earlier struggles. This not only came through in the interviews but is also present in feminist books that frequently cite figures such as Gloria Steinam, Germaine Greer, or bell hooks as inspirational. Perhaps the challenge with inclusivity when it comes to feminist activism, therefore, is not so much in a desire on the part of a younger generation either to reinvent the wheel or to neglect feminist history; rather it is in the absence of conversations regarding those issues which specifically affect older women.

Disability

Although feminist disability scholarship is a burgeoning and critical field with transformative potential for both feminism and for disability studies (Garland-Thomson, 2005), this has yet to translate into the inclusion of disabled women within the wider movement. Issues that are of specific concern to women with disabilities are not mainstreamed within the movement and nor has the full inclusion of feminists with disabilities occurred yet. Writing in 2010, Redfern and Aune observed that full inclusion of feminists with disabilities had yet to be adequately addressed by the movement (215); four years on this remains the case. At the same time, women have felt marginalised and sidelined within the disability rights movement, which only serves to reinforce the sense of marginalisation experienced by women with disabilities, a point articulated by Begum: 'Disabled women have become perennial outsiders, our powerless position has not been seriously addressed by either the disability rights or the women's movement' (1992: 73). In short, exclusion on the grounds of either sex or disability is not only morally wrong but it also serves to highlight the particularly vulnerable position that disabled women occupy.

The discourse surrounding disability is at times complex and difficult to negotiate. The use of the term 'disability' is generally used to suggest a lack or deficiency, whilst it is also used by feminists as a means by which to describe women's condition in society. Both uses of the term are problematic given that disabled feminists seek to counter the representation of disability as a negative (Garland-Thomson, 2005: 1557). Disabled scholars have long advocated a social constructivist model of disability where disability is not individualised but is instead viewed as a form of social oppression (Begum, 1992: 72). Such a framework should be highly compatible with most feminist approaches that seek to emphasise the structural barriers to full equality and liberation. And yet disability as an issue is less readily taken up than sex, gender, and sexuality. Lamp and Cleigh argue that a failure to engage with such ideas in relation to disability has meant that feminists have not always sought to resist manifestations of contemporary eugenics in relation to disabled women and girls, such as forced hysterectomies (2011).

Gender and feminist scholars have been criticised for failing to take up the challenges posed by feminist disability studies (Piepmeier et al., 2014). The extent to which feminists, in their writing and in their activism, take for granted the idea that individuals and groups are without disabilities, either visible or invisible, has recently resulted in charges of ableism in the US or disablism in Britain. The difference in emphasis between US and British discourse on this is telling. With ableism, the charge is aimed at those without disabilities for ignoring the issues facing those with disabilities, whilst disablism is more akin to a form of discrimination such as sexism or racism, where people with disabilities are discriminated against. This suggests that in the US there is a greater emphasis on individual and collective societal failures to address issues affecting disabled people adequately, whilst in Britain it is framed more in legalistic terms. Recently however there has been a turn towards ableism within Britain, with the creation of the twitter hashtag #EverydayAbleism, taking inspiration from #EverydaySexism.

It is hard to find much mention of disability in many popular feminist books. Certainly it does not appear to be a feature of many of the collected editions; notable exceptions include an essay on the intersection of race, mental illness, poverty, and motherhood in Hernández and Rehman's collection (Brooks, 2002) and a chapter on disability as a feminist issue in Findlen's book (Green, 1995). The lack of critical attention paid to disability is striking when we consider comparisons with other forms of identity. The absence of disability as a feminist issue within a movement that has sought to prioritise inclusivity and intersectionality merely serves to underscore the extent to which women with disabilities are marginalised within feminism.

Various women's and feminist groups exist to support women with disabilities but perhaps the most active of these is the deaf women's community which has a range of support, networking and discussion groups, including the British-based Triangle and the US Deaf Women United.[17] Online spaces have provided an important site for feminists with disabilities to discuss issues that have a specific impact upon them and their feminism. The US site GimpGirl also provides a space for women with disabilities to meet virtually through weekly support meetings and they also regularly attend national conferences to raise awareness.[18] The now defunct website FWD (Feminists with Disabilities for a way forward), created an online community for those wanting to discuss issues of disability, feminism, and social justice.[19] FWD also demonstrated its commitment to accessibility for the website by describing images, transcribing text in images and providing audio content. Such issues of accessibility are typically not addressed at all on mainstream feminist websites. Whilst online sites for women with disabilities have been important, these very often rely on the contributions of one or two individuals and are prone to dormancy, unlike say the general feminist websites which do not take a specific interest in disability beyond posting the occasional article.

Whilst it is not now unusual to see people on the stage signing at feminist conferences or video captioning, this is not something that is universal for feminist events. Writing in 2009 about disabled feminism on the British feminist blog *The F Word,* Philippa Willitts argued that a lack of attention to inclusion was inexcusable:

> I appreciate that some groups have limited resources, or not much choice of venue, but seriously, if you are a feminist group and you are not meeting in an accessible place, what are you thinking? Would you meet somewhere that excluded other groups of women? Some kind of white-only venue?[20]

The charge that feminists have failed to take inclusion for those with disabilities seriously is particularly worrying. During the interviews, I asked those who were responsible for organising events at either the local or the national level how they addressed issues of inclusion. When it came to including feminists with disabilities, several interviewees mentioned wheelchair access or the importance of having signers. However, beyond physically ensuring that women with disabilities could attend, there was no real consideration of the extent to which specific issues or a feminist disability perspective had been included, even though the absence of women with disabilities from the platform is something that has long been considered a problem for the feminist movement (Green, 1995: 143).

Conclusion

Feminist approaches to inclusion are patchy when one compares the extent to which some groups and issues are represented and addressed. In part, this reflects either the strength or impact of a particular strand within feminism, such as black feminism, or the extent to which an issue, such as trans inclusion, dominates discussions of inclusion. For women with disabilities and working-class and economically poorer women there is still some way to go in terms of achieving a fully inclusive feminism. Although as previously acknowledged, inclusivity is not a proxy for intersectionality, evaluating the extent to which feminist activism has sought to prioritise issues of inclusivity is instructive as to the extent to which those issues that affect specific groups of women are made a constituent part of the feminist agenda. Of course, when one discusses inclusivity it is not just groups of women that need to be accounted for. The following chapter considers the relationship between the third wave and men through analysis of women-only organising. Additionally, the chapter also develops the themes explored in relation to trans inclusion through the exploration of women-born-women-only organising.

5
The Sisterhood: Inclusivity and Spaces

Sisterhood was a key feature of second wave feminism, providing a collective sense of unity and purpose but also demonstrating the solidarity of the feminist movement (Morgan, 1970). Sisterhood emphasises relationships between women that are horizontal instead of vertical, avoiding the hierarchy inherent in the mother/daughter trope, something that is also sometimes grafted onto the second/third wave distinction (Henry, 2004). Notions of sisterhood are more contested within the third wave because of an emphasis on intersectionality, which exposes the ongoing power dynamics amongst and between women, but also because of the extent to which men are viewed as critical to the feminist movement and to the wider goals of feminism. Hence, a rejection of the term 'sisterhood' is not simply rhetorical but also ideological. The emphasis on inclusivity within feminist praxis has created divisions within the feminist movement, in particular concerning the role of men and the trans community. This chapter explores these debates by mapping out and analysing women, and women-born-women-only activism. This will subsequently allow us to explore the extent to which a sisterhood is still possible or desirable. The chapter begins by providing a brief overview of sisterhood and its attendant problems, before considering the ways in which the term is used by feminist activists.

Sisterhood

Sisterhood was a leitmotif of the second wave; not only did it signify collectivism but it also signified the solidarity amongst women and amongst feminists in particular (Archer Mann and Huffman, 2005). Second wave feminists used the word 'sister' both as a term of endearment but also in recognition of the shared struggle against patriarchy. Sisterhood celebrates the close-knit bond that was in evidence in sections of the Women's Liberation Movement whilst simultaneously conveying a commonality amongst women. The term functions as a bonding mechanism with both an inclusionary and exclusionary sub-text: note the highly gendered nature of the term. To be a sister is to be female; thus to be a proper feminist is to be female. Hence, for some the term is essentialist and therefore problematic. This is compounded by charges of racism underpinning the idea of sisterhood. Indeed, sisterhood can be a dishonest label if it fails to acknowledge not only the heterogeneity amongst women but also the hierarchical structures amongst and between women (hooks, 1991). Indeed, hooks claims that the term is fundamentally flawed, because it emerged from women liberationists who did not acknowledge the extent to which women oppress other women (1991: 29). Such an analysis suggests that sisterhood is used to 'cover up' for the fact that many women oppress and exploit other women. These critiques, and in particular the charges of racism, are important and legitimate.

The term 'sisterhood' is now either historicised through its association with second wave feminism, or it is something that tends to be linked to radical feminist discourse and in particular with the focus on the category of woman. Such an embodied material discourse is not an approach advanced by all within the movement, not least those who wish to see the trope abandoned in favour of something more inclusive. The term 'sister' is frequently deployed with heavy sarcasm by sections of the anti-feminist press; keen to portray high-profile feminists as out of touch with their focus on 'wimmin's issues', it is frequently deployed against them by those who view the idea of female solidarity as outdated in this highly individualistic age.

For some feminists the idea of a sisterhood, based on a specific sex and gender, is highly problematic (Archer Mann and Huffman, 2005). Their unease is not just a reactionary response to the media, but speaks more broadly to their concerns about the exclusionary nature of the term and to their somewhat ambivalent ideas about collectivism. The key concerns with sisterhood are therefore threefold: first, some third wave popular books can often articulate highly individualistic ideas about agency and empowerment which do not sit easily with a notion of collective identity, although as the previous chapter argued, this is not representative of the wider movement; second, the term 'sister' suggests a commonality amongst women that is troubling to third wavers who seek to prioritise intersectionality; and lastly, sisterhood excludes men, whom many third wavers argue are key to feminist success. In order to explore these potential objections to sisterhood, the interviewees were asked for their thoughts on the term.

Some participants used the term 'sister' or 'sisterhood' before being asked, using it to highlight the importance of solidarity and of collective identity. Moreover, for some it was seen as a constituent part of creating and sustaining a group political identity. The interviewees used the term 'sisterhood' and 'sister' in a variety of ways that highlights the flexibility and adaptability of the idea:

> When I think of my sisters facing similar issues and fighting, it gives me strength.
>
> (New York)

> I think having a strong sisterhood is really important – locally and nationally and globally.
>
> (London)

> I may not always agree with the other feminist groups but you know they're not the problem, I don't hate them. They're my sisters.
>
> (Portland)

> Feminism needs a strong sense of sisterhood and solidarity.
>
> (Bristol)

Notions of sisterhood are not simply bound up with the language and discourse determining who constitutes a 'real' feminist. As the above quotations indicate, sisterhood speaks to broader debates concerning collectivism and solidarity as well as offering a means by which to bring feminists together regardless of ideological differences. Those who self-identified as radical feminist and those who had been involved with second wave feminism were more likely to use the term, although there were plenty of other interviewees, including those who identified with no ideological strand and as third wave, who also felt comfortable with it. If we accept that the feminist movement is, in large part, determined by a belief in the importance of collective action and includes a coalition of organisations, groups, and individuals, then the term 'sister' becomes all the more important as it stresses the commonality amongst and between a large and diverse group of activists committed to eradicating sexism.

The term was felt by some to have specific relevance for women of color. Indeed, some white interviewees, particularly in the US, felt that the term was more frequently used by women of color and it made them uncomfortable to be seen to be appropriating it:

> I don't use the term 'sister' personally; my African American girlfriends use it amongst themselves but I think I might feel a bit uncomfortable using it.
>
> (New York)

> I guess you see it more commonly amongst women of color rather than as a generic term for other feminists.
>
> (Portland)

That these feminists perceive it to be a term more widely used by women of color is interesting, not least when we consider the critiques made by hooks in terms of its use amongst feminists. This is not something that was not raised by the British interviewees. The participants I interviewed who identified as black feminists in both Britain and the US were positive about the use of the term, noting its importance as a means by which to connect women.

There were also some who felt less comfortable with what the term 'sisterhood' represented. They tended to be amongst the youngest interviewees. Their views on the term 'sisterhood' largely revolved around it being 'old fashioned', too 'second wave', and a 'bit exclusive':

> Oh no I'd never use the term 'sisterhood', it's really old fashioned. I'd be a bit embarrassed to be honest.
>
> (London)

> For me it's a bit second wave. You know it's not really how I think about my feminism.
>
> (Portland)

> I don't have a problem with anyone else using the term 'sisterhood', although I find it a bit problematic in terms of who's not being included.
>
> (Washington DC)

For some, sisterhood was symbolic of feminist history; a discourse and approach that was no longer fit for purpose. As the interviewee from London observed, she would be embarrassed to use a term that, at least to her mind, no longer had any significant purchase. Some interviewees had not really given the label much thought and it was clear that it did not form part of their feminist vocabulary. Amongst the men that

I interviewed there was a noticeable reluctance to criticise its use. This was not only because they appeared to be reluctant to critique it as a signifier of the second wave but also because they themselves did not feel it was appropriate for men to dictate the terms used by women, as one interviewee articulated:

> I'm always a bit uncomfortable when I hear it used at a feminist event because it makes me feel like I shouldn't be there. But of course women should have the right to use the terms that they want to and I certainly wouldn't want to raise concerns about it.
>
> (New York)

Whilst some rejected the term outright or raised problems with it, at least two thirds were positive about what it implied and its importance for the movement. That so many were comfortable with the discourse and its attendant problems serves to underscore the symbolic value of the idea for feminists. There were no significant differences between attitudes towards the term in the US and in Britain – the differences tended to be generational and ideological: younger feminists were least likely to be comfortable using the term whilst those older feminists who had been active within the second wave were most comfortable; and those identifying as radical, black, or socialist feminists were also comfortable with the term when compared with those who had identified with queer feminism or with no particular ideological strain.

That sisterhood is still a useful trope for feminists is evident when we consider that a number of groups include the term 'sister' in their title, for instance Southall Black Sisters (a London-based black feminist group), Sister Song (a US-based women of color reproductive justice group), Shoreditch Sisters Women's Institute (WI; an East London branch of the national WI), and Sisters of Resistance (an online, radical queer feminist site). In addition, various zines and blogs also frequently refer to sister or the sisterhood. The focus on women that accompanies the idea of sisterhood is clear. That so many of the interviewees were happy with the use of the term raises questions in terms of inclusivity and of the role of men in feminism, a subject to which the chapter now turns.

Men and feminism

Much has been written about the role of men in feminism (Digby, 1998); indeed, whilst long rehearsed, the debates surrounding the relationship between men and feminism and the extent to which men can and should play a role in feminist activism remain contested. The shift in focus from sex-specific policies that sought to advance women's interests has widely been replaced with the more neutral discourse of gender equality (Squires, 1999). The move away from focusing on women per se towards a focus on equality between the sexes has necessarily changed the extent to which men are implicated, and invested, in debates of equality, at least on a rhetorical level. For men, ontological identification as feminist is neither easy nor straightforward: cultural expectations and historical precedent means that the process is fraught with difficulties (Kimmel, 1998). For men who choose to assume the feminist mantle there are additional complications beyond potential hostile reactions from friends and family; there is also the reaction of female feminists which may not always be positive. Whilst many of the interviewees felt that men could identify as feminist, this was not straightforward. Although some suggested that such a question was a thing of the past, others noted how frustrating it was when men 'became' feminists and tried to dominate the movement. This latter point was made more forcefully by British rather than US interviewees. And it has also been the subject of critical attention in Britain, recently featuring in *The Guardian* and also on the *Feminist Times* website.[1]

The level to which men should be involved in feminist campaigning is a debate which addresses the strategic direction of the movement but also its aims and objectives (Kimmel, 1998; Schacht and Ewing, 2004; Kaufman and Kimmel, 2011). The desire to include men in feminism is something that has long become a key feature of popular feminist texts (Wolf, 1994; Redfern and Aune, 2010). Many of the interviewees discussed the importance of involving men, although to varying degrees and with the caveat that women should assume the leadership positions. The role of men was considered in two distinct ways: as feminist activists and as feminist allies. Around two thirds of the interviewees believed that it was vital for men to identify as feminist because gender affects both men and women and in order for change to come about men have to be involved:

> I think it's really important for men to identify as feminist and for us [feminists] to make them feel welcome.
>
> (London)

> Of course men can be feminist; it's a political position not a biological condition.
>
> (Portland)

This view was also (unsurprisingly) supported by the men interviewed for this research, although they did also note the importance of 'allowing women's voices to be heard', as one male feminist from New York put it. Moreover, several of the men had started up groups or campaigns of their own, focusing on issues around male sexuality and the harmful effects of pornography on men. This was considered to be important in order to explore the impact of gender upon men without dominating women's groups. Whilst some feminists talked about the importance of men engaging and participating, at least a third of the interviewees, and particularly those who identified as radical feminists, stressed the need for women's autonomous organising and preferred to frame men's engagement more in terms of being feminist allies:

> Look, everyone has men in their life. I have male friends. I just think there are ways that men can support the feminist movement in more of a backseat way and act as good feminist allies. I want to spend my time focusing on combating violence against women, not worrying whether or not men are feeling sufficiently included.
>
> (London)

> I think it's really crucial that men are feminist allies and that they seek to support us in the work that we do. We need them to be on board and think about the way their own behaviour feeds into patriarchal culture.
>
> (New York)

Thus, the issue of inclusion, specifically of men, can be viewed as an unnecessary distraction from the political goals of feminism (the issue of women-only spaces is returned to later on in this chapter). In discussing men's role as feminist allies, several interviewees highlighted the White Ribbon campaign; the campaign was set up in 1991 in response to the murder of 14 women at a college in Canada and has since spread around the world. The campaign website urges men to, 'Pledge never to comit (sic), condone or remain silent about violence against women.'[2] The campaign is decentralised and is driven by a need for a collective response to end violence against women (Kaufman, 2012); for several of the interviewees this was seen as an important way for men to be good feminist allies:

> I think things like the White Ribbon campaign shows how men can play an important part in feminism.
>
> (London)

> White Ribbon is a good example of men seeing there's a problem and actually trying to do something about it, to talk to other men about violence and rape, which I think is great and really powerful.
>
> (Washington DC)

Whilst there was widespread support amongst the interviewees for men to set up initiatives like the White Ribbon campaign, there was also a recognition from some that such campaigns tended to be paternalistic in nature, specifically in terms of the way in which men were called upon to be 'real men':

> If you rely on paternalistic masculinist stereotypes to try and sell your idea to this assumed audience of men I think it's quite patronising to men: stand up, be a man, are you man enough to stand up to domestic violence. [...] I think sometimes the messages are quite paternalistic and they fall back on this idea that might equals right. You know if you're bigger than someone else you just can't help using violence over them because you're naturally bigger but you should use that power to protect rather than to hurt. That's offensive to all concerned and they use macho narratives to attract young men.
>
> (Bristol)

To this feminist's mind, whilst campaigns can offer the potential to help men resist the hyper-masculinised culture, the White Ribbon campaign's use of phrases such as 'be a man' undermines the broader political point concerning essentialised notions of maleness and femaleness.

A feminism that focuses on the inclusion of men as part of its strategy necessarily provides a challenge to the woman-centred approach of radical feminism and also ultimately to the idea of sisterhood. To consider this tension further and to widen the exploration of essentialism within feminist activism, the chapter now turns to the issue of exclusive spaces, in particular those feminist spaces that are women only and women-born-women only.

Women (and women-born-only) activism

Traditionally, women-only organising has emphasised the need for spaces for women to talk and mobilise in the absence of men. In the words of feminist philosopher Marilyn Frye, 'woman-only meeting is a fundamental challenge to the structure of power. [...] When those who control access have made you totally accessible, your first acts of control must be denying access or must have denial of access as one of its aspects' (1983: 103). For many active within left wing politics during the 1960s and 1970s, there was frustration at the assumption that women were expected to be passive (Harne and Miller, 1996). This frustration led to calls for women-only spaces and women-only organising became a cornerstone of the Women's Liberation Movement (Crow, 2000). Indeed, if one of the intents of second wave feminism was to privilege the voices and experiences of women, then providing safe spaces for women to talk and share was vital. Women-only spaces, centres, conferences, and cultural groups (including reading groups and theatre companies) provided women with an opportunity to unite across the different strands of the Women's Liberation Movement. Although women-only organising occurred at both a formal and informal level, the best known were consciousness-raising (CR) groups.

CR was central to feminist activity in the US and Britain, where women would discuss preselected topics, each speaking in turn and drawing on their own personal experience (Gornick, 2000: 289). Even though the original idea for CR involved mixed groups, women quickly realised that it would be of more use to organise separately (Connell, 1987: 234). CR groups have been celebrated, particularly amongst radical feminists, as the most 'accessible introduction to the women's movement' (Gornick, 2000: 288). The idea of separatism as a strategy facilitated a greater understanding of the various ways in which oppression affected the individual and collective but also provided a safe space within which women could discuss those dual levels of oppression (Leathwood, 2004). Whilst for some they constituted a site where dialogue could be opened up across class and racial barriers (Phoenix, 2011: 60), for others they represented little more than privileged talking shops (Naples, 2011: 184). Moreover, despite the perception of CR groups as a useful way to cut across ideological divisions and to bring together a diverse range of women, research has also highlighted that the majority of those participating in the groups were white middle- to upper-class women who largely identified as liberal feminists (Kravetz, 1978).

The decline in feminist activism that occurred during the 1980s meant that most CR groups eventually disbanded. Furthermore, many of the women-only organisations that operated at both the national and local level were shut down (Whittier, 1995). With the third wave of feminism there has been no wholesale attempt to revive either women-only organising or the CR groups, even whilst some scholars have continued to highlight how women feel safer in women-only feminist gatherings.[3] Popular feminist books have not in general been supportive of women-only spaces, for instance British writer Natasha Walter observes that they provide a 'strong disincentive for men who might want to join in debates about equality' (1998: 147), and that this would be a perverse outcome for feminists given that men must be encouraged to embrace the roles that women want them to undertake (149). Similarly, US writer Jennifer Baumgardner has argued that women-only spaces are seen as anachronistic at best and harmful to feminism's desired goals at worst (2012).

Debates concerning women-born-women-only organising are relatively recent. Put simply, the logic behind excluding trans women is that they are not viewed as women and as such should not be able to access women-only spaces (Raymond, 1979; Jeffreys, 2003). Whilst campaigns surrounding trans inclusion have become more high profile in the past few years, the 'womyn born womyn' policy adopted by the Michigan Womyn's Music Festival has been the longest lasting site of contention regarding trans inclusion. The annual festival, established in 1976, sought to provide an opportunity to promote women's music and the coming together of women in a safe and feminist environment. Wider awareness of the policy came to light in the early 1990s when a trans woman was asked to leave the festival after refusing to confirm whether or not she was a transsexual. Since that time, the festival has maintained its entrance policy and its founder Lisa Vogel has remained committed to the entrance policy, noting in an interview:

> I feel very strongly that having a space for women, who are born women, to come together for a week, is a healthy, whole, loving space to provide for women who have that experience. To label that as transphobic is, to me, as misplaced as saying the women-of-color tent is racist, or to say that a transsexual-only space, a gathering of folks of women who are born men is misogynist.[4]

The festival constitutes one of the most high-profile and contentious debates concerning trans inclusion. It has resulted in a new camp, Camp Trans, which aims to bring together not just trans women but all transgender people and gender queer activists.[5]

Unlike debates surrounding women-only spaces, the decision to exclude those who identify as women stems from both the rejection of trans women as 'real' women and the corollary assumption that they are still men. Thus, women-born-women-only policies are driven first and foremost by a belief in women-only spaces; it does not, however, always follow that those who value the latter accept or champion the former. Indeed, the data discussed later on in this chapter demonstrates that this is not the case, with many supporters of women-only spaces rejecting women-born-women spaces. Support for trans participation is driven fundamentally by a desire to be inclusive, whilst also recognising the fluidity of sex and gender (Serano, 2007). Moreover, many feminists are uncomfortable with the idea of excluding a particularly vulnerable group (Bates, 2014; Penny, 2014).

Opposition to women-only and women-born-women-only organising has a number of different pressure points: *pragmatic* opposition, expressed by those who view expanding the movement as a necessary and vital strategy; *theoretical* opposition, influenced by queer theory and post-structuralism, with many who seek to overthrow, rather than reinforce the sex/gender binary; *generational* opposition, with younger women who had not been involved with women-only second wave organising less likely to view it as important or relevant and the assumption that younger men are more likely to want to engage with feminism; opposition based upon the assumption of *discrimination* through the exclusion of people based on their sex and gender; and an *economic* opposition, with national organisations seeking to raise funds from membership subscriptions whilst governments make cuts to women-only services. Given these pressures, one might have assumed there to be a backlash against women-only spaces per se; this chapter goes on to demonstrate that whilst there is no strong demand from feminist activists today for women-only spaces, this does not necessarily mean that they oppose them in principle. Conversely, there is little support for women-born-women-only spaces.

Mapping out women-only spaces[6]

Despite a move towards online forms of engagement, national interest groups and grassroots organisations still matter for political activism. For nationwide organisations that engage in formal activities such as lobbying and membership recruitment drives, the idea of stipulating a women-only policy makes little sense. For these larger organisations, it is critical to generate resources in order to support day-to-day activities, including the salaries of professional staff members. Hence, excluding men as potential fee-paying members cannot be defended on an economic basis, nor does it help to try actively to reduce the number of supporters a group can claim. Accordingly, even if there were ideological reasons for stipulating a women-only membership criteria, economic opposition would in all likelihood prevail. That said, there are two national women-only organisations in the US and Britain: the WI and Daughters of the American Revolution (DAR).

The WI constitution explicitly states that only women can be members, although it does permit men to attend conferences and training workshops.[7] Neither the WI website nor its associated literature offer a robust defence of the importance of women-only organising, rather it seeks to stress that historically the organisation was intended to be for women only; indeed it notes that the constitution could be amended in order to allow men to join. Founded in 1915, the WI was established in order to 'revitalise rural communities and encourage women to become more involved in producing food during the First World War'. The WI is currently the largest voluntary women's organisation in Britain and has 212,526 members.[8] Similarly there exists only one women-only organisation in the US, DAR. In order to be eligible for membership, applicants must be able to evidence 'direct lineal descent from a patriot of the American Revolution'.[9] Like the WI, the DAR is a historic institution (founded in 1890) with a sizeable membership (177,000); it is a non-profit, non-political volunteer women's service organisation whose aims include the promotion of patriotism, the preservation of American history and championing education standards.

Neither the WI nor DAR self-define as feminist organisations, indeed both are relatively conservative organisations. The exclusion of men stems, therefore, not from a belief in the importance of women-only organising as a means by which to empower women and overthrow the patriarchy, but rather as a means by which to reinforce appropriate roles and levels of engagement for women in public life. Indeed, it is worth reflecting upon the fact that where a women-only membership policy does exist, it tends to be in those organisations which are often antithetical to feminist campaigning, for instance religious groups or sororities. Thus despite the evident legacy of radical feminism in the third wave's focus on objectification and violence against women, the idea of separatism appears now, somewhat ironically, to be championed by more conservative women's groups in society.

Accordingly, the overwhelming majority of national women's and feminist organisations in the US and Britain are open to men, including NOW, the Feminist Majority Foundation and the Fawcett Society. More specifically, even those organisations which were *explicitly* established by and for women have an open membership policy, for instance the League of Women Voters changed its constitution in 1973 to allow men to join its chapters[10] and the National Council for Negro Women (NCNW) also allows men to join.[11] Whilst there are women's caucuses within the legislatures in the US and Britain, there are opportunities for men to join women's groups within political parties, see for instance the Liberal Democrat Women and local branches of the National Federation for Republican Women.[12] Reasons given by these various groups on their websites stress the importance of inclusivity and of the important role that men can play in their organisations.

Although women-only groups can be found at the local level, they are rare. Moreover, in the cities that form the case study analysis for this research, I found evidence of only two feminist groups that explicitly identified as women only, the London Feminist Network (LFN), a broadly radical feminist group and Radical Women Portland, a socialist feminist group. Whilst the Bristol Fawcett Society does not have a rule against men joining, its membership is exclusively female; all members are expected to be active participants who have to demonstrate a certain level of commitment in order to become approved as full members; so far no men have become full members. The LFN is a very active group: it holds regular meetings; runs a book group; and is responsible for organising events such as Reclaim the Night, the Feminism in London conference and the Stop Porn Culture group. The LFN has a very clear statement about its membership policy on its website:

> We are a women-only group because we believe it is vital that women have safe and supportive spaces where we can work together politically to campaign for our rights. We are the experts on our own lives and on what it is to be a woman, in all of our various identities, in a society where we do not have equal political representation, where we are disadvantaged and discriminated against simply because we are women. All too many of us know what it is to experience male violence, including rape, domestic violence, sexual abuse, pornography, prostitution, forced marriage, female genital mutilation and so-called 'honour' crimes.
>
> ('Why Women Only?' London Feminist Network)[13]

Whilst Radical Women, an autonomous women's organisation with links to the Freedom Socialist Party, argues that in order to facilitate women's and feminist voices, separate organising is critical.[14] The feminists I interviewed who were involved with LFN and Radical Women noted the importance of regular face-to-face meetings for women only, not least because with online activism there was the potential for men to join. Indeed, patterns of male domination on the Internet have led some to identify the reactive establishment of women-only groups (Herring et al., 1995). Several interviewees cited the women-only policy as a distinguishing strength of such groups, moreover it was offered as a reason why LFN has so many members (the website states that it currently has nearly 2,000 members).[15] More specifically, younger women in their early 20s who had no previous experience of women-only organising found it to be a refreshing and important way of discussing the impact of sexism at an individual, collective, and societal level, as one feminist articulated: 'I've never been in a woman-only space before, it feels really great to know that you all share something in common and that no one is going to judge you, especially when you're just trying to figure all this stuff out.' For this feminist then, the opportunities afforded to her through women-only organising were invaluable to the development of her feminist awareness.

I could find no evidence of women-only feminist groups in New York (despite it being the home to the pivotal New York Radical Feminists of the 1960s and 1970s).[16] Indeed, the Radical Feminist Activists of NYC states on its Meetup page that the group welcomes 'both women and men as well as transgender, gender queer, and all other gender identities'.[17] One-off women-only events however were more prevalent. For instance, the RadFem Reboot 2012 conference in Portland was billed as 'three days of women only space and rad fem utopia',[18] whilst the North East Feminist Gathering in Britain sought to highlight the diversity of the women attending to discuss feminist strategy.[19] Specific women's and feminist groups and caucuses run women-only panels at feminist conferences and discussion groups, for instance the Black Feminists runs a private black-women-only national discussion group in Britain.[20] Women-only organising can also be found in specific moments of activism. Take for instance the British Aldermaston Women's Peace Camp which campaigns against nuclear weaponry; women camp at the site on the second weekend of every month which has, since its inception in 1985, operated on a women-only basis (although male visitors are allowed during the day).[21] Or the annual Reclaim the Night (Britain) and Take back the Night marches (US), some of which continue to remain women-only despite regional versions of the march being opened to men (Mackay, 2015).

Views of the activists

At a recent conference in London on women-only spaces, speakers frequently articulated the idea that women-only organising was something vital that was missing from this current wave of feminist activism.[22]

For those who were currently involved with women-only organising, or those who had been active within second wave feminism, the value of such spaces was obvious. Indeed, interviewees spoke about wanting to feel safe in spaces without men present and of the empowering nature of a group of women working towards a common end:

> It feels such a relief being in a woman-only space talking about our experiences and working together. It would change completely if men were there.
>
> (London)

> Oh, I think it's a wonderful thing having women all sharing and helping each other, nothing feels quite like it.
>
> (Portland)

Many of those who I interviewed for this research, in particular those who had not been active in second wave feminism, had not been chosen to be part of a women-only group. Whilst many had participated in women-only campaigns and events, this was not a deliberate decision; simply, women tended to be more likely than men were to be involved in feminist activism. This was something several interviewees reflected upon, articulated best by an interviewee from Bristol: 'well sure you could have a policy saying this is women only but really what's the need for that when men don't turn up to get involved anyway?' For many there was simply no need to have a women-only policy because the reality was that men were less likely to participate. Therefore, despite the seeming lack of opportunities for women to organise autonomously, in reality, women-only organising was the norm for numerous feminists.

The absence of men, however, was something that interviewees felt should be addressed for both pragmatic and generational reasons; these views were particularly articulated by those who had identified as third wave and by liberal and queer feminists. Interviewees pointed to the need to expand the movement and to engage men in helping resist gender inequality in all its forms, a view echoed by the men I interviewed:

> We need to make it so men feel like they want to join in. We need as many people on board as possible and young men are really the key to changing things for the future.
>
> (New York)

> Oh, it can sometimes be a bit awkward and there are one or two women who clearly don't think I should be there but men are affected

> by sexism too, not to the same extent but unless we as men change, what hope is there?
>
> (London)

> I think young men really do want to be involved but they don't know how to engage. It can be a bit alienating for guys if they feel like they have to apologise for how women have been treated historically.
>
> (Washington DC)

These interviewees associated the expansion and development of the movement with the inclusion of younger men, many of whom were judged not to hold the same views as previous generations. Although the majority of the interviewees were not in favour of excluding men in toto, at least three quarters of the interviewees recognised that there were specific times when it would be appropriate to have women-only spaces:

> Well, I can see where in certain situations it would be more appropriate for women to meet separately but that should be specific to the issue that is under discussion not just a blanket rule.
>
> (London)

So for this feminist, the norm should be mixed organising but it was also acceptable to have women-only spaces where appropriate. In particular, issues of violence, rape, and body image were considered to be such sensitive topics that some felt it might put women off from opening up if men were present. Of the men I interviewed, all said they respected the right of women to organise autonomously. Therefore, the interviewees whilst broadly very positive about men being involved *also* recognised that in certain circumstances there was a need for women-only spaces.

Only a quarter of the interviewees (all women) were implacably opposed to (by design) women-only spaces; these interviewees were more likely to have identified as liberal and queer feminists. Their opposition was based on the fact that it was detrimental to the feminist movement and was discriminatory. They argued that it shut down debate between the sexes and made it harder to move things forward:

> I don't know why you want to exclude men from this. I mean men are part of the problem sure but they're also part of the solution. I wouldn't ever be involved in anything that deliberately excluded people based on their sex or gender.
>
> (New York)

> It seems a bit strange and old fashioned to insist on women-only spaces, men are affected by patriarchy and so their voices and views need to be heard. I don't know how it makes sense for us to talk about sex discrimination but then impose it when we want to.
>
> (Glasgow)

As the quotations above indicate, for some it appeared to be an outmoded way of campaigning that failed to recognise the importance of 'getting men on board'; opposition therefore being both pragmatic and theoretical.

Despite the appearance of a decline in women-only organising in terms of group type, it was clear that many interviewees had experienced women-only organising albeit often by default. Their experiences were positive, although many were still anxious to ensure that men were not excluded. For one-off events or for discussions surrounding specific issues there was broad support for the idea of women-only spaces; indeed, the support for women-only spaces reflected the extent to which these can be found in contemporary feminist activism. The chapter now turns to one of the most contentious issues associated with women-only organising: the exclusion of those who were not born female but identify as women.

Mapping out 'women-born-women' only

Whilst the data highlights that women-only organising can be found in one-off events and has broad support from feminist activists, the more controversial aspect has been related to trans inclusion, specifically instances where groups or events have operated a female-born-only or women-born-women-only policy. Indeed, this debate has generated much of the heat in the feminist blogosphere recently and also underpins much of the overt hostility towards radical feminism.[23] Ostensibly, the debate is dominated by trans activists and their allies on the one side and radical feminists, referred to as TERFs, who argue that transgender entryism into women-only spaces is harmful for feminism (Jeffreys, 2014: 55); although it is worth stressing the point that not all radical feminists believe in women-born-women-only spaces. The debate has, at least to some extent, become so highly charged that feminists have become increasingly careful about what they say about the issue of trans inclusion for fear of being labelled transphobic.

Whilst there are some fairly bitter and personalised attacks that occur online, there are no trans exclusionary groups (that exist offline) that operate in the US or in Britain; indeed LFN has several trans members.[24] Where trans exclusion occurs is in the organisation of specific events. The Michigan Festival, discussed above, is the best-known trans exclusionary event. In Britain, the debate concerning trans inclusion gained prominence in 2012 with the planned London RadFem conference for 'women born women living as women'.[25] The conference was billed as an event to organise for women's liberation, including workshops and keynote speeches from high-profile feminist scholars such as Gail Dines and Sheila Jeffreys. Outlining their motivation for the conference, the organisers noted:

> Many of us involved in radical feminist organising feel isolated, even within the wider feminist movement. In our experience, the need for an autonomous women's movement and the value of women-only organising are seldom recognised. Women-only spaces are either rare, non-existent or under siege. Radical feminism is often misrepresented and maligned. The trend towards post-modernism and queer theory have marginalised feminist critiques of patriarchy, and rendered lesbian feminism all but invisible.
>
> ('Why RadFem 2012')[26]

As the above statement indicates, part of the rationale for organising the conference was (at least in part) defensive. A defence of radical feminism and a defence of lesbian feminist interests in particular. The reference to post-modernism and queer theory highlights the unease with which these approaches are viewed by some radical feminist activists. Issues that affect trans women are elided with those advanced by gender queer activists; however, trans women are sometimes marginalised in trans activism just as lesbians can be marginalised in gay rights campaigns (Serano, 2007: 5). The response to the RadFem conference, specifically its entrance policy, was such that it united both trans activists and MRAs. In reaction to the acrimonious and high-profile dispute over the entrance policy, the central London venue (Conway Hall) eventually withdrew their support for the conference which had to be hosted elsewhere. On the popular *F Word* blog, one writer opposed to the policy argued that to exclude trans women was particularly egregious given the specific forms of marginalisation and violence that they face:

> Trans women suffer horrifying levels of violence, abuse and discrimination, fuelled not only by the fact that they are women, but by the

> refusal of the vast majority of the cis population to acknowledge and respect their identities. The organisers of RadFem2012 have actively chosen to align themselves with this majority, and in so doing are complicit in trans women's oppression. Radical? Feminism? I think not.[27]

Hence, for this feminist, the fact that trans women would be excluded ultimately undermined the idea that it could be a feminist event. To her mind at least, both inclusion and support for oppressed women should be central to feminist organising; through excluding trans women, the organisers effectively privileged one group of women over another much-abused group of women. RadFem is not an isolated incident, and a recent conference in Portland, where radical feminists sought to explain their position on women-born-women-only spaces, also lost its venue after trans activists lobbied management.[28]

Debates concerning Dyke Marches on both sides of the Atlantic have also resulted in acrimony with both radical feminists and trans activists counter-protesting against each other.[29] The debates over trans inclusion are framed as being between radical feminists and the feminist 'mainstream' and has become a totemic issue, dominating many of the recent online discussions concerning the future direction of feminism. Whilst this has been both distracting and divisive for feminism, at its root are fundamental questions concerning the definition of woman, inclusivity, and feminist priorities. For those who have sought to organise women-born-women-only events, there is both a degree of surprise and frustration at the way in which radical feminism is being portrayed and a reinforced commitment to defending the need for some exclusionary spaces. The elision of 'radical' with trans exclusionary feminism is also extremely unhelpful; not least because plenty of groups using the prefix 'radical' do not agree with the case for women-born-women-only spaces.

Views of the activists

The impact of debates surrounding RadFem in particular were far reaching, indeed during my interviews in New York, Portland, and Washington, feminist activists were keen to ask me about the conference and what was going on in British feminism. Portland's Radical Women (a socialist feminist group) had issued a statement on transphobia in response to the organisation of the conference, something that it considered to be due to the biological determinism of radical feminism.

Stating that (despite its name) unlike radical feminism, socialist feminism had always fought for trans women's rights:

> Radical Women has fought for trans people from the 1973 First West Coast Lesbian Conference to participating in the 2007 United ENDA movement that pushed for inclusion of trans people in the Employment Non-Discrimination Act (ENDA). Radical Women welcomes trans women as members and defends transpeople's right to respect within the queer movement as in society at large.[30]

Opposition to women-born-women-only spaces was conceived of as discriminatory by Radical Women and by a number of other interviewees who highlighted the irony that feminists should seek to engage in such discriminatory practices. Interviewees marshalled a range of arguments in opposition to trans exclusionary policies, including most explicitly a fluid understanding of sex and gender:

> Listen, if we believe de Beauvoir that one becomes a woman then that clearly includes all people. I don't need to know what operations or meds you take to be convinced you're a woman; if you tell me you're a woman then that's enough.
>
> (Portland)

> The whole point of feminism is to overthrow the gender binary. Why would we want to reinforce it with trans women and say you can't come in, you're not really a woman? It kind of undermines the whole thing.
>
> (Bristol)

Unlike women-only organising, the vast majority of interviewees did not think that there would be times at which it would be acceptable to exclude trans women from whole events or groups. The opposition to separate organising was theoretical, and furthermore was reinforced by a belief that it echoed discrimination within the feminist movement that women of color had long since highlighted.

Amongst the interviewees there were only several willing to advocate women-born-women-only spaces and it is certainly true that these interviewees all identified as radical feminist. However, not all of the self-identified radical feminists supported women-born-women-only spaces. The opposition to inclusion of trans women reflected much of the literature and the ideas of scholars such as Sheila Jeffreys:

> I think there are certain circumstances when it is appropriate for women-born-women to discuss things on their own and I think trans activists should accept that. Forcing their way into meetings or trying to get people vilified does not help their cause.
>
> (London)

> The problem comes when you have trans activists that essentially try and take over; they need to organise on their own and stop trying to infiltrate spaces for women.
>
> (New York)

For these feminists there was anger at the way in which both women-born-women policies were viewed but also at the subsequent hostility towards radical feminism. Underpinning this anger was also a sense of disappointment that so many feminists had been quick to portray radical feminists as hateful or discriminatory for wanting to have their own space.

Likewise, amongst the trans women I interviewed there was a sense of anger that they would be considered a threat, particularly given how vulnerable many within the trans community are to outside attacks, as one interviewee noted: 'I don't get it, feminism is supposed to be about liberating women so why would they want to keep certain kinds of women out; thankfully the feminists I work with aren't like that' (New York). On the other hand, one trans woman observed that she was happy for there to be women-born-women-only policies in place for specific events and discussions, and she was unhappy at the way in which radical feminists were being targeted: 'I think we in the trans community should accept that women-born-women do have a right to space, not for everything but for some things. We're doing ourselves no favours in the way we attack radical feminists' (London).

From the interview data, it would be difficult to argue that there was much support for women-born-women-only spaces; moreover, there was no real appetite for advocating for such spaces on a one-off basis. There was a feeling that the current debates over trans inclusion were extremely damaging for the movement and led many to argue that those who sought to exclude trans women were not real feminists.

Is a sisterhood still possible or desirable?

Within third wave feminisms, sisterhood has not proven to be as central a symbol or concept as for second wave feminisms. Part of this is to do with the ongoing contestations regarding essentialism and sex/gender identities. For feminist scholars, the (still) polarised yet intrinsically linked binary between essentialism and social construction has dominated feminist thought (Fuss, 1989). It is this tension that foreshadows debates concerning women-only and women-born-women-only organising, as it seeks to emphasise the importance of sex as a fixed category. The tensions within the debate are of course theoretical but they have practical implications when it comes to debates concerning inclusion. The resurgence of feminist activism has seen a reaction against the perceived exclusivity of second wave feminism (Dicker and Piepmeier, 2003; Redfern and Aune, 2010); this has led many feminists to embrace an intersectional agenda that requires a commitment to inclusivity (Evans and Chamberlain, 2014). The implications of this shift make it harder to operate a discourse that includes within it elements of exclusivity. The increasing popularity of online activism also makes the exclusion of certain groups much harder to achieve.

This means that the notion of sisterhood as espoused by prominent second wavers such as Robin Morgan appears to be of less value, even whilst the need for collectivism has never been greater. The conceptual impact of intersectionality, moreover, has meant that for some feminists, the idea of using the language of sisterhood does not present an honest reflection on power dynamics both within and external to the movement. A reimagined sisterhood that is inclusive of all strands of feminism (including those who reject as essentialist any emphasis on the category 'woman') is not easy to conceive of. Nor would it be clear what it was trying to achieve if not unity amongst feminists. The issue of trans inclusion perhaps presents less of an issue to the idea of sisterhood than inclusion of men, given that those who identify as women would be considered part of the sisterhood. It is clear that the term still has some purchase with feminist activists, not least because women undertake the majority of feminist campaigning and organising.

Conclusion

This chapter has highlighted that whilst women-only spaces may appear to be in decline, there are still opportunities for such activism and more broadly, that it has support amongst feminist activists, even if there is not much demand for it. Despite the high-profile and contentious nature of debates concerning women-born-women-only spaces, there were very few of these occurring; furthermore, there was little support for them amongst the interviewees – such support was to be found amongst the radical feminists. The support for women-only spaces was based on a desire to ensure that women had safe spaces to discuss specific issues and to ensure female leadership, whilst the opposition was driven by pragmatic, economic, generational concerns, and fears of discrimination. Conversely, the support for women-born-women-only spaces grew out of a rejection of the theoretical foundations of queer theory and in particular, the belief that sex is not a movable category. Opposition to women-born-women-only spaces was largely theoretical but underpinned by a desire to avoid discriminatory practices. Hence, the differences between the two discussions signal overlapping yet distinct debates. The book has so far considered issues of inclusivity and modes of activism within the feminist movement. The book now turns towards feminist attitudes towards, and engagement with, the state. In so doing, we consider the extent to which debates surrounding inclusion have shaped the interaction between the movement and formal political institutions.

Part III

6
Feminism and Women's Political Representation

That women remain under-represented in legislatures across the world is a fact readily acknowledged by popular texts on feminism (Wolf, 1994: 11; Banyard, 2010: 5; Bates, 2014: 48). As a feminist issue, it is usually framed as symptomatic of patriarchal power structures, typically appearing as part of a statistical list of gender inequalities (gender pay gap, number of women on executive boards, and so on); as such, it does not often feature as a *main* focus of popular feminist analysis. Although the number of elected women legislators in Westminster and Congress is low, it is not clear whether third wave feminist activists prioritise the issue as part of an overarching struggle to resist gender binaries. In part, this is because many within progressive social movements have viewed national legislatures as neoliberal institutions. Furthermore, it is not obvious how an intersectional approach can be applied to campaigns that essentially argue for an increase in the number of female bodies present. The first half of this chapter maps both the under-representation of women, and of groups of women, and explores feminist campaigns to increase the number of women elected. The second half of the chapter analyses the views of the interviewees towards the issue of women's political representation. The research finds that few of the interviewees were active or particularly interested in campaigns to increase women's representation; this stems both from disengagement with the formal political process and from a perception that such campaigns only serve to benefit white middle-class women.

The case for women's electoral presence

For many, the arguments in favour of increasing the number of women in an elected legislature are axiomatic; however, there remains a degree of hostility to the idea that we should be concerned about *who* our elected representatives are. Whilst some have argued that it matters more what representatives do (Pitkin, 1967: 90), others have sought to demonstrate that voters do not necessarily care about the sex of their representative (Cowley, 2013). Conversely, feminist scholars have marshalled a range of arguments to support the claim that the sex of our representatives matters: first, the symbolic value of women politicians is such that it will encourage other women to consider running for office; second, there are specific women's issues that men cannot adequately represent; third, women will likely engage in more consensual and cooperative styles of governance, thereby enhancing and improving the deliberative process; and lastly, it is simply unfair that women make up half the population yet are largely absent from positions of power (Young, 1990; Phillips, 1995).

That women politicians may have an important role to play in encouraging other women to run for office makes intuitive sense, although it would be difficult to prove the link between the two empirically. However, women often speak of the mentoring role played by senior women politicians (Childs, 2004; Swers, 2013), which suggests that their presence may have an influential role to play in helping determine whether or not women choose to run for office. The second and third arguments in favour of increasing women's representation, that there are specific issues that only women politicians can fully represent and the idea that women will 'do politics' differently, take us into contested debates that raise questions of essentialism and the differences between men and women. The literature exploring the extent to which women represent women's interests has found evidence of a link between the behaviour of women legislators and the pursuit of women's policy interests (Osborn, 2012; Swers, 2013); and feminist views of the links between descriptive representation (who should be present in a legislature) and substantive representation (the representation of women's interests) are considered in the following chapter.

The last argument that women should be present in legislatures as a matter of justice is perhaps the most persuasive claim in favour of increasing the number of women elected. Indeed, the strength of the argument is such that it led Iris Marion Young to argue in favour of positive discrimination as a necessary means by which to redress inherent gendered inequalities (1990). For Young, an approach to political representation solely based upon equality of opportunity, rather than equality of outcome, fails to recognise the significant structural and cultural barriers that face women when seeking out positions of power and influence. Therefore, it is only by discriminating *in women's favour* that we will see greater numbers of women in elected office (Young, 1990). Debates concerning positive discrimination or affirmative action are contentious on both sides of the Atlantic. Opponents of measures designed to *guarantee* women's representation, such as sex-based quotas, frequently cite supply-side factors, tokenism, or a drop in the quality of candidates when not selected from a full field; these factors are also mediated by party ideology and a commitment to women's issues more broadly (Childs and Evans, 2012: 743). Whilst those in favour of quotas are more likely to highlight the efficacy of the mechanism, emphasising how they can be part of a broader 'attempt to redress entrenched privilege' (Bacchi, 2006: 35).

Although the case for increasing women's descriptive representation is compelling, it is not without its problems. Many feminists are rightly critical of the role of the state and its failure to advance the interests of women in society adequately (MacKinnon, 1989); moreover, national legislatures are not always viewed as being particularly active sites of critical political engagement. Thus, campaigning for women's increased presence within such institutions, without the guarantee that they would even seek to advance women's interests, does not, at heart, address the multiple forms of oppression that effect women's lives. In addition to these critiques, one of the central problems with calls for increasing the aggregate number of women politicians is that diversity amongst women is not always addressed. When statistics regarding women's representation are presented, attention to *who* those women are does not always follow. Certainly specific axes of intersectionality have been addressed by scholars, most notably in the work exploring the representation of black women (Hardy-Fanta, 2011; Minta, 2012). But it is not altogether clear what an intersectional approach that can address the complex and varied matrices of oppression would look like. Before we explore the extent to which such concerns are reflected in the views of feminist activists, the chapter firstly sets out the current state of women's representation in the US and Britain.

Women's under-representation

The data on the number of women elected to Westminster and to the US Congress reveals a similar picture; Tables 6.1 and 6.2 highlight the paucity of women elected over the past 20 years.[1] Whilst 1992 may have been heralded as the Year of the Woman, it is clear that progress has been slow on both sides of the Atlantic. In both Britain and the US, women

Table 6.1 Number and percentage of women in the House of Commons, 1992–2010

Election year	Number of women	% of women
1992	60	9.2
1997	120	18.2
2001	118	17.9
2005	128	19.8
2010	147	22.0

Source: Ashe et al., 2010: 407. NB: Total number of MPs = 649, excludes the Speaker who runs as an independent and is not challenged by the major parties. Data for the House of Lords is not included as they are appointed rather than elected.

Table 6.2 Number and percentage of women in Congress, 1991–2013

Congress	Number of women	% of women	Congress	Number of women	% of women
102nd	32	5.9	108th	74	13.8
103rd	54	10.0	109th	82	15.3
104th	57	10.6	110th	88	16.4
105th	63	11.7	111th	90	16.8
106th	65	12.1	112th	90	16.8
107th	73	13.6	113th	99	18.5

Source: Centre for American Women in Politics.[2] NB: Total number of Congressmen and women = 535. Data does not include delegates from Guam or the Virgin Islands but does include Washington DC.

constitute roughly 51 per cent of the population; thus, there is an under-representation gap of around 29 per cent in Britain and 32 per cent in the US.

The aggregate data in Tables 6.1 and 6.2 obviously masks party differentials with regards to women's representation. As Table 6.3 illustrates, both the Democrats in the US and Labour in Britain are 'ahead' when it comes to both the number of women elected and also the percentage of women within their legislative party; there is roughly a gap of around 20 per cent between the parties of the left and right in both countries.

Beyond party differences, which on one level serve to reinforce the idea that leftist parties are more hospitable to women and women's issues, it is important to drill down into the figures in order also to explore the diversity of those women elected. Since the election of Hawaii Representative Patsy Mink in 1964, 51 women of color have

Table 6.3 Number of women elected by party

Party	US		UK*			
	Democrats	Republicans	Consv.	Lab	LD	Other
Number of women	76	23	48	86	7	6
% of women in party	30	8.2	15.7	33.4	12.5	19.3
Total	99		147			

*I am using 'UK' here as I have included data from the whole of the UK Parliament which includes Northern Ireland.

served in the US Congress and only two of these have been Senators: 32 African Americans, ten Latina and nine Asian-Pacific. Of the 51, just two have been elected on a Republican ticket (Ileana Ros-Lehtinen and Jaime Herrera).[3] There are currently 30 women of color serving in the 113th US Congress (30.3 per cent of all women legislators). Diane Abbot became the first black woman MP in 1987 and since then there have been just 12 BME women MPs. Currently there are ten BME women MPs (6.9 per cent of all women MPs): six British Asians, three African Caribbean, and one mixed race. Of those ten, eight are Labour MPs and two are Conservatives (Table 6.4).

There are serious methodological issues with attempting to count or measure sexuality and disability, given that these are not always

Table 6.4 Diversity of women currently serving in the US/UK legislatures

Country/ Party	Number of women	Number of women of color/ BME women	LGBT	Disabilities	Age (ave.)
US					
Democrat	76	28	2	1	61.5
Republican	23	2	0	0	54.3
Total	99	30	2	1	60.1
UK					
Labour	86	8	1	1	51.8
Conservative	48	2	1	0	49.2
L.Dem	7	0	0	0	50.2
Other	6	0	0	0	49.1
Total	147	10	2	1	50.8

reported or obvious. As such, the data in Table 6.4 *only* includes those who have openly identified as LGBT or disabled. To date, only two LGBT women have been elected to Congress (both Democrats) and only two have been returned to the House of Commons (one Labour and one Conservative). Although numbers of LGBT elected politicians are low across the board, women are also under-represented amongst that group, constituting two of the nine LGBT Congressmen and women. In Britain, parties do not release figures on the number of LGBT MPs (nor does the Parliamentary diversity unit collect this information); however, a BBC report claimed that there were around 22 LGBT MPs and women constitute just two of these.[4] There are no transgender politicians serving in either the House of Commons or Congress. Age is also a salient characteristic when we consider diversity of women. The youngest woman MP is 29 (Pamela Nash) and the oldest is 77 (Glenda Jackson), and the average age of women MPs in the House of Commons is 50.8; whilst in Congress, the current youngest woman is 32 (Tulsi Gabbard) and the oldest is 80 (Diane Feinstein), and the average age of women in the House of Representatives is 59.3 whilst it is 60.9 in the Senate.[5] There is one registered disabled woman member of the House of Commons (Anne Begg) and given the difficulty of monitoring disabilities, not least because of unseen disabilities, it is impossible to provide aggregate data or percentages.[6] In the US, Representative Tammy Duckworth (8th District Illinois) is the sole registered disabled woman in Congress.

The glaring omission from the above data is of course class. In terms of social class and economic conditions, it is hard to provide any meaningful measure; however, given the importance of money, particularly in US electoral races, it is perhaps relatively safe to assume that many come from more affluent backgrounds. In the British context where class has historically been of greater importance, there is no satisfactory way of getting a proper sense of the backgrounds of MPs; in part, this is to do with the complex and fluid nature of the class system but also because of the politics that accompanies an individual politician's claims to be of a specific class background (particularly important for some Labour candidates seeking selection and election in traditional working-class communities). Despite strict spending legislation to regulate the amount spent on elections in Britain, candidates do need sufficient economic resources to support themselves in the run up to an election where oftentimes they are expected to work full time on the campaign (candidates in target seats will often be selected as much as three years out from the next election).

The data discussed above indicates that the overwhelming majority of women politicians are white with an average age between 50 and 60; few have identified as LGBT, and even fewer are registered as disabled. Hence, the representativeness of women politicians does not reflect the diversity of women in either country. The fact that 'woman politician' appears to be coded as white, able-bodied, and heterosexual is problematic. Of course simply counting numbers of LGBT women or women of color present in a legislative chamber does not provide us with a full intersectional account of descriptive representation. If the very point of intersectionality is to consider the overlapping and multiple points of oppression, then counting numbers is insufficient; however, it can still act as a reliable indicator for assessing the extent to which diversity amongst and between women is visible in powerful places. This is particularly true when we consider the idea that ethnicity, sexuality, age, and disability necessarily intersect with gender when evaluating the various ways in which politicians substantively represent group interests. Although it is not clear how political scientists reconcile the need for diversity whilst trying to adopt such an intersectional lens.

Explaining women's under-representation

There are a number of interrelated factors that shape women's descriptive representation: political systems, candidate selection processes, and the extent to which women's groups are active in the area. This section explores these causes in order to both highlight the differences between the US and Britain but also to provide the political context within which feminists construct their attitudes towards women's representation and the extent to which they consider the issue to be a priority.

Political systems

At the legislative level, both the US and Britain use the first past the post electoral system (a simple majoritarian system of one member one district), which is assumed to be unfavourable to women candidates, it being the case that women traditionally lose out (at the point of selection or nomination) when there can only be one winner (Norris, 2004). Parties do not assume the same type of gatekeeping role in the US as they do in Britain; at first blush, this may indicate an easier route to candidate selection. However, the significant resources required to launch a nomination bid can be prohibitive for many women (Lawless and Fox, 2005), particularly as money and networks are more likely to be readily available to male aspirant candidates (Darcy et al., 1994). Extant research also demonstrates that women in the US are less likely to run for office because they are more likely to under-estimate their own abilities (Lawless and Fox, 2005). Whilst in Britain women are less likely to be selected by the party gatekeepers, at least in part because the role of politician is traditionally coded as male (Norris and Lovenduski, 1995; Lovenduski, 2005). Thus, the interaction between both supply- and demand-side factors creates and recreates a pattern of women's under-representation. Moreover, the power of incumbency in both the US and Britain is such that traditionally male-dominated institutions are slow to change. The various rules and processes in place for candidate selection shape women's chances of success. The role of political parties and the use of primaries in particular are important factors to consider when exploring the opportunities and barriers facing aspirant women candidates; these factors differ in the US and Britain.

Candidate selection

Despite a decline in vote share for the two main parties, MPs at Westminster are still overwhelmingly likely to be either Conservative or Labour, although at the time of writing the Liberal Democrats (the third largest party in Britain) are currently in coalition government with the Conservatives. In order to become an election candidate, aspirant MPs must first win their party's nomination through an internally run election. Traditionally, candidates are shortlisted by the local party and then selected by local party members following a nomination campaign. Recognising that women have long been under-represented across the political spectrum, the main parties have experimented with different selection processes in order to increase women's representation in addition to running equality training sessions for local selectors across the parties. Following internal party campaigns from women activists, the Labour Party introduced all-women shortlists (AWS) in order to guarantee the election of women MPs; this has been a successful strategy (Lovenduski, 2005). The Conservatives, who are less comfortable with the idea of sex-based quotas, have experimented with less prescriptive approaches to increasing diversity: the creation of an 'A' list of candidates including women and ethnic minorities, from which local associations were encouraged to select; and the use of primaries to open up the process of selection to all in the constituency. Neither of these have yielded the results that David Cameron had hoped for, although primaries have to date only been used in a few selections (Childs and Webb, 2011). For their part, the Liberal Democrats have rejected the use of quotas at the point of selection, although they use a sex-based quota at the point of shortlisting to avoid all-male shortlists, and have sought to place greater emphasis on equality training and promotion; this approach has yet to produce any tangible results (Evans, 2011). Thus, for women in Britain, the journey to elected office is mediated by 1) which party they choose to join and subsequently, 2) by the specific mechanisms that party chooses to adopt in order to increase its number of women MPs.

In the US, it is less about party mechanisms and processes and more about political opportunities and individual resources that help shape women's chances of winning their party's nomination. For aspirant candidates seeking to run for office at the national level, they face a range of different selection processes: open primary, where all registered voters can cast a ballot for the candidate regardless of their own party affiliation; closed primary, where only registered party members can vote; and the party caucus, where registered party voters meet to vote for the party candidate. These different options clearly allow for greater participation of those beyond the party; the use of the open primary in particular is markedly different to the British selection process which more closely resembles the closed primary (although as noted above the Conservatives have to date used the full open primary in a handful of seats). The literature on women's electoral fortunes in the US has identified a number of factors that significantly influence whether or not women choose to run in a primary, are successful in a primary and then get elected at the general election. These include whether or not the woman candidate is running as an incumbent, a challenger, or for an open seat (Welch and Studlar, 1996); candidates standing for re-election face a 95 per cent chance of being re-elected in the House and 84 per cent in the Senate, which leads to a very low rate of turnover (Ondercin and Welch, 2009: 595). The partisan context of the race also matters, with women faring better in Democrat districts (Darcy et al., 1994). Although research has shown that women candidates raise as much money as male candidates (Seltzer et al., 1997: 8), it is also true that incumbents raise more money than challengers do and that there are more male than female incumbents.

Campaigns to increase women's representation

Women's political representation is a key theme for national women's civil society organisations in the US and Britain as well as for long-established feminist media outlets such as *Ms Magazine* in the US and the daily Woman's Hour Radio programme in Britain (Farrell, 1998; BBC, 2006). The largest feminist organisations that seek to campaign on this issue include NOW, who has its own NOW Equality Political Action Committee (PAC) to help fund feminist candidates,[7] and in Britain, the Fawcett Society, which campaigns to improve opportunities for aspirant women candidates and seeks to lobby political parties to select more women. Of course, the approach to increasing women's descriptive representation differs in the US and Britain, not least because of the very different party and candidate selection processes. As discussed above, in Britain the provision for political parties to introduce sex-based quotas at the point of selection has only been undertaken by the Labour Party, whilst in the US, with the primary selection system and a strong incumbency bias, there are fewer opportunities for political parties to manipulate the process and outcome (Darcy et al., 1994). Therefore, in the US, the potential for external women's organisations (read those with sufficient funds to spend supporting specific candidates) to influence the number of women elected is more significant than in Britain, where the political parties keep a tighter control over the selection process. Whilst organisations like Fawcett lobby the political parties to take action with regards to selecting women in winnable seats, it is arguably more important to have internal women's groups pressurising from within.

Perhaps the most high-profile partisan women's group in the US that seeks to increase the number of women is Early Money Is Like Yeast's List (EMILY's List), which seeks to promote the election of pro-choice Democrat women.[8] On the contrary, the Republican equivalent, the Women in the Senate and House (WISH) List is neither as well known nor as powerful within its own party (Day and Hadley, 2002).[9] In addition to these groups, there are also specific leadership training programmes for women in the US run through non-partisan organisations such as the Center for American Women in Politics at Rutgers and Running Start which seeks to help mentor and train young women for political office.[10] More broadly there is also the Women's Campaign Fund, a non-partisan group set up in 1974 to provide research and funding into the issue.[11]

In Britain, the leading women's civil society organisation, the Fawcett Society, has a long and established interest in women's political participation; having been set up by one of the leading women's suffrage campaigners Millicent Garret Fawcett. Fawcett reports on the number of women selected and elected in UK general elections and in the wake of 2010, Fawcett launched the Counting Women In campaign to push for greater action concerning the issue of women's under-representation. The campaign is linked with other organisations who do not have a specific remit for addressing women's issues (such as the Hansard Society, a political research and education charity) in order to frame the issue as one of a 'democratic deficit'.[12] Fawcett neither has the funding nor the resources of its US equivalent (NOW), but operating in a smaller political system does mean that it has purchase with the main political parties (although questions have been asked about its closeness to the Labour Party).[13] Because of the difference in terms of the scale of money required, there are no British equivalents to either the WISH List or EMILY's List; instead, the impetus and training for women comes specifically from within the political parties, including the Centre for Women and Democracy (which has close ties to the Labour Party), Labour Women's Network, Fabian Women's Network, the Conservative group Women2Win, and the Liberal Democrat's recently formed Liberal Democrat Women (which was an amalgamation of Women Liberal Democrats and the Campaign for Gender Balance).

Leading women's civil society organisations who seek to campaign on the issue typically provide at least a nod to the importance of encouraging and empowering a diverse range of women to run for office. For instance the Fawcett Society's Women and Power campaign notes that the 'barriers are even greater for ethnic minority women and women from other marginalised groups such as women with disabilities, Lesbian, Bisexual and Transgender women and women from lower socio-economic backgrounds'.[14] Whilst Feminist Majority promotes 'non-discrimination on the basis of sex, race, sexual orientation, socio-economic status, religion, ethnicity, age, marital status, nation of origin, size or disability', offering a comparatively wider range of identity markers.[15] For both of these organisations, the explicit recognition of the importance of diversity is clear; however, it is less obvious the extent to which that translates into specific strategies, which were not highlighted on their websites. The chapter now turns to analysis of the interview data, exploring feminist views on political institutions and women's representation.

Feminist approaches to legislative politics

To contextualise the views of the activists on the issue of women's electoral presence, we must first establish their attitudes towards Congress and Parliament. Given longstanding critiques from radical feminists that such sites merely serve to advance men and male interests (Millett, 1970; Crow, 2000), it is worth reflecting on the extent to which those views are echoed in contemporary opinion. The US self-identified third wave literature does not really explore the scope of such spaces for feminist activists. Indeed, Baumgardner and Richards interpret traditional forms of political participation, such as contacting politicians, as encouraging 'passivity in the would-be activists' (2005: 13). Conversely, some British texts have noted the benefits of lobbying politicians, for instance the successful campaign led by Object to get lap-dancing clubs re-licensed as 'sexual entertainment venues', which means that local councils have greater control over the application and regulation of such sites (Banyard, 2010: 214).[16] In general, popular British feminist texts are much more likely to promote feminist engagement with formal political institutions, perhaps reflecting the tendency of US texts to be comprised of multi-authored individual accounts, but is also suggestive of a feminist movement that is more focused upon achieving legislative change.

During the interviews, participants were asked for their views on Parliament and Congress and whether they considered these as important sites for feminist engagement. For some, formal political institutions were viewed as the hollowing out of politics:

> Congress is hardly what I'd call political. It's all about money, in order to get there and stay there, and in terms of who and what you represent.
>
> (Portland)

> I suppose I don't really think of Parliament as being a particularly effective way of trying to overthrow patriarchy, which as a feminist is my ultimate goal.
>
> (London)

> I guess I see my feminism as being more grassroots-based; I'm more interested in bottom-up rather than top-down approaches.
>
> (New York)

For these feminists, the legislature is viewed as a site that dilutes the potential for transformative change: in short, they are a distraction from more radical forms of politics. Those who expressed these kinds of sentiments were as likely to have identified as third wave as those who rejected such a label and identified as radical feminist. Particular criticisms of Congress and Parliament were also made by those who identified as black feminists, with interviewees explicitly stating that they were more interested in grassroots activism rather than political lobbying.

Conversely, other feminists, specifically liberal feminists and those who were involved with national organisations, saw the potentially transformative nature of legislatures, hence the need for feminists to engage with them:

> Yeah, sure Congress has its problems but whilst we do our politics in this way, we have to make sure we advocate on behalf of women and we can only do that by engaging with the process.
>
> (Washington DC)

> I know it can feel a bit like tinkering around the edges but it is important to lobby MPs or to sign petitions because Parliament's where big decisions get made.
>
> (London)

So, despite problems with the political institutions, for these feminists the recognition of *realpolitik* trumped any ideological frustrations with the political institutions. In addition, several interviewees spoke about the need to contact city councillors, state-level representatives, and, in Glasgow, Members of the Scottish Parliament (MSPs). This was an approach stressed by interviewees in Glasgow, Bristol, and Portland, where distance from the national legislature made it appear remote.

> I've been to quite a few city council meetings; it's really important that we show up and have our voices heard in decisions that affect our community.
>
> (Portland)

> It's easier having the Scottish Parliament, it means we can work closely with MSPs on issues effecting women in Scotland.
>
> (Glasgow)

Whilst there were those who were willing to articulate a more positive approach to political institutions, many expressed scepticism, even whilst some of those did recognise the value in working through them as necessary sites for advocating feminist change. It was clear that there were interviewees who were not very interested in formal politics, whilst others critiqued the institutions as representative of the (male) elite. In sum, there was a widely expressed sense, amongst both US and British interviewees, that legislatures and formal political institutions do not provide an adequate site for the contestation of feminist politics.

Reflecting upon why this might be the case, we might look to the broader neoliberal context, not necessarily as an explanans, but in order to situate such sentiments. Disengagement from formal institutions of politics within a neoliberal context can take three forms: 1) a critical and reflective disengagement which posits Parliament as a hollowed out shell advancing neoliberal goals (for instance, the ideas espoused by the Occupy movement, which is a left critical active disengagement); 2) there are those who disengage because, in effect, they have absorbed neoliberal values which are also a rejection of politics, the idea that you should not get involved with the state (collective political activism is not important, hence a more individualistic disengagement); and 3) there exists a more, what we might call grassroots approach to feminist activism which sees collective action as a good thing but looks to focus more on bottom-up campaigning rather than a top-down statist approach to change.

All three sentiments were expressed by the interviewees, although individual feminist ideology mediated the extent to which the participants articulated such views. Those who identified as third wave and queer feminist were most likely to espouse views similar to the second form of disengagement. Whilst radical and black feminists were most likely to voice sentiments more in line with the third form of disengagement and socialist feminists the first. Of course, the three approaches should not be viewed as mutually exclusive and it is clear that a prioritisation of the third form of disengagement could be motivated by an attendant acceptance of the first. However, perhaps of most concern for those keen to see feminists actively engaging with the political sphere is the second form of disengagement, which not only reflects a tendency to reject engagement with the state, but is also imbued with a sense of atomisation. In a survey of UK feminist activists, Redfern and Aune's data reveals that only 7 per cent of respondents viewed politics, law, or government as one of their priorities (2010: 232); despite the breadth of this category, it is perhaps indicative, along with the interview data discussed above, of the fact that for many feminists the fight for gender equality lies elsewhere. However, when considering the need for legislative change in order to address more pressing feminist concerns, such as funding for rape prevention or prostitution laws, it is clear that the formal spheres of legislatures and executives are necessarily brought into the picture.

Views on women's descriptive representation

There has been (to my knowledge) no grassroots organising around the issue of women's political representation; such campaigns are usually directed through political parties, branches of national organisations (e.g. the Bristol Fawcett Society, Oregon's NOW), although an exception to this appears to be Bristol Women's Voice who is currently campaigning on the issue at a local level. Where there is activity around this issue, it tends to be led by the political parties themselves and in particular, by those within political parties who have long campaigned on the issue. If the broader neoliberal context can, at least in part, help situate feminist responses to national legislatures, it is intersectionality that can help us explore why increasing women's presence in national legislatures is an aspect of feminist campaigning that does not appear to spark the interest of many feminist activists. The subject is notable by its absence in many of the popular feminist texts published in the US and Britain. When campaigns call for an increase in women politicians, those who wish to apply an intersectional lens to their feminism will want to ask further, *which* women? Although it is certainly true that campaigns for increasing women's representation do not argue solely for increasing the presence of white heterosexual women, it is nevertheless true that they are more likely to be the ones who end up in office. Such issues, along with a lack of critical engagement with the formal political sphere, can help us understand why the issue is not prioritised by activists.

If opportunities to actively campaign on the issue of women's representation outside of the formal party structure are somewhat limited, then it may come as no surprise that feminist activists themselves have not shown as much appetite for engaging with the issue. The strong association between liberal feminism and electoral and partisan politics is also perhaps an explanation for why more grassroots activists are not engaged with the issue, at least amongst the participants I interviewed for this research. Moreover, it also highlights a problem for those organisations who are promoting the issue in terms of soliciting the support of feminist activists. Although previous research has observed that the US women's movement places a high priority on electoral and partisan politics (Young, 2000: 27), this is not necessarily true for feminist activists beyond those involved with the major women's organisations. When asked about women's representation, many of the interviewees in both the US and Britain noted that it was important but not necessarily a high priority:

> Yeah, it's important to mobilise on this. Representation is important, but it's just not my priority, I'm more interested in helping women directly.
>
> (Portland)

> I am interested in getting more women MPs, I think it's really important for there to be more women in Westminster, I suppose it's just not my number one concern, I mean I'm not a member of a political party myself so I suppose I don't feel there's an obvious way to be involved.
>
> (Glasgow)

The sentiments expressed in the above quotations were fairly reflective of the responses of other feminists interviewed, although it is worth noting that the majority of those who could be identified as third wave and those who identified as radical feminist were distinctly less interested and engaged in the issue. Many saw descriptive representation as important but perceived it to be a broader national campaign and one that did not really engage them vis-à-vis their activism. There was a sense that the campaigns surrounding women's representation were the preserve of women in Westminster or Washington or specifically for those women who wanted to run for office. Whilst the majority of interviewees agreed that increasing women's representation was important, if not their priority, some sounded a note of caution regarding the emphasis on descriptive representation when there were more structural inequalities to tackle:

> The structure of this country was set up such as to minimise participation and engagement, so what's happening in the halls of Congress and who's there, whilst really important to me, is not really what I would stake out as the key battlegrounds. You know it's been only still less than 50 years that African American people have gotten the right to vote [...]. There's a huge amount of voter disenfranchisement.
>
> (New York)

As this interviewee noted, the problems of representation in Congress can seem far removed from the more fundamental problems of inequality facing African Americans. Hence, the issue of women's representation was perceived as something privileged by 'white middle-class women', whilst for her the focus of the feminist movement should be on grassroots activism. In her response to the question of women's representation, this interviewee highlighted the already competing demands of adopting an intersectional approach when considering the importance of descriptive representation. This was a view reinforced by several other US self-identified black feminists:

> Well, when you talk about getting more women elected, which women do you mean? It seems to me that women of color are pretty absent from the discussions that take place amongst white women in DC.
>
> (Portland)

For this feminist, the issue of women's representation was perceived to be an issue of concern to white women who are not necessarily invested in ensuring diversity amongst those women seeking office. Perhaps this returns us to the problem of adopting a woman-centred approach to the issue of women's representation, one that can evade discussions of inequality amongst and between women. Part of the problem lies at the discursive level but also in terms of the actors involved with devising the strategies to advance women's representation.

Of course, the solutions to addressing the under-representation of women in politics differ greatly. In Britain, debates concerning women's representation at Westminster have been dominated by demand-side solutions such as party quotas; whilst in the US there has been greater emphasis on fundraising for women candidates and tackling supply-side constraints through the promotion of EMILY's List (Lawless and Fox, 2005). Feminists in both the US and Britain discussed a general lack of willpower on the part of political parties to do enough about increasing the number of women:

> Well it's obvious that the parties don't take it seriously, I mean Labour have quotas which is great but there are very few prominent women MPs that I can think of [...] women just seem to be absent.
>
> (Bristol)

> The Democrats are way ahead on this but there's still a really long way to go but I guess it just doesn't feel like anyone is really taking the issue seriously you know? We have all the economic debate and so on that just kind of dominates.
>
> (New York)

Both US and British feminists highlighted the inter-party differences and were aware of the fact that Labour and the Democrats seemed more committed to increasing women's electoral presence. When pushed on how this under-representation might be addressed through the use of quotas (something that can more readily be applied in Britain), there was more division amongst the feminists:

> Labour's done a great job with all-women shortlists – they've really led the way.
>
> (London)

> My issue with quotas and things like positive discrimination is that it only really seems to address one aspect. So where is the focus on race or on class? As far as I know things like the Labour Party's policy on women shortlists really only seems to benefit certain types of women.
>
> (Glasgow)

The latter quotation resonates with some of the themes that emerged particularly strongly from the US interviews. Namely that quotas, and indeed the broader issue of women's representation, seem to be conflated with the increased election of white middle-class women. Reluctance to endorse quotas wholeheartedly was more apparent in the responses of the third wavers; this, in part, is unsurprising given the extent to which their analysis of quotas was determined both by a noticeable lack of interest in the issue but also by the adoption of an intersectional lens. When pushed about what an intersectional approach to descriptive representation might look like, several US feminists argued that it was about a 'mind-set' and a specific approach to women's representation. Thus, to them, intersectionality need not necessarily result in what John Adams described as mirror representation, whereby the legislature should be a microcosm of society (Pitkin, 1967), but rather should constitute a willingness to acknowledge that political structures privilege certain types of women over others.

At a discursive level, the use of the term 'all-women shortlist' was felt by one London interviewee who identified as a queer feminist to be essentialist: 'I think probably gender quotas is better than all-women shortlist – it's a bit cis-centric.'[17] For this interviewee, it was a term that smacked of cis-privilege and was a term that demonstrated 'a complete ignorance' of the issues faced by those who consider themselves to be women when society does not. An intersectional approach to political representation would require, as one interviewee put it, 'an awareness of the intersecting forms of oppression and privilege that we represent'. This, in part, reinforces the difficulty with which feminist activists themselves can put their intersectionality into practice.

If we accept that intersectionality is about recognising the multiple and overlapping points of oppression, then such a lens raises a number of problematic questions: surely it is not just enough to look at the dual axes of oppression, for example gender and ethnicity (or more obviously race)? How then do we campaign for increasing the number of female bodies whilst also being sensitive to the fact that it matters who those women are? An intersectional approach that accounts for underlying power dynamics and structural oppression cannot truly be identified by simply counting the LGBT women present in a legislature. How can equality guarantees work so as to ensure that it is not just white middle-class women who benefit?

At this point, it might help to return to Crenshaw's work on the concept in which she sought to distinguish between structural and political intersectionality. Structural intersectionality refers to the experiential differences in the way multiple points of oppression affect an individual, whilst political intersectionality refers to the ways in which institutions seek to respond to the interaction between different inequalities. Hence, in this dichotomy, we have both an individual- and institutional-level response (Crenshaw, 1991). It is understandable why scholars have sought to privilege political intersectionality as a means by which to explore issues such as political representation (Krizsan et al., 2012: 20). A political intersectionality speaks to the specific strategies adopted by institutions to respond to the plurality of women's experiences; however, given that there are a limitless number of axes that could be accounted for, this is in some respects inadequate. In short, an intersectional lens pushes at the limits of descriptive representation.

The problem lies partly in the theorisation and operationalisation of intersectionality vis-à-vis descriptive representation. Parties, institutions and campaign groups could have an infinite number of axes on which to develop affirmative action measures; whilst this can capture some groups, it does not in truth speak to the more complex idea at the heart of structural intersectionality. Whilst one might wish to see an intermediary level of intersectionality, a meso level for instance that bridges the divide between individual experiences of structural oppression and institutional strategies designed to address discrimination, it is not altogether clear how that would differ from political intersectionality. For instance, the challenges facing Congress or Parliament in increasing the diversity of women is something that is replicated in feminist reading groups and women's civil society organisations. Therefore, intersectionality begs questions of descriptive representation because institutions cannot address oppression simply through reflecting different groups.

Attitudes amongst feminists towards the importance of women's presence in legislatures can be understood in two different ways: on the one hand, there are those for whom the legislature is an important and legitimate site for furthering the goals of gender equality (alongside the pursuance of neoliberal goals); whilst others are critical of the institution qua institution, specifically for the reasons that it pursues a distinctly neoliberal agenda, even whilst accepting that because it exists it is important for women to be included. Thus, the discourse surrounding campaigns for increasing women's representation can be broken down into more of a leftist and centrist feminist approach to political institutions. This distinction is important in terms of thinking through how national campaigns might better engage with feminist actors. Indeed, it might necessarily require a short-, medium-, and long-term approach to transforming feminist politics that begins with increasing women's presence but ultimately leads to the possibility of more radical feminist advances.

Conclusions

For those who are keen to campaign for women's descriptive representation, the lack of evident engagement, and interest in the issue on the part of feminist activists should be of concern, particularly given the energy and wide range of actors involved with this third wave of feminism. In particular, analysis of the empirical data above suggests a couple of issues for those seeking to engage feminist activists in the campaign for women's increased electoral presence: first, a lack of interest in engaging with the formal political process; and second, the 'problem' of how to advance a more intersectional framework for women's representation. I would suggest that both of these issues require attention in order to harness the involvement of the wider movement in such campaigns. Having the support and engagement of grassroots activists is important when one considers the need for large feminist organisations to remain responsive to and grounded within the feminist movement. Pushes to increase women's representation have disproportionately helped white, heterosexual able-bodied women who, in the US in particular, are likely to have access to independent wealth to fund expensive campaigns. For feminists, issues of political involvement in existing male-dominated institutions have always been a contested issue: on the one hand, feminists argue that women should be where power lies, whilst on the other, feminists seek to overthrow institutions and cultures that have long preserved patriarchal norms that serve to exclude women – merely joining men in these institutions is not sufficient to bring about radical change. As such, the following chapter explores how well feminist issues are advanced and represented through the substantive action of elected politicians and how feminist activists interpret those actions.

7
Representing Women's and Feminist Interests

Hillary Clinton and Margaret Thatcher are perhaps the two most widely known female politicians in the US and Britain. Whilst the former is often observed to be an important advocate for women around the world, the latter, despite being Britain's first female prime minister, had a less than straightforward relationship with feminism and the women's movement. These two politicians symbolise some of the problems underpinning assumptions about what women will do in office once elected; whilst Clinton sought to use her position as First Lady, New York Senator, Presidential hopeful, and then Secretary of State to articulate and advance women's interests, Thatcher is regularly cited as an example of a woman politician who did nothing to encourage or promote women's interests (Campus, 2013; Genovese, 2013). Thus, whilst both *descriptively* represented (white, heterosexual, able-bodied) women, only one is deemed to have *substantively* represented women. In short, the relationship between descriptive and substantive representation is not straightforward. Nor are politicians, even feminist politicians, necessarily those best placed to represent the interests of marginalised groups, something that is better advanced by social movements and civil society organisations (Weldon, 2012: 5). In order to explore these ideas, this chapter considers feminist attitudes towards the substantive representation of women and feminists. Interviewees were asked to identify women's and feminist interests and the extent to which they considered them to be well represented in the House of Commons or Congress. Before moving on to the empirical analysis, the chapter begins with a brief overview of the feminist scholarship on substantive representation.

Substantive representation

Rather than focusing on *who* the representative is (descriptive representation), substantive representation focuses on *what* the representative does and whether those actions are in line with the wishes of the represented. Those who claim to either be acting on behalf of a group, or whose actions are interpreted as such, can be seen as acting in the interests of the represented (Pitkin, 1967). The representative should therefore act as a substitute for the represented. This is not to say that the representative should not use their own judgement but neither should they be consistently at odds with the wishes of the represented (Pitkin, 1967). As the previous chapter highlighted, part of the argument in favour of increasing the number of women politicians is that they are better suited and more likely to advance issues of specific interest to women. Feminist scholar Jane Mansbridge developed this argument by claiming that in order to improve conditions for under-represented groups it is not simply about increasing numbers but also about *increasing the diversity* within those groups (1999). Such a claim is important, not least when we consider how substantive representation can be interpreted through an intersectional lens.

Dominant shifts within the gender and politics literature have precipitated a move away from simply counting the number of women politicians to exploring how, what, when, where, and why the substantive representation of women's interests occur (Weldon, 2002; Dovi, 2007; Celis et al., 2009). In expanding the way in which we think about the links between descriptive and substantive representation, scholars have emphasised anti-essentialism and ideological plurality: thus, female bodies do not equal feminist minds (Childs, 2007); male bodies do not necessarily equal anti- or non-feminist minds (Evans, 2012); and Conservative or centre right women can claim to act on behalf of women and feminists (Celis and Childs, 2012). A focus on multiple sites of representation has the potential to provide a better fit with an intersectional framework as scholars move beyond counting roll call votes to undertake more in-depth institutional and extra-institutional analysis. Such an approach should also ideally allow for more interaction between the research on women and minority representation and intersectional research that addresses specific populations of women (Hancock, 2007: 249; Minta, 2012: 542).

The idea that increased numbers of women *alone* will result in more attention being paid to women's and feminist interests is not an argument that has convinced gender and politics scholars (Childs and Krook,

2006; Weldon, 2012). Instead, various factors are important in shaping the representation of women's and feminist interests, including the actions of critical actors who initiate policy proposals specifically designed to further women's equality and who may also encourage others to promote women's interests (Childs and Krook, 2006); differences in partisanship and ideology (Reingold, 2000; Sanbonmatsu, 2008); and seniority of service, attendance rates, and the legislative process can all help shape and determine how and when women's interests are articulated (Childs and Krook, 2006; Grey, 2006). Additionally, our understanding of how the substantive representation of women's and feminist interests occurs can be further developed by distinguishing between process and outcome: the difference between the actual process (debate) which does not necessarily require an outcome (legislation) (Childs, 2004; Franceschet and Piscopo, 2008). This becomes particularly important when considering how an intersectional approach might be identified. For instance, the preliminary debates that occur in committees but that do not make it into the final wording of the bill might mean that attempts to apply an intersectional frame might not always be obvious.[1]

Understanding how feminists view those who claim to speak on behalf of women and feminists (and indeed exploring who is 'permitted' to claim to speak for women and feminists) has implications for those interested in exploring gendered and feminist political representation. If we accept Saward's model of the representative claim, in which the representative creates the framework (and conditions) within which a set of claims are constructed (Saward, 2006), then both the descriptive and substantive representation of women need to be understood as a dynamic process of engagement between representatives and the plurality of feminist groups and activists; hence, the need for greater engagement with feminist activists. Indeed, given the lack of consensus surrounding what constitutes the women's movement and feminist movement (McBride and Mazur, 2008: 219), it is vital that gender and politics scholars investigating women's substantive representation seek to engage with a wide range of feminist viewpoints.

Representing feminisms

There exists an imbalance in terms of feminist representation, reflected by the fact that large national women's organisations are frequently assumed to speak for the movement (Weldon, 2012: 22). Previous research has highlighted that all types of interest groups, from large to small, use a range of tactics to lobby members of Congress (Kollman,

1998: 15) and the use of online technologies to disseminate calls for consultation has undoubtedly opened up a process that was once the preserve of insider interest groups (Grant, 2004). And yet large liberal civil society women's organisations tend to dominate public policy discussions concerning women's issues. This means that marginalised sub-groups within the movement, particularly identity-based feminist groups, who also lack sufficient descriptive representation, may feel excluded from consultative processes. Hearings, testimonies and requests for written evidence can still act as a barrier for some feminist groups who do not have the necessary experience or confidence to submit formal responses.

Beyond the dominance of large organisations, representing the full panoply of feminist views is no easy task, either for gender scholars or for those seeking to advance a feminist agenda. Indeed, I would argue it is only possible for a limited number of issues where there is consensus amongst feminists, for instance the liberalisation of abortion laws or equal pay for women. The *realpolitik* of the lobbying process and the subsequent horse-trading would necessarily privilege certain types of feminism. By this, I mean that it is more likely that a large liberal feminist organisation will have both the resources and the connections to advance its specific causes, whilst those feminists who identify and organise as queer feminists, as distinct from the LGBT lobby, are less likely to 1) engage with such processes and therefore 2) are less likely to have their voices heard. And it is not just within women's groups where we see liberal feminist demands equated with feminist representation; it also underpins the policy responses of the state to women's and feminist demands.

Shifts in policy discourse from women's rights and mother's rights towards human rights and parental rights have to some extent already detracted attention away from the focus on women per se. The turn towards gender mainstreaming in the 1990s marked a new way of advancing equal opportunities and those policies previously categorised as women's issues. It is worth noting that analysis of gender mainstreaming has been more widely studied and analysed in a European rather than a US context. Judith Squires outlined three distinct and, at times interrelated approaches towards gender mainstreaming: *inclusion*, associated with a liberal feminist approach to equality where men and women should be treated equally; *reversal*, where there is a greater emphasis on rectifying historic and current inequalities facing women specifically, usually associated with a radical feminism; and *displacement*, which seeks to prioritise diversity and break down gender stereotypes, associated with a post-modern approach (Squires, 1999; Squires, 2005: 370). The first of these, inclusion, typically dominates much policy discussion in Britain and the US, reflecting the liberal approach towards gender equality typically adopted by the state.

For some, such an approach is problematic as it necessarily involves pursuing the interests of men and masculinity (Eveline and Bacchi, 2005: 505): in short, it moves the policy focus away from women. Such an approach not only reflects a liberal approach to gender equality but also provides some crossover with a conservative agenda. Although claims made by those who seek to articulate a conservative feminism are often met with a degree of suspicion, conservatism not being known for its attention to or advancement of women's rights (Bryson and Heppell, 2010). However, the liberal and conservative emphasis on equality of opportunity is underpinned by a rhetorical focus on individual rather than structural inequalities. Such individualist discourse predominates policy discussions surrounding issues of equality and makes it difficult for other more radical, and arguably more challenging, forms of feminisms to be included. This in turn has implications for which kinds of feminism are represented. In order to evaluate state representation of women's and feminist interests, the chapter firstly considers how the interviewees interpret those interests, before moving on to explore where they consider such representation to occur.

Defining women's and feminist issues

Underpinning the idea of women's substantive representation is of course the assumption that women have a set of issues that politicians can claim to be advancing. There has been extensive debate within the gender and politics scholarship regarding what precisely constitutes women's interests (Sapiro, 1981; Chappell and Hill, 2006; Vickers, 2006) and it is important to note the danger of researchers basing their studies into the substantive representation upon an essentialised interpretation of women's interests (Celis, 2006). Indeed, coming up with a prescriptive list of 'women's issues' is clearly problematic. However, to suggest that there is no such thing as 'women's interests' is equally problematic. There is also the need to distinguish between women's and feminist issues; whilst they have some overlap, they are not the same thing. Feminism is a political ideology that not all women subscribe to and to suggest that feminists are acting on behalf of women who are suffering from a sense of false consciousness would be a difficult claim to support. That said, those feminist campaigners who seek to lobby parties and governments do themselves frame the issues as women's (rather than feminist) interests and are clearly motivated by a belief in the collective set of interrelated challenges facing women.

The plurality of women's experiences necessarily makes the job of defining women's interests a difficult and challenging one. Any attempt to define women's issues should also recognise diversity amongst and between women; more specifically, we should be critical of attempts by states, politicians, or social movements to portray or reduce women's issues to those issues which predominantly concern middle-class, white elite women. Additionally, a sole focus on those issues that affect women's bodies clearly runs the risk of excluding trans women, and moreover does not adequately deal with the range of political, cultural, and economic inequalities that affect women's lives, albeit to differing degrees. The dangers of creating a list so broad as to be of little political value means that feminists have to tread a fine line between marshalling the case for an all-inclusive category of women's interests, whilst still retaining the focus on specific campaigns and policies.

Interviewees were asked to consider the idea of women's and feminist issues. Many of the interviewees were comfortable with the term 'women's issues' and were willing to identify several specific issues that they considered to fall within such a category, including childcare, abortion, violence against women, and equal pay. Such issues chime with academic analysis of what might constitute women's issues (Lovenduski, 2005). The label 'women's issues' was considered to be important as a means by which to articulate the collective nature of the issues.

Conversely, around a quarter of the interviewees expressed some unease at the use of the term, with some raising the potential danger of separating out women's issues as distinct from 'normal' or 'mainstream' policy issues:

> Well, I guess I feel a little bit uncomfortable about giving a list of women's issues, I mean these are issues that affect all of us, not just women. So childcare is an issue not just for women but for men too. (London)

> I think of women's rights as human rights, you know? Sure, there are maybe specific things that we [*as women*] might think about more, but I think we should make those mainstream and not isolate them. (Portland)

> I suppose my issue with the label 'women's issues' is that it suggests a kind of reductive form of politics. It's not outward or expansive

> enough in its remit to include most of the issues that me and my friends or other gender-queer folk identify with. It's not good enough to say women's issues equals biology.
>
> (New York)

Such ideas were more obvious in the responses of those who had explicitly identified as third wave feminists and black feminists, whilst none of those who identified as radical feminists expressed such concerns. All of the male interviewees problematised the category of women's issues. Moreover, some interviewees highlighted the difficulty of producing an exhaustive 'list' because some women's concerns would inevitably get lost, as one feminist from New York argued: 'Well, when people say women's issues I always think what women do they mean? Most of the time they mean white women's issues not the specific issues facing women of color.' So for those who expressed concern about the idea of women's issues, there were four main concerns: 1) that calling issues 'women's issues' would inevitably set up a binary whereby they were distinguished from 'normal' or 'mainstream' policy areas; 2) that such a label suggests that they do not affect men; 3) that such an umbrella term fails to recognise the experiential differences between women and can be read as synonymous with the concerns of white women; and 4) the label 'women's issues' is a particular challenge to those who seek to reject gender binaries.

Whilst the empirical data reinforces the importance of adopting a reflexive use of the term 'women's issues' (Celis, 2006), it also indicates a high degree of support for the use of the term. Indeed, three quarters of interviewees were happy to identify issues that they considered to constitute women's issues, reflecting the purchase that a woman-centric approach has, even if this is not reflected at the policy level. Unsurprisingly, all interviewees were comfortable discussing feminist issues, although there was plenty of discussion concerning the plurality of feminist positions. In some instances, these issues overlapped with those that many had identified as being women's issues, notably reproductive rights. Interviewees were asked what they considered to be feminist priorities: most of the participants named two or three issues, although some only mentioned one. The interviewees were not provided with a list; instead, the data in Table 7.1 below illustrates the top-five feminist issues cited by country.

The issues listed in Table 7.1 below illustrate some differences in prioritisation between feminists in the US and Britain. Although there were other specific priorities listed by the interviewees, such as issues

Table 7.1 Most frequently cited feminist issues

	US	**Britain**
1	Reproductive rights	Violence against women
2	LGBT rights	Pornography
3	Women in poverty	Abortion
4	Women of color rights/anti-racism	Equal pay
5	Cultural stereotyping (TV/film/media)	Global feminism

affecting disabled women, employment rights, and the environment, the issues listed in the table above were those most widely cited by the interviewees. Indeed, virtually all of the same issues were named across the two countries, but in terms of frequency, there was a difference. It is unsurprising that reproductive rights should be a more commonly cited example of a feminist issue in the US than in Britain because of the relentless campaigns to restrict access to abortion (discussed in greater detail in the following chapter). What is more striking about the differences between the US and British feminist issues is the inescapable fact that inclusion and issues facing specific groups were more likely to be highlighted by US feminists, in particular the emphasis on LGBT inclusion and an emphasis on women of color. The issues cited in Table 7.1 above reinforce the influence of intersectionality on feminist praxis in the US; this suggests that marginalised groups within the feminist community are more widely recognised as being central to the overarching aims of the movement. The category of 'feminist issue' lends itself to a more analytical approach that can encompass an intersectional framework; moreover, it allows for a less restrictive interpretation of the issues that affect women (and men).

Conversely, despite British feminists citing global or transnational feminism, the focus was directed more towards specific issues rather than particular groups. Those who identified issues that affected specific groups in the US were more likely to have identified as third wave feminists and as black feminists, whilst in Britain there was relatively greater consensus regarding the issues amongst feminists regardless of waved and ideological identities. Although ideological influences could be identified in both the US and Britain, with those identifying as socialist feminist much more likely to talk about global campaigns to tackle women's poverty, whilst radical feminists were much more concerned about violence against women. A distinction can also be drawn between the ways in which British and US feminists talked about objectification.

For the US interviewees the issue was inextricably bound with cultural representations of women through the media. Whilst amongst the British feminists the emphasis on objectification was linked with a critique of pornography. The two quotations below illustrate the difference in tone and emphasis in the interviewees' discussion of the term 'objectification':

> Also, we really need to tackle the objectification of women and girls. I don't want my daughter growing up in a world where TV shows portray women as sex kittens or as passive or not as smart as the guys.
>
> (Portland)
>
> The objectification of women that's now popularised and normalised through online porn is so harmful. Kids can get this stuff on their phone and they don't even need to go looking – porn has become mainstream.
>
> (London)

The difference in terms of the discursive use of the term 'objectification' is telling; whilst a few US interviewees discussed pornography, it was nowhere near as widely cited as an issue as it was amongst the British interviewees. Of course, pornography is an issue that can be divisive for feminists; those who articulate a radical feminism tend to be more critical of the harmful effects of pornography on women, whilst others seek to explore the potential of erotica or feminist porn as a means by which to achieve female sexual empowerment. That said, amongst the British interviewees there was a greater degree of unanimity with regards to the dangers posed by pornography and objectification, and it is clear that large parts of feminist activism in Britain have been motivated by campaigns against the mainstreaming of pornography. This was less evident in the US, where it was mainly those who identified as radical feminists who considered pornography to be an important feminist priority.

When we think about some other controversial debates within contemporary feminism it is clear that there are disagreements over the extent to which certain issues can or should be considered feminist issues. For example, recent debates on both sides of the Atlantic about trans inclusion have precipitated discussions amongst feminist activists regarding the extent to which this should be constituted as a *feminist* rather than LGBT issue, as one interviewee from London argued: 'I guess sometimes I hear issues being talked about as feminist issues and sometimes I'm not really sure if they are feminist issues? Sometimes it's just a distraction and I guess I feel that way about trans inclusion.' The fact that the example given in this quotation is trans inclusion is not unimportant, as it encompasses a whole set of contested ideas concerning inclusion and feminist identification.

So whilst all were happy to give examples of feminist issues, there were a few that reflected upon the existence of divergent feminist views as problematical:

> There are so many different feminist arguments on so many different issues that sometimes it's hard to know what is and what isn't a feminist issue and what is and isn't a feminist response.
>
> (Portland)

> I suppose the problem with the idea of feminist issues is that they are driven by your own particular political beliefs and opinions and they don't always chime with what others think.
>
> (Bristol)

A plurality of ideas, campaigns and objectives is of course an indication of a healthy and pluralistic political movement. Notwithstanding this, it is worth remembering that this can make it hard to measure or evaluate the extent to which politicians and extra-Parliamentary actors are advancing feminist issues. It returns us to the idea of claim making and of the ongoing iterative process of defining, redefining, and defending specific issues or positions as feminist.

The issue of exclusion, which had been much more apparent in the discussions concerning the descriptive representation of women, became less prominent when interviewees were asked to consider women's and feminist issues. In Britain, particular biological concerns (specifically those concerning women's health) were discussed, often interchangeably, as 'women's' or 'feminist' issues. This differed in the US, where several interviewees sought to identify which types of women might be excluded from certain discourses:

> I mean take reproductive rights, you know we can't just talk *Roe v. Wade* [...] we need to go beyond that and address the continued inequality that women of color face when going through childbirth. These issues aren't championed by the national women's groups because they only represent a certain type of woman.
>
> (Portland)

> What we don't want is to assume that women's issues are all the same; issues affecting me as a young white college graduate living in New York are very different from those experienced by say women of color in the south who may be struggling to pay bills on a low-wage job. Their interests and rights have to be championed too.
>
> (New York)

The interaction between race and sex was a leitmotif throughout many of the US interviews in their discussions of both descriptive and substantive representation (although many also mentioned other points of intersectionality). This dual approach to understanding the feminist issues meant that many of the interviewees automatically considered the racial dimensions of any given issue that one could reasonably claim to be part of a women's or feminist agenda. This same attention to, and awareness of, race was not as apparent in the interviews with British feminists. Having explored how activists interpret the terms 'women's' and 'feminist' issues, the chapter now turns to look at the representation of women's and feminist issues in the US and Britain and more broadly considers the extent to which interviewees were able to identify instances where the substantive representation of women and feminists had occurred.

Locating sites of substantive representation

If as Kantola and Squires have argued (2012) there is a marketplace of feminist ideas, then this makes it hard to provide aggregate analysis of the substantive representation of feminist issues. Debates surrounding the claim making of specific acts of representation (Saward, 2006) also make it difficult, not least when they are often filtered through the media, which can often be keen to label actions as feminist or otherwise. This means there are multiple layers of interpretation that need to be understood. Whilst a politician may claim an act as feminist, it is not always interpreted as such either by feminist groups or by feminists individually. In order to explore this further we can consider the ways in which the interviewees discussed the multiple sites in which the substantive representation could be expected to occur: 1) at the institutional level, 2) at the individual level, and 3) in the wider feminist and women's movement.

Institutional

At the institutional level, there is a variety of sites where the representation of women's issues can, at least potentially, be advanced. At the federal level in the US, there exists a number of different agencies and bureaus that are specifically focused upon policies for women including, inter alia, the Women's Bureau based in the Department of Labor; the Office of Global Women's Issues based in the Department of State; the Office on Women's Health based in the Department of Health and Human Services; Women, Children, and Infants based in the Department of Agriculture; and the Office on Violence against Women based in the Department of Justice.[2] There also exists at the executive level a White House Council on Women and Girls, created by President Obama, that seeks to ensure that all agencies take into account 'the needs of women and girls in the policies they draft, the programs they create, the legislation they support'.[3] Additionally, the US Commission on Civil Rights which considers 'deprivations of voting rights and alleged discrimination based on race, color, religion, sex, age, disability, or national origin, or in the administration of justice'.[4]

Conversely, the UK government has a single office to address women's issues, the Government Equalities Office. It has been based in various different government departments and is currently housed within the Department for Culture, Media and Sport. The first Women's Unit was created by Prime Minister Tony Blair in 1997 and was based in the Cabinet Office. However, it attracted criticism from some for its failure to have any serious impact, this despite the fact that it was under-resourced (Squires and Wickham-Jones, 2004). It was subsequently renamed the Women and Equality Unit in 2001, which was shortened to the Equalities Unit in order to reflect the fact that it sought to promote equality between the sexes. Controversies regarding the role of the Minister for Women, how much they are paid, whether their role is combined with another government portfolio and whether or not that politician is a full member of the Cabinet have also often detracted attention away from the work undertaken by the office.

The plurality of sites seeking to address women's interests in the US is a marked contrast with the single, often beleaguered, office in Britain. Whilst there are certainly arguments to be made in favour of centralisation, along the lines of the British model, the presence of the Women and Girl's Office contained within the executive branch suggests a possible site for proper scrutiny with subsequent impact. Whilst in the US there has been no attempt to shift away from women as the focus of policy development, this has not been the case in Britain. Why though should this make a difference in terms of evaluating the substantive outcomes for women? If we return to the three approaches to gender mainstreaming outlined by Squires at the start of this chapter, we can see that maintaining a focus on women is aligned with a radical feminism, whereas a focus on equality is more likely to be pursued by liberal feminists or gender equality advocates. Now, this does not obviously mean that US bureaucracies are chocked full of radical feminists, but the retained emphasis on women and girls rather than on equality is interesting for two reasons: first, it does not reflect predominant discourses in US feminism to discuss equality and inclusion of men; and second, it does not necessarily facilitate intersectional policy development.

It is certainly true that few, if any, of the popular feminist texts address the various agencies and offices at the national level that effect women's equality. Additionally, during the interviews when I asked participants about where they saw change occurring for women at the legislative level, none mentioned the work of the various agencies. This in itself is no surprise. In the US, there are lots of different potential points of entry and pressure; whilst in Britain, the work of the Equalities Office does not tend to attract much high-profile media attention, at least not in terms of substantive outcomes. It is also true that the relationships between the government agencies and individual grassroots organisations are, at least to some extent, mediated by the larger national women's civil society organisations. Moreover, the 'revolving door' sees the movement of those who had worked for such large women's organisations move into governmental positions, for instance the current director of the Women's Bureau at the Department of Labor, Latifa Lyles, was formerly vice president of NOW.[5] Such a fluid movement between women's organisations and agencies of the state can of course also give the impression that such individuals (and offices) are disconnected from grassroots feminism.

Critical actors

Identifying critical actors and the various processes, formal and informal, by which politicians are able to advance women's interests has become a useful way in which to explore how and where the substantive representation of women occurs. However, such a focus on the actions of individuals, and their seniority and networks within a legislature, risks focusing too much attention on the actions of elite individuals who are not necessarily representative of the wider feminist movement. If bureaus and offices can appear remote in terms of observing where the representation of women's and feminist interests occurs, then individual critical actors should in theory be easier to identify. Interviewees were asked if they could identify particular politicians who had advanced women's and feminist interests. Several names were given and in particular, Senator Diane Feinstein (D, California), Harriet

Harman MP (Labour), Fiona MacTaggart MP (Labour), and Senator Patty Murray (D, Washington) were named by a number of interviewees:

> Well, I think it's clear when you look at someone like Patty Murray that she's really stuck her neck out for women in Congress.
>
> (Portland)

> I think you only have to look at the way that the right wing press write about Harriet Harman to know that they're doing that because she is willing to stand up for women's rights.
>
> (London)

For these interviewees it was about being seen to be standing up for women; in fact, this perception, which was not in fact always accompanied by specific examples of legislation or policy proposals, underscores the symbolic importance of feminist leadership in national legislatures. The interviewees were clear that it was likely tough for women, and for feminists in particular, in such male-dominated institutions.

A number of the feminists interviewed in both the US and Britain were also open to the idea that men could represent women's interests: 'for sure men can represent women, I mean women can represent men so the reverse must be true' (Washington DC) and 'of course men can represent women on a whole range of issues especially if they're of the same political viewpoint as you' (Bristol). Indeed, in discussing how men could help represent women's interests, some interviewees claimed that some male politicians, such as feminist men and pro-choice men specifically, might be preferable to some women politicians:

> I'd rather vote for a pro-choice man than a pro-life woman. For me that's the line in the sand.
>
> (New York)

> Yes I think some men do take an interest, although probably not many male MPs [...] maybe around issues to do with childcare, there are younger men who get that it shouldn't just be the women's responsibility?
>
> (London)

For these interviewees, sex, and gender did not necessarily preclude politicians from acting on behalf of women. Indeed some thought it would be a good thing if more men felt like they wanted to take an interest in women's issues. For many of the feminists there was no sense of 'ownership' over the issues, although some interviewees did raise objections to the idea that men would simply 'take over' the women's agenda, leaving women completely disempowered: 'I think it would be great if male politicians started speaking to the interests of feminists but it should be women at the forefront, the last thing we want are just male solutions to the problems raised by feminists' (Portland).

US feminists sought to highlight Obama's work for women, comparing it to the 'anti-feminist' stance of women like Michelle Bachmann who claim to be feminist. This suggests that for feminist activists at least, the substantive representation of women does equal the substantive representation of feminists. For them, issues of representation appeared to be much more closely bound up with an intersectional approach and one that was ultimately less dependent on the sex of the elected representative. Whilst none of the British feminists mentioned by name any male politicians who they considered to have acted on behalf of women, the overwhelming majority believed that men could be feminist and that, more importantly, the gendered nature of all issues meant that it should not just be women that are thought about: 'it can't just be about representing women; we also need to think about how men and masculinities are impacted by the law and the people that make it' (Bristol).

Whilst the interviewees were happy to talk in general terms about the representation of feminist and women's issues, it was also clear that many could not name specific politicians or tended to use 'party' as a proxy for talking about women's issues; this was particularly true of the US interviewees who regularly noted the anti-feminist/anti-woman nature of the GOP and the subsequent importance of the Democrats. In Britain, the size and relatively centralised nature of the political system perhaps enabled interviewees to have a greater knowledge of those politicians who had specifically sought to represent women and feminists, with MPs from the backbenches also being cited by some as being important advocates for change. It was also clear that there was a general sense of pessimism on both sides of the Atlantic regarding the status of women's and feminist issues and a pervasive feeling that the issues themselves were not deemed as important as other issues to either governments or the women politicians:

> I just don't see them [politicians] speaking to a feminist agenda; you know they'll do it when it suits them but otherwise they're in it for themselves.
>
> (Portland)

> I can't say I've really picked up on many MPs actively trying to pursue issues that are important to feminists, but then maybe the media don't report it or it's because I'm not that into Westminster politics.
>
> (Glasgow)

As the above quotations highlight, there was a degree of cynicism regarding politicians (including women politicians), and how and when politicians might choose to engage in feminist representation. Moreover, the point raised by the Glaswegian feminist regarding media coverage is particularly salient given both the under-representation of women politicians in the media and the heavily gendered coverage they receive when they do appear (Bligh et al., 2012; Ross et al., 2013).

Women's movement

Given the emphasis in the gender and politics scholarship on the role of critical actors, identifying specific politicians who are seeking (or have sought) to advance feminist agendas can help shed light on the ways in which activists make judgements about which politicians can be deemed to be acting on behalf of feminists. Indeed, and returning to the kinds of women who get elected, there was a sense that women politicians sometimes reinforced the idea that all that feminists are concerned about is white middle-class women's issues; there was a strong desire to focus more on the grassroots as the *real* manifestation of feminist activism, where the real representation (in terms of outcomes) of women's interests occurs.

> I think we should be focused more on getting the next generation of women activists trained up to work for women's rape crisis centres or pro-choice campaigns. You know, campaigns on the ground that actually make a difference to women's lives rather than lobbying Congress when it takes so long to get anything changed.
>
> (New York)

> I think it's great that there are people who care enough to campaign to get more women elected and that some of those women might introduce legislation to make our society more feminist. But for me, the real feminist work is done working at a more localised and grassroots level, delivering services, speaking to schoolchildren about objectification and so on.
>
> (Bristol)

This supports claims made in the academic literature which has sought to identify the women's movements and extra-legislative activities as being an important site of women's representation (Weldon, 2002), but begs questions of association and mobilisation between the sites.

The interviewees highlighted several campaigns that had been established by feminist groups outside of the legislative sphere as having had a critical role to play in advancing feminist interests. For instance in Britain, the campaign group Rewind&Reframe has been raising awareness of the need to introduce age classifications for music videos in an attempt to tackle the sexual objectification of women that is so often a constituent part of such videos; a campaign that the government has subsequently responded positively to.[6] Meanwhile in Portland, one interviewee told me about a grassroots campaign that she had been involved in to reopen a 'johns' school' which was shut down over a decade ago, which had taken years of hard work and activism on the part of local activists with little interest from politicians.[7] Both of these examples illustrate the ways in which the feminist movement has brought about effective change, either through raising awareness of the need for change in the British case or by focusing on community responses to dealing with men who buy sex. Of course, both of these campaigns are directed from a particular feminist position, one that perceives the sexual objectification of women and the selling of sex as part of a continuum of violence against women. To that end, there will inevitably be feminists who disagree with such positions. However, given the prominence of anti-porn feminism in Britain, we would be on relatively safe grounds interpreting this as evidence of the movement acting on behalf of feminist interests. Whereas in the US, where debates around sex workers' rights have gained prominence, campaigns and strategies to advance an abolitionist agenda do not necessarily represent feminist interests.

Both of the organisations and campaigns cited above have, however, effectively set the terms of the debate; legislators at the local and national level have been forced to respond to the debate, which places them in a more reactive rather than proactive role. National campaigns, oftentimes started online, have also had demonstrable effects. In Britain, the campaign PinkStinks has lobbied shops and advertising agencies to change the gendered stereotyping evident in the marketing of clothes and games for girls.[8] Whilst in the US, the SPARK movement (Sexualisation Protests: Action, Resistance, Knowledge) made up of girls between the ages of 13–22 was established as a grassroots campaign to target the sexualisation of girls in the media.[9]

It is not just at the level of awareness raising that feminists can advance feminist interests; it is also at the service level. Women's groups, and in particular feminist volunteers, are responsible for delivering services for women, with feminists in the US often volunteering to help staff abortion clinics or to help women with the travel to their nearest clinic. In Britain, the austerity measures brought in after 2010 meant the closure of a number of women's centres.[10] Those that do still exist, such as the Nottingham Women's Centre, do so in large part because of the commitment of feminists to help run them. Groups that have a specific advocacy remit for black women or women of color also provide important outreach services for women who are experiencing domestic violence, such as London's Southall Black Sisters or the Dominican Women's Development Center, which provides holistic support for women from the Dominican community. During the interviews, participants explicitly highlighted the importance of grassroots groups and organisations that were advancing feminist and women's interests as being more important than what goes on in Congress or Westminster:

> When I think about what's important for feminist issues, I look around at the amazing work being done by volunteers helping women deal with rape or sexual assault and that's really so much more important than what politicians say and do.
>
> (New York)

> Look, we have an Equal Pay Act in this country and yet we don't have equal pay, for me that kind of sums up the limitations of the lobbying and legislative approach. I'm much more interested in what goes on at the local and grassroots level, opposing the opening of a new strip club or saving a rape shelter from closing.
>
> (London)

The second quotation in particular highlights the perception of some that the legislative mode of representation is limited compared with the more tangible impact that grassroots campaigns can have. As several interviewees pointed out, the grassroots nature of feminist campaigning as a means by which to advocate for women's and feminist interests was also more democratic, as it allows for, and indeed requires, the involvement and engagement of a larger number of people.

Conclusion

This chapter has sought to problematise and explore the idea of women's and feminist issues. The fact that neither are, always, straightforward to define makes it much harder to not only explore the representation of women's and feminist interests but also to consider how critical actors, institutions and the wider movement can be judged to be 'acting on behalf of' feminists or women. Such a claim would necessarily be contested by some of those on whose behalf the claims are being made. Although most of the interviewees were happy with the idea of women's issues, there were some concerns with it as a label, not least in terms of the need to reframe issues as also affecting men and exploring the specific impact of that. Discussions of feminist issues and their relative importance to activists revealed differences between British and US activists, with issues of inclusion broadly conceived, being more obviously important in the US than in Britain. There was symbolic value in the importance of specific politicians who were felt to be feminist advocates but very often, especially in the US, parties were used as proxies for critical actors as a way for activists to discuss who represents women's and feminist interests. Interviewees were more able to articulate clearly the important contributions that the wider movement had made to bring about change at various levels, including extra-legislative organisations. The findings from this research support calls from within the gender and politics literature to explore the representation of feminist interests beyond explorations of the behaviour of female legislators (Weldon, 2002; Dovi, 2007; Celis et al., 2009). This expansion has included the recognition that the substantive representation of women occurs in places other than, or in conjunction with, legislatures (Weldon, 2002); as such, the following chapter considers debates and campaigns that are focused on a specific issue that has attracted widespread attention in the US and Britain: abortion and reproductive rights.

8
Abortion and Reproductive Rights Activism

Feminist movements necessarily have to fight on multiple fronts; some issues rise and fall in terms of their prominence and political saliency, whilst others, such as abortion, have been an almost permanent feature of twentieth and (to date) twenty-first century feminist campaigning. There has been some speculation in the media regarding an 'Americanization' of the abortion debate in Britain;[1] this refers both to the presence of US anti-abortion campaigns now active in Britain but also to the idea that the issue is becoming a 'political football'. This chapter presents analysis of the ways in which feminist campaigns have responded to the state's attempts to roll back abortion provision. In doing so, the chapter highlights the different role that the issue plays in feminist discourse and activism within Britain and the US. Focusing on one specific high-profile policy issue also enables us to consider more fully the ways in which feminist positions are framed by activists, the various groups campaigning on the issue and politicians and political parties. Abortion is a longstanding feminist issue and it is one that typically unites feminists: it has not emerged with this third wave of feminism and it is for that very reason that it provides a useful way of thinking through the points of continuity and divergence between feminist campaigning in the US and Britain. As a policy issue, abortion also provides a focus for analysis of women's role in the political process and the extent to which the state is responsive to women's interests (Marx Ferree et al., 2002: 6).

There are significant political, religious, and economic differences between the US and Britain. These differences are particularly pertinent to the issue of abortion. The multiple windows of opportunity afforded by the US federal system, both at a legislative and judicial level, facilitate the anti-abortion movement, whilst making it harder for activists to oppose incremental reforms of existing provision. This is not simply to state the obvious but rather helps us understand the importance of political systems to the success of anti-abortion movements. Meanwhile, in the predominantly unitary UK system, abortion rights activists can focus their attention on Parliamentary debate.[2] That said, much of the movement and counter-movement activity occurs beyond the legislative sphere, amongst competing social movements, interest groups, and religious factions. The chapter firstly sets out the 'state' of abortion legislation in Britain and the US in order to provide the context for contemporary analysis. We then go on to explore some of the key differences between the US and British abortion rights campaigns and anti-abortion movements, highlighting both the discourse that surrounds the debates and also the types of groups active in the area. The chapter finishes by considering the views of the interviewees and the extent to which abortion is central to third wave feminist writing and activism.

An overview of abortion legislation in the US and Britain

A woman's right to choose has been a key demand of subsequent feminist movements in the US and Britain (McBride Stetson, 2001; Amery, 2014). It has clearly been more controversial in the US where the 1973 Supreme Court *Roe v. Wade* ruling has long faced sustained attacks from anti-choice interest groups and individuals.[3] Indeed, comparative research has noted the intensity of the debate surrounding the issue of abortion in the US and its ability to mobilise actors on both sides of the divide (Marx Ferree et al., 2002). Abortion is an issue that speaks to debates concerning women's bodily autonomy and the extent to which the state seeks to influence and intervene in a woman's decision-making process. Of course, the political systems and the difference between a federal and unitary state (albeit one with substantial devolution) shape any comparative analysis of this issue. Whilst *Roe v. Wade* was a decision taken by the Supreme Court at the federal level, individual states in the US have considerable scope to enact abortion restrictions at various stages of pregnancy and can limit availability of public funding for abortions. In the British context, abortion remains the purview of Westminster, excepting Northern Ireland where abortion is still illegal. Whilst the twentieth century witnessed the passage of key pieces of legislation that allowed women to access abortion legally, the twenty-first century has seen a concerted effort by the anti-choice lobby to restrict those rights. The politics of abortion therefore is contingent upon political, cultural, and social norms which are refracted through the various institutions that take an interest in forms of social control over women's bodies. These influences are not always obvious from simple analysis of bills that have been enacted, but tracing legislative and judicial developments in abortion law over time does provide the context for contemporary comparative analysis.

Abortions are provided free by the NHS in England, Scotland, and Wales, although private abortion providers are also in operation. Whilst provision is guaranteed by the NHS, there have been concerns about patchy delivery, for instance there have been reports that women in Wales have been unable to access contraception or abortions. Looking at Table 8.1 below we can see that the fight for, and subsequent defence of, abortion rights has been a regular feature of Westminster debate, with various unsuccessful attempts made by politicians to restrict availability and access.

In 2012, the then Secretary of State for Health, Andrew Lansley, ordered emergency inspections of abortion clinics after receiving reports that medical consent forms had been pre-signed. In 2013, Conservative backbench MP Fiona Bruce led an inquiry into foetal disability, recommending that Parliament reviewed the law allowing abortion on such grounds, despite strong evidence from those in the medical profession who noted the importance of the upper limit of 24 weeks for parents who receive a late diagnosis of foetal abnormality. Whilst in 2014, reports that doctors had been willing to accept sex selection as a reason for abortion led the new Secretary of State for Health Jeremy Hunt to issue government guidance making clear that sex-selective abortion was illegal. Despite these regular attempts to restrict and police abortion law in Britain, the main story has been one of success for the pro-choice movement, insofar as its defence of the 1967 Act remains robust. Indeed, as will be explored below, activists in Britain are now turning their attention to the campaign to decriminalise abortion in Britain rather than having to defend the 1967 Act. As Table 8.2 indicates, the same cannot be said for the US, where campaigners have arguably been facing a losing battle since abortion was declared constitutional in 1973.

The sustained attacks on *Roe v. Wade* and the incremental restriction of women's access to abortion is in part facilitated by a federal political system, whereby states' rights to determine the law regarding moral issues is enshrined in the constitution; indeed, research has shown that anti-abortion activity is most engaged and effective at the local level (Ginsburg, 1998: 8). The 2003 Partial Birth Abortion Ban Act and the subsequent *Gonzalez v. Carhart* ruling have clearly been

Table 8.1 Developments in British abortion law

Date	Act
1803	The Ellenborough Act defined abortion as a criminal act. Abortion after 'quickening' (when movement is felt at 16–20 weeks) carried the death penalty.
1861	Offences Against the Person Act. Amended to criminalise the procurement of drugs or instruments to obtain an abortion. Performing an abortion or trying to self-abort carried a sentence of life imprisonment.
1929	Infant Life Preservation Act. Criminalised the act of killing a viable foetus (at that time 28 weeks) unless the life of the mother was in danger.
1938	The Bourne case. Following an abortion performed by Dr Alec Bourne on a young woman who had been gang raped, a judge ruled abortion to be lawful if continuation of the pregnancy would wreck a woman's mental or physical health.
1967	The Abortion Act. Provided a legal defence for those practitioners carrying out abortions up until 28 weeks. The law does not legalise abortion, rather it provides exceptions to the illegality of abortion. Abortions can only be performed under certain conditions (i.e. when continuing the pregnancy would result in a greater risk to the physical and mental health of the woman).
1980	Corrie Private Member's Bill to reduce the time limit available for abortion to 20 weeks – defeated.
1990	Human Fertilization and Embryology Act. Time limit for abortion reduced from 28 weeks to 24 weeks. Although abortion after 24 weeks is allowed if the woman's life is in danger.
1990	Alton amendment to the Human Fertilization and Embryology Act to reduce the time limit to 18 weeks – defeated.
2008	Dorries Amendment to the 2008 Human Fertilization and Embryology Act to reduce the time limit to 20 weeks – defeated.
2011	Dorries and Field Amendment to the Health and Social Care Bill to stop charities offering independent counselling to women seeking abortion – defeated.
2012	Backbench debate held by Dorries to reduce the time limit – defeated.

Source: Education for Choice.[4]

decisive moments in abortion legislation, with the restrictions enacted offering encouragement to those who would seek to restrict women's rights even further. In addition to the introduction of ultrasound laws and foetal pain laws, various states have also sought to introduce a raft

Table 8.2 Developments in US abortion law

Date	Ruling/Act
1850–1900	Most US states passed laws to ban abortion throughout pregnancy, in some instances excepting where a woman's life was in danger.
1963	*Griswold v. Connecticut*. Supreme Court struck down an anti-contraceptive law on the grounds that it intruded on the right to marital privacy.
1973	*Roe v. Wade*. Supreme Court ruled that the constitutional right to privacy and liberty protected a woman's right to terminate her pregnancy.
1976	*Planned Parenthood v. Danforth*. Supreme Court overturned a Missouri law which required married women to have the permission of their husband before terminating their pregnancy.
1980	*Harris v. McRae*. Supreme Court upheld the restriction on Medicaid funding (medical assistance for those from low-income households) for abortion except in cases of rape, incest, and life-threatening illnesses.
1989	*Webster v. Reproductive Health Services*. Supreme Court upheld a Missouri ban on the use of public employees and facilities to perform abortions.
1990	*Hodgson v. Minnesota*. Supreme Court struck down a Minnesota law that required minors to notify both parents before obtaining an abortion.
1992	*Planned Parenthood v. Casey*. Supreme Court ruled that states are allowed to enact laws requiring pre-abortion counselling and waiting periods. Court also overturned decision banning states from requiring minors to get parental consent before obtaining an abortion.
2000	*Stenberg v. Carhart*. Supreme Court struck down a Nebraska law prohibiting partial birth abortion through the use of the dilation and extraction (D&X) method.[5]
2003	Partial Birth Abortion Ban Act. Bans the use of the D&X method, the primary method of abortion during the second trimester.
2007	*Gonzalez v. Carhart*. Supreme Court upheld the 2003 Partial Birth Abortion Ban Act.
2007–	Following the *Gonzalez v. Carhart* decision, a number of states have increased the regulation of abortion, including ultrasound laws, requiring a compulsory ultrasound procedure prior to an abortion, and foetal pain laws, which prohibit abortions at 20 weeks and in some states, even earlier.

Sources: Pew Forum on Religion and Public Life and Baumgardner, 2008: 145–147.[6]

of other measures that could inhibit or prevent women from accessing abortion services, including a proposed database of women who have had an abortion (Louisiana), the introduction of admitting privileges for doctors (Texas) and an extra healthcare-coverage insurance policy requirement for abortion (Michigan). Such ongoing incremental attacks on *Roe v. Wade* have led some to argue that attempts to overturn the ruling could result in women who have abortions being sent to jail (Paltrow, 2013).

Comparatively, the US and Britain do not have much in common when it comes to abortion politics; although there are some areas of overlap, the differences between the two countries go beyond general pieces of legislation or judicial rulings. There are important variances in the ways in which abortion is framed – in terms of public discourse, pro-choice activism, and the strength of unity amongst and between feminists on the issue. These differences are instructive as they not only tell us something about the way in which abortion as a policy issue is conceptualised but also about the multiple ways in which feminists active in this third wave seek to engage with the state and with the various institutions that exercise influence over the issue. In order to explore some of the differences between US and British campaigns around abortion, the chapter focuses on four key areas: discourse, pro-choice activism, anti-abortion activism, and politicisation.

Discourse: Third wave reframing

In the US, third wave feminists have reframed abortion politics in terms of reproductive rights or reproductive justice; it has gone from being a single morality issue to one that speaks to a much broader agenda. The term 'reproductive justice' came chiefly from women of color in the US who wanted to expand the movement to include a range of related issues that specifically affect non-white women. This was partly in response to the sense that black women's concerns were peripheral to abortion rights campaigns, what Angela Davis described as the 'lily-white complexion' of the second wave abortion rights movement (1982: 203). Davis noted that whilst many women of color were in favour of abortion rights and accessed abortion services, they were not 'proponents of abortion' (204). Such a distinction is important, she argued, because of the large number of black and Latina women whose need for an abortion arises because of 'the miserable social conditions which dissuade them from bringing new lives into the world' (204).

Historically, the racialised dimensions of birth control in the US, as a means of compulsory sterilisation, disproportionately affected black women (215). Indeed, President Roosevelt's plan to reduce the population in Puerto Rico led to a sterilisation campaign which meant that by the 1970s, 35 per cent of Puerto Rican women of childbearing age had been sterilised (219). For women of color, abortion is an issue that cannot be divorced from the racial and economic inequalities inherent within the US. Davis' critique has been taken up by third wave activists who have sought to widen the scope of the abortion rights movement. The third wave shift from abortion to reproductive rights to reproductive justice situates the agenda within a broader holistic framework that seeks to protect women and girl's health, spiritual and economic well-being (Ross, 2006).

SisterSong, a women of color reproductive justice collective, argues that the switch to reproductive justice represents, 'a shift for women advocating for control of their bodies, from a narrower focus on legal access and individual choice (the focus of mainstream organisations) to a broader analysis of racial, economic, cultural and structural constraints on our power'.[7] Specific issues that were not previously addressed by a sole focus on abortion but which have specific pertinence for women of color include access to birth control; HIV/AIDs; and fibroids, which disproportionately affect African American women in the US. Indeed, shifting the discourse away from a sole focus on abortion to the much more inclusive reproductive justice also allows progressives, who might shy away from the loaded politics of abortion, to champion the cause (Joffe, 2005). Such a shift in discourse and focus is illustrative of how intersectionality has become a part of third wave praxis.

In Britain, reframing abortion as part of a wider reproductive justice agenda has not really occurred.[8] For instance, Abortion Rights, the national pro-choice campaign, makes no mention of reproductive justice on its website or in its literature. Furthermore, there have been no discussions of reproductive justice on the most popular feminist blogs in Britain – *The F Word, Vagenda,* and *Feminist Times*. Sarah Jackson, writing on British feminist blog *Bad Reputation,* got in touch with several pro-choice campaigners in Britain to ask whether or not a shift to reproductive justice would be useful for the British movement.[9] The responses to Jackson's question are instructive and reveal that neither Abortion Rights, Education for Choice nor the Abortion Support Network thought the US model of reproductive justice would be a useful or appropriate model to import to Britain. Such a position was justified because of the specific focus of British activism around defending the 1967 Act but also because of the perceived relative lack of racial inequality in accessing healthcare services. And yet, the fact that within Britain abortion rights are relatively safe compared with the US makes it somewhat surprising that a move towards expanding the focus of the movement has yet to occur.

Reflecting further upon why British activists have not sought to reframe the debate, there could be several additional inter-connected reasons: first, abortion is not constantly under threat in Britain and so whilst most activists are pro-choice, it is not necessarily something that has resulted in much debate amongst feminists; second, abortion is not the 'political football' that it is in the US where some pro-choice politicians prefer to articulate their support for a woman's right to choose through the use of the phrase 'reproductive justice'; and third, the particular influence that women of color and intersectionality have had upon US feminist praxis relative to Britain suggests that as an approach, reproductive justice would more likely gain traction in the US.

Third wave abortion rights activism[10]

For feminist activists in the US, reproductive justice is a top priority (see Table 7.1 in the previous chapter); this is largely due to the fact that campaigners constantly have to defend *Roe v. Wade*. In many respects this has led to the stalling of the wider feminist movement in the US, at least when compared with Britain. Pro-choice groups in the US are numerous (with 22 operating at the national level) and highly active, with a mixture of advocacy and service providers operating at the national, state, and local level. The most high profile of these organisations were established long before the emergence of the third wave. For instance, Planned Parenthood was founded in 1916, combines healthcare provision with abortion rights advocacy and operates 68 state and local offices; it has an online Planned Parenthood Action Network which enables activists from across the US to get involved and claims seven million activists, supporters, and donors.[11] Whilst NARAL (currently the National Abortion and Reproductive Rights Action League) was formed in 1969, has 20 state affiliates and claims to have more than one million members and supporters.[12] There are a plethora of other pro-choice groups that operate across the US that reflect the diversity of the movement, including Choice USA, which promotes and encourages the diverse and upcoming generation of reproductive choice activists; the Feminist Abortion Network, which acts as both an abortion provider and as a public policy advocate; and Catholics for Choice, which operates in the US and internationally to campaign for equal access to reproductive healthcare services.

In Britain, there are five pro-choice organisations, the majority of which are either direct or indirect service providers. Abortion Rights is the only national membership-based group and its remit largely revolves around defending the 1967 Abortion Act.[13] The organisation was formed in 2003 following the merger of the two longstanding and influential abortion rights campaigners: the National Abortion Campaign (NAC) and the Abortion Law Reform Association (ALRA). The coming together of these two groups in 2003 is of course no coincidence, as leading pro-choice campaigners witnessed a stepping up of anti-abortion activity in Britain after the successful signing of the Partial Birth Abortion Ban Act in the US. The unification of the group in 2003 also indicates a recognition by the newly resurgent feminist activists that a united resistance was necessary to defend the 1967 Act. Other groups active in Britain include Doctors for a Woman's Choice for Abortion, which campaigns for a change in the law to allow women to decide whether or not to have an abortion, rather than having to secure the signatures of two doctors; Antenatal Results and Choices, which supports and advocates on behalf of women who, as a result of screening, are told that there is a risk their baby is not developing as expected; and bpas, the British Pregnancy Advisory Service, which advocates for access to abortion as well as being the largest single abortion provider in Britain. British pro-choice activists, in addition to defending the 1967 Act, tend to focus their attention on the case for extending the provision of the Act to Northern Ireland. Moreover, a new activist group, My Belly is Mine, was established in support of Spanish women against a proposed reform to abortion law which sought to allow abortion only in cases of rape or where there were serious mental or physical health risks to the mother.[14]

Pro-choice groups in the US are much more explicitly and actively engaged in lobbying politicians and in trying to influence the outcome of primary or general elections. For those well-funded pro-choice groups, an election can be an important window of opportunity to influence an individual politician or the tone of the debate. Despite the Democrats being more closely associated with pro-choice politics, there are those within the GOP that also seek to pursue a pro-choice agenda, for instance Republicans for Choice or the WISH List. Because of differences in campaign financing and also because of the relative lack of wealth of pro-choice groups in Britain, there is not that same opportunity for influence at the point of nomination and election. Indeed, Abortion Rights has recently had to launch a fundraising campaign to maintain its website. Whilst the opportunity to have such purchase with a specific group of elected politicians who have pledged to run on a pro-choice ticket is clearly a boon for the cause, the same is also true of those who receive funding from anti-choice groups and organisations. In Britain, this lack of clear financial links between specific 'wings' of the abortion debates and policy preferences of legislators makes for a different relationship between the campaigning groups and elected politicians.

US pro-choice groups provide rankings of politicians depending on how they have voted on the issue of abortion; for instance Planned Parenthood publishes a Congressional 'scorecard' where visitors to the site can look up Senators and Representatives by name to see how they voted on issues pertaining to women's healthcare and rights.[15] British-based Abortion Rights has recently started to ask members and supporters to send in details of how their MP voted in order to help build the database, although so far this has not resulted in the same 'ranking' of individual politicians. Previous research has highlighted the implications of the ranking of politicians on this issue, with some female Senators losing funding for not voting in line with EMILY's List on 100 per cent of votes (Swers, 2013). In Britain, whilst information regarding how an individual politician may have voted in relevant lobby divisions is available on the Abortion Rights website, the limited capacities of the organisations means that it has yet to be translated into the same campaign strategy. Indeed, at a recent Abortion Rights event there was discussion about the need to create a database with the views and voting records of members of the House of Lords, which despite being an unelected chamber, has an important influence on legislation.

Despite the energy and number of pro-choice organisations in operation in the US, there are divisions within the movement. NARAL was criticised following the 1992 election for using focus groups to generate frames more likely to appeal to the public; this was deemed by some to be a watering down of the need for an aggressive counter to the mobilisation of anti-abortion activists. Whilst Planned Parenthood, following the use of focus groups, has also decided to drop the label 'pro-choice' because it creates an unhelpful binary between pro-life and pro-choice. Similarly, there has also long been division within the anti-abortion movement concerning the use of polemical or overtly religious rhetoric (Meyer and Staggenborg, 1996: 1653). In Britain where there is less controversy over the issue, there is less division amongst the pro-choice movement. US pro-choice groups are arguably more plugged in to the various opportunities for influence and engagement with the formal political process, whilst British activists can afford to give relatively less attention to the legislative process and can mobilise resistance as and when necessary.

Anti-abortion activism

Just as there are more national pro-choice groups in the US than in Britain, there are also more anti-abortion groups active in the US. Not only are the US organisations numerous but they also vary in terms of the strategies and repertoires they adopt in their campaigning. Some 66 anti-abortion organisations operate at the federal level with many more local campaigns and evangelical groups in existence. There is a wide range of anti-abortion groups representing various political and ideological views. The National Right to Life is the largest US anti-abortion organisation, with affiliates across all 50 states; it seeks to influence debate and decision makers through education, legislation, and political action.[16] At the other end of the anti-abortion spectrum sits the Christian terrorist group Army of God, who have claimed responsibility for nail bombing abortion clinics and targeting individual abortion providers (Smith, 2008). The anti-abortion movement in the US includes both liberal Catholics who view abortion as a strict religious issue and those Christian fundamentalists who oppose abortion as part of a symptom of a wider decline in 'family values' (Staggenborg, 1987). Also noteworthy are the Feminists for Life, a group particularly active on college campuses across the US, who serve as a symbolic riposte to the claim that the anti-abortion movement is anti-women.[17] US anti-abortion campaigners have also tried to target particularly vulnerable women in their efforts to restrict the numbers of terminations carried out. Indeed, there was a recent attempt to target 'undocumented Asian women' who were allegedly going to California to have abortions; the accompanying claims that were made regarding the scale of the 'problem' were ill-founded and the proposed new tightening of restrictions was abandoned.[18] This illustrates the importance for US abortion rights activists to understand the ways in which specific groups of vulnerable women and girls can be targeted.

There are at least ten anti-abortion groups active in Britain. The Society for the Protection of the Unborn Child (SPUC) is the oldest of these, established in 1966 to oppose the introduction of the Abortion Act. In addition to educational awareness and political lobbying, SPUC also holds an annual public witness event on the anniversary of the introduction of the Abortion Act to highlight the 'loss of life and harm to women' brought about by abortion.[19] In addition to individual members and local groups, SPUC also has a Muslim division intended to encourage more Muslims to engage with anti-abortion activism. As in the US, there are a range of groups that campaign to end abortion in Britain, not all of whom undertake political lobbying; Abort 67 is a hard-line group which shows graphic images and videos of abortion procedures in order to try and make abortion 'unthinkable' for women and girls. Whilst UK Life League has used extreme tactics from time to time, including targeted hate campaigns against a headmistress who was accused of 'child abuse' for providing sex education to her pupils at a Catholic girl's school.[20]

There has been much consternation that US-style tactics are being deployed by the anti-abortion movement in Britain. Part of that inevitably flows from the boost given to anti-abortion activists in Britain upon the passage of the Partial Birth Abortion Ban Act in 2003. Moreover, the increased use of new social media has made it easier for campaign tactics and rhetoric to transcend national boundaries, as well as the funding that has flowed from the US-based Center for Bio-Ethical Reform to British groups.[21] At least one of the US anti-abortion groups, 40 Days for Life, has become active in Britain with its tactic of holding 'peaceful' prayer vigils outside abortion clinics. Its website highlights where vigils have been held, which demonstrates both the national and international spread of the campaign. Indeed, there have been vigils held across seven cities in Britain.[22] The arrival of 40 Days for Life in Britain has to some extent re-mobilised the abortion rights movement where, unlike their US counterparts, they have had to be less vigilant about the activities of anti-abortionists. The East London Feminists counter-protested the 40 Days for Life vigil in Hackney, until the latter abandoned its post. Of course, responding effectively to anti-abortion activists is in some respects easier in Britain with its smaller landmass. The more densely populated areas including London, Birmingham, and Sheffield have allowed pro-choice campaigners to mobilise quickly and in sufficient numbers to counter protests outside of abortion clinics. This is much harder for US activists to achieve, who are fighting on many fronts over a much greater geographical area.

Politicisation

Abortion is typically considered by public policy scholars to be an 'easy issue' (Arceneaux, 2002), one which most citizens understand and feel able to proffer an opinion on. The increasing prominence of abortion in US political debate over recent years has been compounded by the fact that citizens tend to have strong opinions on the issue (Mooney, 2001); as a result, US activists have to be vigilant about safeguarding the gains won by second wave feminists, despite only a third of US citizens wanting to see *Roe v. Wade* overturned (a figure that has remained stable for the past 20 years).[23] It is not uncommon for abortion to feature in US election campaigns and the issue is viewed as a salient policy value for voters at both the state and federal level (Abramowitz, 1995). Abortion has also largely become a partisan issue in the US, with Republicans more likely to be anti-abortion than the Democrats. In 2012, several Republicans gave interviews in which they outlined variations of abolitionist rhetoric: Missouri Senate candidate Todd Akin claimed that in cases of 'legitimate rape', women's bodies have a way of blocking unwanted pregnancies, thereby making the case for abortion redundant; Indiana Senate hopeful Richard Mourdock claimed that the only justification for abortion was in order to save the mother's life; whilst Washington's John Koster, running for a seat in the House of Representatives, condemned abortion, including in cases of rape and incest.[24] All of these claims, in addition to the GOP's introduction of the Partial Birth Abortion Ban Act, form part of what some Democrats, women's organisations, and feminist groups have been calling the 'War on Women'.

The War on Women is crystallised around the issue of abortion, although analysis of the 2012 Presidential election has found that the impact of the rhetoric on voter choice was confined to the issue of insurance coverage for birth control rather than abortion (Deckman and McTague, 2014). That the GOP is now positioned as leading the War on Women is ironic, given that historically the Republicans were more likely to be pro-choice than their Democratic counterparts were (Williams, 2011). However, the contemporary GOP has sought to advance both an incremental policy approach to restricting access to abortion through Congress (Ainsworth and Hall, 2011) alongside introducing key pieces of legislation, such as the Partial Birth Abortion Act. It is not just the GOP that has been the sole determinant of legislative change: the Supreme Court's upholding of the Partial Birth Abortion Ban Act means that the courts have also been steadily depriving women of their right to bodily control since *Roe v. Wade* (Oshana, 2011: 46). Hence, the nexus of the courts, GOP opposition, and anti-abortion activism all create a political context within which it is hard for third wave abortion rights campaigners either to defend *Roe v. Wade* or to push forward in terms of liberalising abortion laws.

Anti-abortion campaigners in the US have attempted to bring in 'personhood' bills, which could ultimately make some types of birth control illegal. So-called personhood bills are pieces of legislation that define human life as beginning at the moment of fertilisation. In short, the bills attempt to confer constitutional rights on embryos. The slew of bills that have been drafted across the US have been introduced directly into the state legislature and have been the subject of state ballot initiatives. The campaign group Personhood USA, originating in Colorado, has been the main driving force behind this movement.[25] The first attempt to introduce such legislation formed part of a ballot initiative in Colorado in 2008, where it was rejected by the voters and it was rejected again when it was introduced in 2010. To date, no personhood bills have passed; the implications of such a bill passing would of course mean overturning *Roe v. Wade,* as it would no longer be legal to terminate the life of a 'citizen'. Moreover, it has implications for the types of operations that could be performed on women and the extent to which infertile women are able to access fertility treatment.

Conversely, abortion does not typically feature in UK elections and has yet to become the partisan political football that it is in the US. Whilst abortion does make infrequent appearances during electoral campaigns in Britain, it tends to constitute an individual politician or party leader making their views clear rather than as part of inter- or intra-party debate. For instance, during the 2010 general election campaign, David Cameron vocalised his support for a reduction in the time limit available to 22 or 20 weeks.[26] Where abortion is clearly linked to electoral politics in Britain is through the ProLife Alliance Party; the party was formed in 1996 and has fielded candidates at local, regional, national, and European elections and was established as a political party to put abortion 'back on the political agenda'.[27] The electoral support garnered by the ProLife Alliance Party is negligible and it is very much on the fringes of party politics in Britain. Broadcasters refused to show the party's election broadcasts in 1997 and 2001, as they contained images of aborted foetuses, leading the party to sue the BBC. Whilst the Court of Appeal ruled in favour of the ProLife Alliance Party, this was subsequently overturned by the House of Lords.[28]

Indeed, Conservative backbench MP Nadine Dorries, who seeks a restriction on the time limit available for abortion, has spoken in Westminster about her frustration that Parliamentary debate on abortion is seemingly prohibited:

> Abortion law is made in Parliament, and there should be no taboo on discussing it in Parliament. Abortion law should be debated and

reformed here, yet each and every time I have raised an abortion issue in the House, one MP after another has risen to comment that this is not really the place to discuss abortion.

(Nadine Dorries MP, Hansard: 31/10/2012)

The views of Dorries chime with the claims that have long been made by the ProLife Alliance Party. Its 1997 election manifesto explicitly identified the problem of individual MPs voting with their parties rather than with their conscience. This, according to the ProLife Alliance Party, is disingenuous, as those who attempt to amend the Abortion Act have either been talked out or denied government support; furthermore, it claims that pro-life MPs have been 'subjected to disgraceful bullying, or have faced deselection'.[29] Claiming certain issues as 'conscience issues' is clearly a movable feast and one that is inherently problematic, not least because issues such as decisions whether or not to go to war are not considered matters of conscience (Cowley, 1998). Nonetheless, abortion has remained a matter for individual MPs despite the partisan and gendered patterns that are identified in roll call analysis. The defence of current abortion legislation has overwhelmingly relied on the support of Labour women MPs (Childs et al., 2013). And there has been some suggestion that had the 2010 general election returned a Conservative majority then we may already have seen restrictive changes to the current abortion law.

Within Britain, struggles over abortion policy are more likely to occur at the movement level rather than in legislative debate and this is something that corresponds with Meyer and Staggenborg's characterisation of the relationship between movements and counter-movements: 'Direct and indirect interactions between movements, in which the state may only be an occasional actor and target, are increasingly common' (1996: 1630). However, it would be a mistake to suggest that anti-abortion activism has not resulted in frequent attempts to restrict access to abortion in Britain incrementally, as Table 8.2 illustrates. None of these has passed, but each time they have been introduced they are accompanied by a media-led public debate about the nature of British abortion law. The most recent controversial example being the accusation that doctors were signing off on abortions on the basis of sex selection. This put pro-choice feminists in a difficult position, with many wanting to defend a woman's right to choose, whatever the motivation, whilst others worried that unborn girls would be disproportionately aborted.

Here we return to the role of women politicians. In both the US and Britain, female legislators tend to hold more liberal positions on abortion: in the US, female legislators are shown to enact less restrictive abortion policy (Berkman and O'Connor, 1993), whilst in Britain, female Parliamentarians are traditionally those who most vocally defend the Abortion Act (Childs et al., 2013). For abortion rights campaigners then, it is not just about getting 'more women' into the national- and state-level legislatures but it is also about getting pro-choice women elected. Having established the significant difference in the ways in which abortion is both framed and considered politically in the US and Britain, the chapter now turns to the interpretation of abortion both as a feminist issue and as a priority for third wave campaigning. The next section of the chapter draws upon the data gathered from the interviewees as well as reflecting on the way in which abortion is written about in popular feminist texts and online blogs.

Feminist activists and abortion campaigning

As Table 7.1 in the previous chapter identified, for the US feminist activists, abortion and reproductive justice was their most important priority, and, given the scale and intensity of the anti-abortion rights movement, this is not surprising. Some of the US activists were fairly despondent about the successful attacks waged by those who would like to see access to abortion restricted; indeed, for some, there was a sense that it was effectively holding back the momentum of wider feminist demands:

> Reproductive justice is my number one concern. It has to be. We're constantly fighting for our right to choose.
>
> (Portland)

> It's just so sad, all those gains that we thought we had made are now steadily being lost. I can't believe we're having to fight the same battles as my mom. It feels like I'm going to so many pro-choice meetings and fundraisers at the moment.
>
> (New York)

> Abortion is such a touchstone issue that if we lose on this, who knows what we'll have to concede to next.
>
> (Washington DC)

For these feminists then, abortion is an ongoing battle. There was a sense of frustration that the focus on abortion was so important that it all but prevented much progress on other fronts. In other words, the wider feminist movement has effectively been stalled by the need to defend existing gains. There was a sense of disbelief amongst some interviewees that in the US in the twenty-first century, women still had to fight for their basic right to have an abortion. Indeed, in their criticism of the Partial Birth Abortion Act, interviewees expressed anger and disappointment at elected politicians and the courts alike.

Many noted the difficulties facing the abortion rights movement in taking on the strength and financial resources of the anti-abortion movement, as one Portland interviewee observed: 'it's hard to see how we can win back those rights that are being taken away from us. They have much better resourced campaigns.' The financial disparity between the abortion rights movement and their opponents was a recurring theme. For the US abortion rights movement there were a plethora of activities that activists engaged with, including contacting state- and federal-level Congressmen and women, attending fundraisers, and helping to organise transport and accommodation for women who needed financial support in order to have an abortion. In 2013, Stop Patriarchy launched a National Abortion Rights Freedom Ride which travelled across 15 states; its accompanying statement called for abortion on demand and without apology, arguing that 'how one thinks and feels about abortion flows fundamentally from how one views women'.[30] US feminist magazines and blogs have repeatedly reported on the War on Women and in particular, the attacks on women's bodily autonomy. There was also extensive coverage of the controversy surrounding the comments made by radio host Rush Limbaugh, who labelled Sandra Fluke a 'slut' for wanting to ensure that birth control was covered by employer insurance. The response to Limbaugh was encouraging for reproductive rights advocates, as sponsors pulled their advertising from his show.

Conversely, British feminists, whilst all noting their support for abortion rights campaigns, were far less likely to be actively involved in campaigns concerning abortion. Moreover, there was less anxiety concerning the security of the provisions of the Abortion Act. Although they were all aware of the recent Parliamentary attempts to reduce the time limit available and of the increased presence of anti-abortion campaigns such as 40 Days for life, they did not express concern that this would actually happen:

> Of course, I'm pro-choice, although I suppose my activism on the issue consists mainly of emailing my MP or signing a petition. Apart from people like Nadine Dorries who are always trying to restrict the

> time limit, I feel fairly safe. We know we have public opinion on our side.
>
> (London)

> I email my MP whenever there's a vote on abortion but she's pro-choice anyway. I think we're fairly lucky in the UK, I mean it's not as much of an issue as it is in America.
>
> (Bristol)

> I went to a counter protest to 40 Days for Life when they were in Bedford Square [London], it was awful to see how they use children to try and make out that abortion is evil. We had a really good turn out on our side which is important and I think there were easily more of us than them.
>
> (London)

For the British activists, then, abortion rights campaigning tended to consist of contacting MPs or attending counter-protests (although this was relatively rare). There was not the sense of pessimism surrounding the issue that was clearly articulated by the US activists nor was there a sense of urgency regarding the need to defend the Abortion Act. The language in the quotations above marks a sharp contrast with that used by the US activists in terms of both their tone and their fears regarding access to abortion. Several interviewees highlighted that abortion was not as much of an issue as it was in the US. They variously spoke about the role of the religious right in the US and the fact that in Britain, popular opinion is fairly solidly in favour of a woman's right to choose. There was a sense of anger that groups such as 40 Days for Life were trying to import 'US-style tactics', as one interviewee put it, to Britain, and a feeling that this style of campaigning was not well suited to the British political context.

Indeed, Abortion Rights has recently been debating the need to go beyond defending the 1967 Act in order to push for the decriminalisation of abortion; at the moment, doctors are still liable to prosecution. Moreover, there are many within the abortion rights movement who want to see an end to the medicalisation of the abortion process by removing the need for the signatures of two doctors. Recent guidelines issued by the government now allow for midwives and nurses to take a 'leading role' in administering the drugs used for medical abortions, something that bpas has long supported given that family planning trained nurses already carry out such duties in their clinics.[31] Moreover, some interviewees noted their support for campaigns to help abortion rights activists in Northern Ireland campaigning to legalise abortion.

During the discussion of abortion, participants were asked whether or not they thought feminists could be anti-abortion. For many US and British interviewees, there was a clear sense that opposing a woman's right to choose was distinctly 'un-feminist'. Indeed, only a couple of interviewees was willing to defend the idea of a feminist opposition to abortion. This clearly raises a number of issues, not least concerning the dilemmas facing those feminists who have strong religious beliefs. Jennifer Baumgardner's book on abortion reflects on the idea that feminists can hold anti-abortion views. Indeed, she claims that 'It's a stultifying myth of feminism that prioritizing abortion rights is the most significant test of your commitment to women' (2008: 65). For Baumgardner then, it is a mistake to argue that it is oxymoronic to be what she calls a 'pro-life' feminist; that said, she critiques Feminists for Life for failing to provide sufficient emphasis on how to make political structures easier for women (64). She offers a series of recommendations that 'pro-life' feminists can adopt including, inter alia, supporting birth control and sex education (along with abstinence); advocating early abortions; and condemning the violence and extremist acts carried out in the name of the pro-life movement. The idea of teaching abstinence, which is usually associated with attempts to exert more social control over young women's sexual behaviour, is clearly problematic (Herzog, 2008). Moreover, her position marks a distinct shift in emphasis from the importance of pro-choice activism that was identified as one of the key points in the third wave seminal text *ManifestA* (Baumgardner and Richards, 2000). The idea of feminists also holding anti-abortion views is not something that has attracted much significant discussion elsewhere; research has highlighted the strength of the views held by those on both sides of the debate as effectively disbarring any meaningful dialogue (Vanderford, 1989).

Conclusion

Despite attempts to roll back abortion law in Britain and to import certain US-style tactics, it is clear that there is a gulf between the US and Britain when it comes to abortion policy and activism. Incremental changes to abortion law have been successful in the US but not in Britain. Anti-abortion activism is undertaken by a wide range of well-funded and well-organised groups in the US whereas this is yet to be the case in Britain. Abortion rights and reproductive justice remains the most important issue for US feminists whereas British activists can be comparatively 'relaxed' about attacks on abortion provision. Whilst the federal political system in the US in theory provides for less government intervention and control of individuals' lives, it has also proven to be far more interventionist in curtailing women's bodily autonomy than the British government has. The effects of all of these differences are significant for feminist activism and for the movement more broadly: in short, the US feminist movement has effectively been stalled by the issue, whilst in Britain, activists are able to concentrate their efforts on a wider range of issues and policy areas.

Conclusion

Feminist activism is thriving in both the US and Britain. The movement is ideologically diverse and continues to fight on many fronts. The continuity with previous waves of feminism is striking. Flourishing feminist campaigns targeting a range of social, political, and economic inequalities are indicative of the successful growth, and current depth, of the movement. Although there are certainly those who espouse a more individualistic, consumerist, or lifestyle mode of feminism, grassroots activists continue to engage with the politics of resistance. At times, activists seek to engage with the reconfigured state in order to advance feminist concerns, whilst at others they seek to resist and critique those very same institutions. Feminists are, therefore, both critics of the patriarchal power structures that reinforce gender inequality and are also, at times, beneficiaries of the decisions taken by those in power. Ideological plurality within the feminist movement prevents us, for the most part, from making sweeping generalisations about feminist successes; instead, a more critical and reflective analysis of what we might consider to be the gains and losses of the third wave is needed. Exploring the third wave of feminism comparatively through the prism of a 'long wave', one that covers a chronological period of over 20 years, allows us the opportunity to evaluate multiple theoretical and empirical accounts of feminist discourse and praxis. Such an approach also helps illuminate the, at times, gulf between popular representations of feminism and grassroots activism.

By analysing the long third wave of feminism, this book has demonstrated how feminist discourse and praxis differ between the US and Britain, both in terms of grassroots activism and in wider attitudes towards, and engagement with, the state. The research has mapped feminist activity and debate, examined feminist attitudes, and theorised the various challenges and opportunities that the neoliberal context and the turn towards intersectionality present for feminists. We have explored the political environment within which feminism has been resurgent; a situation which has made it difficult to establish group solidarity and collective action. And yet feminists, despite ideological differences, have sustained this current wave of resistance. Ironically, the need for recognising difference amongst and between women has also helped reinforce the collective nature of the movement, as feminists examine both what separates and divides but also what *unites*. In order to draw together the key findings of the book and to elucidate the principle differences between the US and Britain, this concluding chapter addresses the five research questions set out in the introduction.

How might we theorise a third wave feminist framework?

The typology, as set out in Chapter 1, identified five approaches to third wave feminisms: chronological, oppositional, generational, conceptual, and activist. Such a typology provides a framework for comparative research as it accounts for differences in temporal moments whilst also reflecting intellectual trends and movement dynamics. The typology draws upon the dominant frames in the academic literature but also upon popular feminist writing on third wave feminisms. The empirical application of such a typology demonstrated that most understood the third wave to constitute a chronological moment, closely aligned with the concept of intersectionality. A third wave conceived of primarily through a chronological lens with the additional recognition of the turn towards intersectionality is a useful way of approaching the third wave (not least when we consider continuity between the waves).

'Third wave' was a term more widely used and commonly understood amongst the US interviewees; this meant that at times, British feminists used US feminist popular texts as an interpretive proxy. Such a reading does to some extent help explain why some have sought to identify a fourth wave of feminism in Britain that reflects the particular concerns of the British movement. That feminists still seek to situate their feminism within waved and ideological frames demonstrates the purchase that both have on the feminist imagination. Whilst such narratives may be considered unhelpful for feminism, it may also be the case that those same categories and frames have an important heuristic role to play in developing and sustaining a feminist politics that seeks to prioritise links with previous iterations of feminist activism. Moreover, the ideological subjectivities of the activists can also be read as an important means by which to theorise the multiplicity of third wave feminism. Exploring contemporary feminism through a wave framework which encompasses ideological positioning not only allows us to consider points of continuity but also avoids reductive interpretations of feminist praxis.

Is the term 'Anglo-American feminism' useful?

The term 'Anglo-American feminism' provides an additional descriptor that can be read alongside the wave and ideological narratives. It is used as shorthand both as a way of signifying a certain type of feminism and as a way of thinking about feminism. Such a term relies upon historical similarities between US and British feminism, and yet this belies the various important political differences and points of emphases between the two movements. For sure, both movements have campaigned for women's suffrage and sought to fight for equal opportunities, but this is not something unique to Anglo-American feminism. Moreover, ideological debates and the role of race and class have shaped the feminist movements in the US and Britain in different ways, whilst radical feminism appears to play a more dominant role in contemporary British feminist activism. In short, imposing a term such as 'Anglo-American feminism' on either historical or contemporary analyses of feminism is problematic. Anglo-American feminism also relies, at least on one level, on both a shared language and the broader political narrative of the 'special relationship' and its use is perhaps in need of more critical reflection.

It is clear from the empirical analysis undertaken for this research that there are significant differences between US and British feminisms at both the level of discourse and praxis. The priorities of the two movements, whilst at times similar, differ according to the wider context and the internal dynamics of the movement. The significant emphasis on intersectionality within a US context means that the narratives, discourses, and campaigns necessarily take on a different complexion in the US than in Britain; the divisive debate over trans inclusion within Britain is a good example of this. Feminist priorities differ between the two states, with abortion having effectively stalled the ability of the US movement to move forward. Partisan politics also shapes the ways in which feminists seek to engage with the formal political process, with the GOP's 'War on Women' providing a much more explicit anti-feminist agenda than any mainstream party in Britain is currently advocating. Whilst there was a shared sense of cynicism towards legislative politics, it would be hard to argue that this view is distinct to the US and Britain.

What are the particular effects of neoliberalism on US and British feminism?

Feminist discourse and praxis are affected by the neoliberal context, in which group identity and collective action are difficult to establish and sustain. Although frequently interpreted as being about the limited role of the state, it is clear that an increased role for the markets can *only* be achieved through an increased role for the state. The mutually reinforcing neoliberal practices and values pursued by both states and markets have particular implications for women and for feminists. Within this current economic climate of austerity, neoliberal institutions are invested in promoting the idea of citizens both as consumers but also as autonomous self-reliant individuals. Such a strategy fosters a sense of alienation, particularly when we consider the extent to which activists seek to engage with the formal institutions of the state. It is perhaps understandable that there are those feminists who have sought to highlight the opportunities that a neoliberal context offers for women, particularly those concerned with the rights and equal status of professional women. Whilst feminist buzzwords such as individual choice and autonomy have now been co-opted to such an extent as to render them all but useless in terms of advancing feminist aims.

However, the political and economic realities of the neoliberal regime have, to some extent, sustained the movement. The multiple sites of opposition and resistance that constitute feminist campaigning are testament to the varied ways in which feminists have sought to oppose the main tenets of neoliberalism, even whilst some feminist writers have co-opted neoliberal frames to promote a conservative version of feminism. The neoliberal emphasis on the individual has implications for feminism, and yet there are reasons to be optimistic about the solidarity that exists amongst and between feminists. We might here consider that the idea of a sisterhood still has purchase amongst some feminists. Multiple sites of resistance are illustrative of the solidarity within the British and US movements, for instance in the reproductive justice movement or campaigns around sexual objectification. Calls from some to 'rebrand' feminism have largely been met with criticism from the wider feminist community who have rightly identified it as a neoliberal strategy in and of itself. And despite the ongoing influence of post-structuralism within the Academy, it is clear that grassroots activists remain committed to tackling the material inequalities facing women and girls.

How and when do activists adopt an intersectional feminist lens?

Intersectionality has come to dominate much framing and analysis of feminist praxis in recent years. Although it would be unfair to suggest that previous generations of feminists did not address the problems of race and class, the current emphasis on intersecting identities within both the feminist movement and the wider patriarchal context speaks to the centralisation of such debates. Theoretical work on intersectionality has been a key feature of gender scholarship, although empirical applications are made problematic by methodological complexities. The problems faced by gender scholars in applying an intersectional lens are mirrored within feminist activism, where it can be difficult to identify what an intersectional approach might look like. The potential atomising effects of such a lens also make it a challenge for those who seek to articulate a common agenda rather than a set of disparate accounts. Moreover, the attendant language of privilege has the potential to cause divisions and hierarchies within the movement, leading to a silencing of some voices and a shutting down of debate.

The emphasis on intersectionality is where we can identify quite a bit of distance between US and British feminists. In the US, debates concerning intersectionality are perhaps less controversial than in Britain – partly, this is because of the specific impact of black feminism in the US but it also perhaps speaks to a greater cultural acceptance of individualism and hence, individual circumstances. Although it is certainly true that feminist groups in Britain are developing a greater awareness of adopting an intersectional lens, it has remained a contentious issue. For the interviewees, the idea of intersectionality could be promoted through inclusivity in feminist events and conferences, but when considered in application to political representation, the issue became less straightforward. Moreover, it is not always clear how an intersectional feminist approach to understanding the ways in which the state represents feminist interests could be either properly implemented or understood. Despite this, the priorities of the feminists in both the US and Britain do centre largely on women's bodies, whether that is in terms of reproductive justice or violence against women.

What are the attitudes of feminists towards state representation of feminist issues?

Feminists have long had a complicated relationship to the state, first seeking to gain access to, and then equality within, institutions. Activists have long critiqued the patriarchal nature of the state. For some this has led to a focus on alternative ways of organising. For others, who have sought to work from within in order to reform, the state offers the best site for the further advancement of feminist aims and goals. Debates concerning representational claims are contentious not only in terms of specific policies and those seeking to champion them, but also with regards to the extent to which national legislatures are suitable locations of resisting and contesting patriarchy. Cynicism surrounding the formal political process has led many to disengage with electoral politics; this is shaped both by an adherence to a more radical politics but also by a sense of disengagement that is encouraged by neoliberal institutions. The resurgent feminist movements themselves are therefore important alternative sites for action and contestation.

Many of the interviewees were hostile towards, or at least sceptical of, the role of the state in advancing women's and feminists' interests. And yet, it is clear that feminists of all ideological strands were willing to work through the official channels in order to bring about change; this was more notable amongst grassroots activists in Britain than in the US. The energy within the feminist movements and their various constituent parts suggests that it is outside the state that many choose to focus their attention. Such an approach means that the state and legislators, particularly those who seek to advance a feminist agenda, adopt a more reactive role, responding to the demands of the movement rather than providing leadership. In many respects, such a situation is to be welcomed, with the power to set the agenda firmly located in the grassroots.

Conclusion

This book has sought to flesh out some of the political debates and controversies within the third wave of feminism in two different states. In so doing, it has highlighted the importance of the neoliberal context within which such activism is occurring and also the influence of intersectionality in shaping feminist discourse and praxis. Of course, such a research project can never hope to provide an exhaustive or definitive account. The ideas explored in this book could certainly be further developed through the addition of other case studies, not least in reflecting upon how well such a typological approach works for feminist movements in countries that do not neatly fall into the first/second/third wave categories. Future research would also benefit from undertaking some complementary quantitative research, alongside in-depth qualitative research, in order to broaden the scope of issues that could be explored; this would be particularly important in terms of specific policy areas. Thus far, the third wave of feminism has been sustained; however, reflection on previous periods of abeyance should caution against an overly optimistic reading of the potential for ongoing high-profile feminist activism. Nonetheless, the fact that the movement has continued to flourish during a difficult political and economic context with a revived anti-feminist lobby should be an encouraging sign.

Appendix A: Interviews Undertaken with Feminist Activists

The timing and the number of interviews undertaken with feminists are set out in the table below. Interviews were conducted in public spaces, such as coffee shops, or, less frequently, in the interviewee's home or office. A few interviews were conducted via email and additional email questions were sometimes sent to participants in order to clarify or follow up on specific points.

Semi-structured interviews were conducted which allowed for a degree of flexibility in the direction of the discussion. Full anonymity was guaranteed to the interviewees; hence, no further biographical data regarding age, sex, sexuality, or ethnicity, inter alia, is provided here, as participants (particularly from the smaller cities) might be easier to identify.

Table A.1 Interview schedule

City	Number of interviews	Dates
Bristol	13	November 2012–March 2013
Glasgow	4	February–October 2012
London	22	January–May 2012
New York	17	July–August 2012
Portland	14	June–July 2013
Washington DC	3	March 2014
Total	73	January 2012–March 2014

Appendix B: Interview Guide

How do you define feminism? How do you define *your* feminism?

What do you think of when you think about third wave feminism? Do you identify as third wave?

What are your thoughts on attempts to rebrand and reclaim feminism?

What, if any, are your views on intersectionality and its place within feminism?

How inclusive do you think that the movement is? What could the movement do to become more inclusive? (For those involved with organising events: what steps have you taken to become more inclusive)?

What are your thoughts on the term 'sisterhood'? Do you use it?

What are your views on women-only organising? Women-born-women?

What are your thoughts on the term 'women's/feminist issues' for policy discussions? Which do you consider to be feminist priorities?

Are you active within abortion rights campaigning?

Do you identify with a political party? Are you active in that party?

Do you think that feminism is well represented in mainstream politics? How well do you think women are represented in Parliament/Congress?

Can you name any politicians that represent feminism?

Notes

Introduction

1. I use the term 'Britain' rather than 'the UK' because my interview data and analysis of feminist groups does not include Northern Ireland. When referring to Parliament however, I use 'UK' rather than 'British'.
2. Indeed, it is worth stressing that whilst calls for a third wave of feminism originated in the US amongst women of color (Orr, 1997); it quickly became synonymous with white, middle-class women (hooks, 1994; Hurdis, 2002). Despite scholars highlighting the coterminous rise of the third wave with black feminist jurisprudence, it is typically an area largely ignored by key third wave texts (Taylor, 1998), even whilst third wave texts have claimed to be more explicitly concerned with inclusion of all women.
3. The recently created online magazine the *Feminist Times*, which had attempted to attract financial support in order to move to a print-based model, announced in July 2014 that it had not generated sufficient income, see the statement on their website available online: http://www.feministtimes.com/ Date accessed: 1st August 2014.
4. The Equal Rights Amendment was written in 1923 in order to guarantee the equal application of the constitution to all people, regardless of their sex. It was passed by Congress in 1972 but has failed to gain the support of the required number of states (38) necessary in order to ratify the change to the constitution.
5. > All persons born or naturalized in the United States, and subject to the jurisdiction thereof, are citizens of the United States and of the State wherein they reside. No State shall make or enforce any law which shall abridge the privileges or immunities of citizens of the United States; nor shall any State deprive any person of life, liberty, or property, without due process of law; nor deny to any person within its jurisdiction the equal protection of the laws.
   >
   > (The Constitution of the United States of America: Amendment XIX)
6. The National Coalition for Men was formed in 1977 in order to provide a 'unified voice' for men and boys, their website is available online: http://ncfm.org/lead-with-us/chapters/ Date accessed: 27th July 2014. Fathers 4 Justice was established in 2001 in order to change a perceived bias in the family court system that denied fathers access to their children, their website is available online: http://www.fathers-4-justice.org/our-campaign/our-campaigns/#anti-male-discrimination Date accessed: 27th July 2014.

1 Understanding Third Wave Feminisms

1. There has been much coverage of the tension within contemporary feminism in the UK over the past couple of years; this has crystallised around

the implications of intersectionality and of trans inclusion in particular. There have been several conferences and online debates, organised by self-identified radical feminists, which have had a woman-born-woman-only policy. The debates between trans feminists and their allies who seek to promote full inclusion and the so-called trans exclusionary radical feminists (TERFs) has come to dominate discussions of feminist praxis. See for instance: http://www.theguardian.com/commentisfree/2014/mar/07/international-womens-day-defence-feminist-dissent-argued-priorities and http://www.newstatesman.com/helen-lewis/2014/02/uses-and-abuses-intersectionality.

2. Throughout the book, when I refer to those who could be identified as being third wave I am referring to those who either answered yes or yes, but (N=38).
3. Here, liberal feminism as a comparable strand of feminism is understood as distinct from the different uses of the term 'liberal' in US and British political traditions; in the US, it signifies a leftist approach, whilst in Britain it can be viewed as a centrist position. The understanding here is that liberal feminism is a widely used frame in the US and Britain and refers to a similar approach and set of ideas.
4. The term 'johns' is used here to refer to the men who buy sex from prostitutes.
5. Throughout the book, the 'third wave' will be used to refer to feminism from the early 1990s onwards, whilst third wave feminisms (plural) will be used to discuss the various ideological strains and themes within the third wave. Reference is also made to 'self-identified' third wavers, which refers to those writers of popular feminist texts who described themselves as such.

2 Conceptual and Contextual Framework: Intersectionality and Neoliberalism

1. See Laurie Penny's article for *The Guardian* which argued that David Cameron's introduction of porn filters was a response to demands from government agencies and private companies to control and monitor the online activity of citizens, available online: http://www.theguardian.com/commentisfree/2014/jan/03/david-cameron-internet-porn-filter-censorship-creep Date accessed: 14th August 2014.
2. In 2013, Women's Aid, Britain's largest domestic violence charity, declared a 'state of crisis' in domestic violence services as a result of the cuts introduced since 2010. These included a loss of 112 specialist posts, with 48 per cent of services running with no funding at all, see its website for further details, available online: http://www.womensaid.org.uk/domestic-violence-press-information.asp?itemid=3194&itemTitle=Women%92s+Aid+warns+of+crisis+in+domestic+violence+services&section=0001000100150001&sectionTitle=Press+releases Date accessed: 27th August 2014.
3. Equal Pay Day was established in 1996 and is marked around the world as a way of raising awareness about the continuing pay gap between men and women, the official website is available online: http://equal-pay-day.com/ Date accessed: 28th August 2014.
4. Sheryl Sandberg's book *Lean In*, published in 2013, encouraged women to pursue their ambitions and stop holding themselves back.

5. There have been reports of sexual harassment and rape at various Occupy camps including those held at Glasgow and New York. Subsequent accusations of victim blaming, cover-ups, and attempts to present it as a means by which to undermine the credibility of the camps and the failure to take the issues seriously undermined the extent to which they constituted safe, let alone feminist, spaces. For further analysis see the blog post on the LSE website by MSc student Emily Miles, available online: http://blogs.lse.ac.uk/gender/2011/12/05/occupy-lsxual-harrassment/ Date accessed: 12th May 2012.
6. Gender mainstreaming refers to an approach that ensures that gender perspectives are taken into account during policy creation, development, and implementation processes.
7. This is a relatively new phrase within the feminist lexicon, and refers to those who are not transgendered and who assume the privileges of those whose birth at sex matches their gendered identity. It is a highly contested term and has generated much debate amongst feminists online, with high-profile activists disclaiming the term as it is dismissive of the various ways in which female bodies are subjected to male scrutiny and violence on a daily basis, see the blog post by Caroline Criado Perez, available online: http://weekwoman.wordpress.com/2014/08/01/what-does-being-cis-mean-for-a-woman/ Date accessed: 2nd August 2014.
8. Standpoint theory refers to the fact that knowledge and understanding are socially positioned. In theory, it allows for the voices of more marginalised women to be heard. It starts from the premise that feminist research and understanding should begin with the lived experiences of women; it grew out of Marxist feminist scholarship that prioritised the importance of the social and historical.
9. See her interview with S. Danius and S. Jonssson. 1993. 'An Interview with Gayatri Chakravorrty Spivak', *Boundary* 2 (20): 24–50.
10. See Louise Mensch's article for *The Guardian* which critiqued the introspective nature of intersectionality, available online: http://www.theguardian.com/commentisfree/2013/may/30/reality-based-feminism-louise-mensch Date accessed: 30th May 2013.
11. In Britain, a debate emerged between several journalists over the use of the term 'intersectionality' which resulted in allegations of transphobia, see the article in *The Independent*, available online: http://www.independent.co.uk/news/people/news/dont-get-mad-get-even-paris-lees-responds-to-julie-burchills-attack-about-the-concept-of-intersectionality-9146871.html Date accessed: 24th February 2014.
12. A recent interview with Kimberlé Crenshaw by *Feminist Times* asked her about the idea of intersectional feminism:

    > I heard about that about four months ago. That intersectionality was being used as an adjective or a noun – a kind of feminist. It's interesting. I've never called myself an intersectional feminist. I'm a black feminist that does intersectional work. I don't have a strong sense one way or the other about how people self-identify.

    The full interview is available online: http://www.feministtimes.com/call-yourself-an-intersectional feminist/#sthash.KuwJt62S.dpuf Date accessed: 30th August 2014.

3 Reclaiming and Rebranding Feminist Activism

1. Two feminist media groups in Britain, *Vagenda* and *Feminist Times*, and one teenage feminist campaigner were paired up with advertising agencies to rebrand feminism, something that *Jezebel* criticised in a blog post, available online: http://jezebel.com/new-issue-of-elle-u-k-tries-its-darnedest-to-rebrand-1435416217 Date accessed: 6th January 2014.
2. See *Jezebel*'s blog post on why high-profile women choose not to identify as feminist, available online: http://jezebel.com/the-many-misguided-reasons-famous-ladies-say-im-not-a-1456405014 Date accessed: 25th July 2014.
3. See Mary Elizabeth William's piece for *Salon* which criticises the way in which high-profile women mis-characterise feminism, available online: http://www.salon.com/2014/06/03/shailene_woodley_still_thinks_feminism_discriminates/ Date accessed: 25th July 2014.
4. See for instance a post by Charlotte Raven for *Feminist Times*, arguing that wearing high heels is incongruent with being a feminist, available online: http://www.feministtimes.com/a-feminist-in-high-heels-is-like-dawkins-in-a-rosary/ Date accessed: 17th June 2014.
5. See the debate in *The Guardian*, available online: http://www.guardian.co.uk/lifeandstyle/2008/aug/22/women Date accessed: 10th May 2012. Also see the official website of The Subversive Cupcake Company, available online: http://subversivecupcakes.co.uk/?page_id=28 Date accessed: 12th August 2012. And also see the blog post on *The F Word*, available online: http://www.thefword.org.uk/features/2012/08/cupcake_feminis Date accessed: 20th September 2012.
6. See the BBC coverage of Tom MacMaster, the US student who presented to be a gay girl in Damascus, available online: http://www.bbc.co.uk/news/uk-scotland-13747761 Date accessed: 10th September 2012. And see *The Guardian* coverage of the man pretending to be 'Paula Brooks', executive editor of LezGetReal, available online: http://www.theguardian.com/world/2011/jun/14/lesbian-bloggers-revealed-men Date accessed: 10th September 2012.
7. Isabella Sorley and John Nimmo were found guilty of sending abusive and threatening tweets to Criado Perez and were sentenced to jail for 12 weeks and 8 weeks, respectively, see the BBC coverage of the story, available online: http://www.bbc.co.uk/news/uk-25641941 Date accessed: 10th January 2014.
8. Jaclyn Munson, founder of the *Onward and F-Word* blog received abusive tweets, neither Twitter nor the NYPD took her complaints seriously, for coverage of this see *The Daily Beast*, available online: http://www.thedailybeast.com/witw/articles/2013/09/05/my-run-in-with-anti-feminist-twitter-death-threats.html Date accessed: 12th December 2013.
9. See the SlutWalk Toronto FAQs, available online: http://www.slutwalktoronto.com/about/faqs Date accessed: 6th July 2013.
10. See for instance the then Conservative MP Louise Mensch on NewsNight 14th June 2011 and Labour MEP Mary Honeyball's blog, available online: http://thehoneyballbuzz.com/2011/06/10/dont-slutwalk-this-saturday/ Date accessed: 9th September 2012.
11. Greer defended the SlutWalks in a piece for *The Telegraph* in which she argued that it was about women reclaiming the right to be dirty in sexual terms but also in terms of cleaning, the full article is

available online: http://www.telegraph.co.uk/women/womens-health/8510743/These-slut-walk-women-are-simply-fighting-for-their-right-to-be-dirty.html Date accessed: 9th October 2013.

12. See *Jezebel's* piece on the man behind Femen: http://jezebel.com/the-man-behind-femen-is-no-friend-of-the-movement-1251310779 Date accessed: 22nd September 2014. See also the Feminists against Femen Facebook campaign, available online: https://www.facebook.com/FeministsAgainstFemen/info?ref=page_internal Date accessed: 20th September 2014.
13. See the Rock the Slut Vote website, available online: http://rocktheslutvote.blogspot.co.uk/ Date accessed: 9th October 2014.

4 Feminist Inclusivity

1. A note on the terminology: whilst 'women of color' tends to be the predominant term used within the US, within Britain 'black' tends to be used by feminists, as British group Black Feminists outline: 'We use the word "black" in the political sense to denote women who self-identify, originate or have ancestry from global majority populations (i.e. African, Asian, Middle Eastern and Latin America) and Indigenous and Bi-racial backgrounds', further details are on its website, available online: http://www.blackfeminists.org/about-us/ Date accessed: 10th May 2014. Given that the ideological and theoretical strand tends to be described as black feminism, rather than women of color feminism, I use the term 'black' exclusively to talk about the strand of feminism. Elsewhere, I have used the terms to some extent interchangeably although have sought where possible to use them discretely when referring to US or British feminism.
2. The 2014 NOW annual conference was held in New Mexico and the conference website stated that the organisers wanted the speakers to 'represent and are relatable' for members, the programme is available online: http://now.org/about/conference/ Date accessed: 10th July 2014.
3. *The New Black Woman* blogged in 2011 that 'Feminism as it stands is unwilling to accommodate, reach out and consider itself an effective ideology for women of color and other women who don't identify as cisgendered, straight and middle-to-upper middle-class white women', the full blog post is available online: http://newblackwoman.com/2011/12/03/i-am-no-longer-a-feminist/ Date accessed: 16th January 2014.
4. See the blog post on *Salon*, available online: http://www.salon.com/2009/09/05/veil_debate/ Date accessed: 12th November 2013.
5. See The United to End Female Genital Mutilation website, available online: http://www.uefgm.org/About-The_END_FGM_European_Campaign,EN.ABOUT.01,EN Date accessed: 17th April 2014.
6. Collection of zines available at *Bitch office*, *In Other Words* (Portland), *Bluestockings* (New York) and at the *Women's Library* (London).
7. See the article in *Bitch Magazine*, available online: http://bitchmagazine.org/post/the-long-history-of-transgender-exclusion-from-feminism Date accessed: 1st March 2014.
8. See for instance the decision by the University of Manchester to ban longtime feminist campaigner Julie Bindel from speaking at a debate, covered by

The New Statesman, available online: http://www.newstatesman.com/sarah-ditum/2014/03/when-did-no-platform-become-about-attacking-individuals-deemed-disagreeable Date accessed: 12th April 2014.

9. See for instance the blog post on *The F Word* about working-class women's views on the feminist movement, available online: http://www.thefword.org.uk/features/2012/03/feminism_still_ Date accessed: 10th June 2014.
10. A historical overview of the National Welfare Rights Organization is available online: http://www.blackpast.org/aah/national-welfare-rights-organization-1966-1975 Date accessed: 1st June 2014. For details of the Coalition of Labor Union Women, see its website, available online: http://www.cluw.org/?zone=/unionactive/view_page.cfm&page=About20CLUW Date accessed: 2nd June 2014. See the official TUC equality pages, available online: http://www.tuc.org.uk/equality-issues Date accessed: 2nd June 2014.
11. See for instance the London meeting of the Women's Assembly against Austerity, details are available online: http://yorkpeoplesassembly.wordpress.com/2014/03/01/womens-assembly-against-austerity-meets-in-london/ Date accessed: 10th September 2014.
12. Details of NOW's campaign for economic justice are available online: http://now.org/issues/economic-justice/ Date accessed: 17th August 2014.
13. Fawcett was unsuccessful in its claim against the government; for an overview see *The Guardian* coverage, available online: http://www.theguardian.com/lifeandstyle/2010/oct/22/yvette-cooper-fawcett-society-cuts Date accessed: 1st September 2012.
14. UK Feminista's press release explaining its protest is available online: http://ukfeminista.org.uk/news/press-releases/feminists-target-nike-ahead-of-olympics-over-firms-exploitation-of-women/ Date accessed: 10th July 2012.
15. The Older Feminist Network's website is available online: http://www.olderfeminist.org.uk/ Date accessed: 20th November 2013.
16. The official website of the Veteran Feminists of America is available online: http://www.vfa.us/History.htm Date accessed: 5th July 2014.
17. For further detail see The Triangle website, available online: http://thetriangle.yolasite.com/ Date accessed: 1st July 2014 and also Deaf Women United's website, available online: http://www.dwu.org/#!about_us/csgz Date accessed: 1st July 2014.
18. Set up in 1998, Gimp Girl aims to create an online community for disabled women and is available online: http://www.gimpgirl.com/about-us/ Date accessed: 1st July 2014.
19. FWD was a group blog roll written by feminists with disabilities, the archive of which is still available online: http://disabledfeminists.com/ Date accessed: 1st July 2014.
20. The full blog post is on The *F Word* website, available online: http://www.thefword.org.uk/blog/2009/11/disabled_femini Date accessed: 12th June 2012.

5 The Sisterhood: Inclusivity and Spaces

1. See the article on the *Feminist Times* website and in *The Guardian* on men using feminism to sleep with women, available online: http://www

.feministtimes.com/space-invaders-men-in-feminist-spaces/ Date accessed: 1st June 2014. http://www.theguardian.com/commentisfree/2014/jan/09/not-a-feminist-move-on-men-women Date accessed: 10th January 2014.

2. The official website of the White Ribbon campaign, including the pledge, is available online: http://www.whiteribbon.ca/pledge/ Date accessed: 20th November 2013.
3. See the interview with academics Ruth Lewis and Elizabeth Sharp on the *Feminist Times* website, available online: http://www.feministtimes.com/whats-so-safe-about-feminist-women-only-space/ Date accessed: 1st May 2014.
4. The interview with Amy Ray is available online: http://www.indigogirls.com/correspondence/2005/2005-06-13-a/interview03.html Date accessed: 13th February 2014.
5. The official website of Camp Trans is available online: http://camp-trans.org/about/ Date accessed: 13th February 2014.
6. I have excluded religious, professional groups, and sororities from this analysis.
7. See the frequently asked questions section of the WI website, available online: http://www.thewi.org.uk/faqs Date accessed: 10th February 2014.
8. See the About US section of the WI website, available online: http://www.thewi.org.uk/about-the-wi Date accessed: 10th February 2014.
9. See the frequently asked questions section of the DAR, available online: http://www.dar.org/natsociety/faq.cfm Date accessed: 10th February 2014.
10. The League of Women Voters website is available online: www.lwv.org Date accessed: 2nd March 2014.
11. The official website of the NCNW is available online: http://www.ncnw.org/e3org/becomeamember.aspx Date accessed: 2nd March 2014.
12. See the official website of Liberal Democrat Women, available online: http://www.libdems.org.uk/ldw Date accessed: 1st May 2014. And for details of the Austin Texas chapter of the National Federation of Republican Women, see its website, available online: http:/austinrepublicanwomen.org/ Date accessed: 26th September 2014.
13. See the LFN page explaining why it is women only, available online: http://londonfeministnetwork.org.uk/home/why-women-only Date accessed: 1st March 2013.
14. The Radical Woman manifesto is available online: http://www.radicalwomen.org/intro.shtml#purpose Date accessed: 17th August 2013.
15. See the homepage of the LFN website, available online: http://londonfeministnetwork.org.uk/ Date accessed: 1st June 2012.
16. This does not mean that there are no small feminist groups operating as women only, but the groups were not large enough for their presence to be identified.
17. For details of the Radical Feminist Group in New York, see its Meetup page, available online: http://www.meetup.com/Radical-Feminist-Activist-Meetup-Group/photos/2558391/43093601/ Date accessed: 1st May 2012.
18. For details of the RadFem Reboot conference see the *Liberation Collective* blog, available online: http://liberationcollective.wordpress.com/2012/04/22/rad-fem-reboot-2012/ Date accessed: 3rd March 2014.

19. The website for the North East Feminist gathering is available online: http://www.nefeministgathering.com/ Date accessed: 10th June 2014.
20. For details of the Black Feminists, see its website, available online: http://www.blackfeminists.org/meetings/ Date accessed: 20th May 2014.
21. The official website of the Aldermaston Peace Camp is available online: http://www.aldermaston.net/camp/all Date accessed: 10th May 2014.
22. The Women's Spaces conference was held at Queen Mary, University of London, 16th May 2014.
23. See Laurie Penny's blog for *The New Statesman*, available online: http://www.newstatesman.com/society/2014/06/laurie-penny-what-transgender-tipping-point-really-means Date accessed: 26th June 2014.
24. Although we can probably assume that DAR has no trans women as members as there is no official policy on this, I have not included it. Whilst some individual chapters of the WI explicitly state on the website that they welcome all those who identify as women.
25. The official RadFem conference is no longer available online.
26. See the *GenderTrender* feminist blog for details of the RadFem conference, available online: http://gendertrender.wordpress.com/2012/05/18/radfem-2012-first-speakers-announced/ Date accessed: 7th February 2014.
27. See the *Feminist Times* article 'There's nothing radical about transphobia', available online: http://www.feministtimes.com/whats-so-safe-about-feminist-women-only-space/ Date accessed: 19th June 2012.
28. See *The New Yorker's* coverage of the disagreement between radical feminists and trans activists, available online: http://www.newyorker.com/magazine/2014/08/04/woman-2 Date accessed: 7th August 2014.
29. See a blog post on the London Dyke March protest, available online: http://www.sarahlizzy.com/blog/?p=236 Date accessed: 30th August 2014. See the *GenderTrender* blog for coverage of the New York Dyke March, available online: http://gendertrender.wordpress.com/2012/06/27/full-video-nyc-dyke-march-2012-transgender-attack-on-lesbian-feminist-cathy-brennan/ Date accessed: 30th August 2014.
30. See Emma Allen's *Unpacking Transphobia* blog on the Radical Women website, available online: http://www.radicalwomen.org/transphobia.shtml Date accessed: 20th August 2013.

6 Feminism and Women's Political Representation

1. Data correct as of February 2014.
2. Factsheet on Women in Congress is available via the Center for American Women in Politics website, available online: http://www.cawp.rutgers.edu/fast_facts/levels_of_office/Congress-HistoricalInfo.php Date accessed: 4th March 2014.
3. For data and further analysis see the History of the House website, available online: http://history.house.gov/Exhibitions-and-Publications/WIC/Historical-Data/Women-of-Color-in-Congress/ and also the data on women of color produced by the Center for American Women in Politics, available on its website: http://www.cawp.rutgers.edu/fast_facts/women_of_color/elective_office.php Date accessed: 4th March 2014.

4. See the BBC coverage of the new 2010 intake, available online: http://news.bbc.co.uk/2/hi/uk_politics/8673167.stm Date accessed: 3rd March 2013.
5. It is worth remembering that the US Constitution requires members of the House of Representatives to be at least 25 years old and 30 for the Senate. In Britain, there is a minimum age of 18, which in part explains why at the aggregate level, women MPs are younger than Congresswomen.
6. Moreover, there has been no systematic attempt to collect the data on this, despite the introduction of the Access to Elected Office Fund which is in part designed to help people with disabilities run for office in the UK. Scope, a leading disability rights organisation in the UK, estimates that to be fully representative of the population there should be around 65 (or 10 per cent) MPs with disabilities. See the Scope press release on the Access to Elected Office, available online: http://www.scope.org.uk/About-Us/Media/Press-releases/July-2012/Access-to-Elected-Office-Fund Date accessed: 11th July 2012.
7. A PAC is a way of collecting and donating political fundraising to either specific candidates or groups of candidates. There is a limit of $5,000 to individual candidates per election and $15,000 annually to a national party committee. For further information see the Open Secrets website, available online: https://www.opensecrets.org/pacs/pacfaq.php Date accessed: 21st December 2012.
8. EMILY's List was created in 1985 in order to help fund pro-choice women candidates, although since then it has expanded its remit to recruiting candidates and mobilising voters. See the mission statement on its website, available online: http://emilyslist.org/who/mission Date accessed: 2nd April 2013.
9. The WISH List was established in 1982 to recruit and help fund the campaigns of 'mainstream' Republican women to all levels of political office. In addition to fundraising activities, it is also involved in the identification and recruitment of potential candidates. Its website is available online: http://www.thewishlist.org/ Date accessed: 2nd April 2013.
10. The Center for American Women in Politics runs a number of non-partisan training and leadership programs aimed at encouraging and preparing women to run for elected office, details are available online: http://cawp.rutgers.edu/education_training/index.php/ Date accessed: 9th January 2014. There is no such equivalent provided by any British university. Running Start was an initiative started in 2007 that grew out of the Women Under 40 PAC, it helps fund young women running for federal office in addition to providing training and mentoring to the next generation of young women leaders; its website is available online: http://runningstartonline.org/about-us/historymission Date accessed: 9th January 2014. Again there is no such British equivalent specifically targeted at young British women.
11. The non-partisan Women's Campaign Fund was founded in 1974 in order to promote women and encourage women's leadership at all electoral levels in order to achieve gender parity. Described on its website as 'political venture capitalists', it has an associated PAC and seeks to support women who want to advance the health of the nation, including reproductive health. Its website is available online: http://www.wcfonline.org/ Date accessed: 12th September 2014.

12. The Counting Women In campaign is pushing for 50/50 gender representation across all electoral levels in British public life. The campaign asks followers to sign up to a mailing list and sign a petition to show their support. Its website is available online: http://www.countingwomenin.org/ Date accessed: 10th January 2014.
13. In 2012, a group of Conservative women complained that the Fawcett Society, which is supposed to be politically neutral, was too closely tied to the Labour Party and had insufficient representation from Conservative women on its board. For coverage of this see *The Telegraph* article, available online: http://www.telegraph.co.uk/women/womens-politics/9605196/Women-Tory-MPs-plot-revolution-at-150-year-old-Fawcett-Society.html Date accessed: 1st June 2014.
14. See the Fawcett Society website, available online: http://www.fawcettsociety.org.uk/our-work/issues/power-influence/ Date accessed: 19th September 2014.
15. See the Feminist Majority website, available online: http://feministmajority.org/about/ Date accessed: 19th September 2014.
16. For further details of the lap-dancing campaign, see the Object website, available online: http://www.object.org.uk/campaign-update Date accessed: 1st October 2014. Petitions have become increasingly popular in Britain over the past few years; successful feminist campaigns include the addition of mothers' names on marriage certificates and the Bank of England's decision to put an image of Jane Austen on the £10 note following their decision to remove the only woman (apart from the Queen) featured on UK currency.
17. 'Cis' is a term used by some to denote those who do not identify as trans.

7 Representing Women's and Feminist Interests

1. It is for instance obvious that an intersectional approach underpinned the Dual Discrimination clause in the UK's 2010 Equality Act which would have allowed claimants to pursue two claims of discrimination, for example race and sex; the clause was not passed (Krizsan et al., 2012: 17).
2. Details of the Federal Agency Resources for Women are available online: http://www.dol.gov/wb/otherfedagencies.htm Date accessed: 1st July 2014.
3. Details of the President's Council on Women and Girls are available online: http://www.whitehouse.gov/administration/eop/cwg/about Date accessed: 1st July 2014.
4. The US Commission on Civil Rights official website is available online at: http://www.usccr.gov/about/index.php Date accessed: 1st July 2014.
5. A brief official biography of Latifa Lyles is available online: http://www.dol.gov/wb/LatifaLyles.htm Date accessed: 9th September 2014.
6. Rewind&Reframe was a one-year funded project that ran between February 2013 and January 2014 that aimed to challenge sexism and racism in music videos. Whilst the campaign has now officially ended, the website is still active and available online: http://www.rewindreframe.org/ Date accessed: 7th September 2014.

7. For details of the 'johns' school' see *Oregon Live* available online: http://www.oregonlive.com/portland/index.ssf/2012/02/52_portland_men_undergo_johns.html Date accessed: 11th August 2013.
8. PinkStinks was established by two sisters who were angry at the explicitly gendered toys and clothes aimed at children in the UK. Its website is available online: http://www.pinkstinks.org.uk/about-us.htmlxplanation Date accessed: 10th September 2014.
9. The SPARK movement was created by two psychology professors in response to the American Psychological Association Taskforce Report on the Sexualisation of Girls; following an initial summit, the organisation brings together leaders, progressive organisations, media experts, and policy makers committed to creating the enabling conditions for healthy sexuality by pushing back on media sexualisation of girls and young women. Its website is available online: http://www.sparksummit.com/history/ Date accessed: 1st September 2012.
10. Various women's centres around Britain have been forced to close due to funding withdrawal, such as the Lambeth Women's Project in South London, the Willow Women's Centre in Hull, and the Swansea Women's Centre. For coverage of the cuts, see *The Guardian* article: http://www.theguardian.com/society/2011/feb/02/womens-groups-funding-cuts for an overview of the impact of funding cuts to women's groups in Britain. Date accessed: 17th July 2013.

8 Abortion and Reproductive Rights Activism

1. See for instance *The Atlantic* coverage of the rise of anti-abortion activism in London, available online: http://www.theatlantic.com/international/archive/2012/04/the-americanization-of-the-uk-anti-abortion-movement/255409/ Date accessed: 4th September 2014. And *The Guardian's* reporting on the US-influenced tactics and claims made by the anti-abortion lobby, available online: http://www.theguardian.com/world/2012/mar/23/abortion-what-children-schools Date accessed: 1st March 2014.
2. Abortion is a reserved matter for the UK Parliament, apart from in Northern Ireland. This means that neither the Welsh Assembly nor Scottish Parliament can legislate on the matter.
3. *Roe v. Wade* was a 1973 ruling by the Supreme Court that a woman's right to choose could be defended under the First Amendment. Abortion was subsequently legalised in all 50 states; however, statutory time limits on when abortions can take place vary from state to state. Under *Roe v. Wade*, abortions are generally permitted until the foetus is considered viable or able to live outside the womb. Some states have no time limit, whilst others allow abortion up to the end of the second trimester, about 27 or 28 weeks into the pregnancy.
4. The history of UK abortion law is available on the Education for Choice website: http://www.efc.org.uk/young_people/facts_about_abortion/uk_abortion_law.html Date accessed: 27th February 2014.
5. D&X extraction refers to the method by which a pregnancy is terminated by partially extracting a foetus from a uterus. It is usually performed during the second trimester between 20 and 24 weeks.

6. The Pew overview is available online: http://www.pewforum.org/2013/01/16/a-history-of-key-abortion-rulings-of-the-us-supreme-court/#roe Date accessed: 14th August 2014.
7. SisterSong was founded in 1997 to educate, advocate on behalf of, and give a voice to women of color in the US. It is made up of a number of local, regional, and national groups and organisations. See its website for information about Reproductive Justice, available online: http://www.sistersong.net/index.php?option=com_content&view=article&id=141&Itemid=81 Date accessed: 28th February 2014.
8. The blog hosted by the Institute for Advanced Studies at the University of Birmingham is available online: http://savinghumans.org/tag/reproductive-justice/ Date accessed: 15th August 2014.
9. Sarah Jackson's research into reproductive justice and pro-choice activism in Britain can be accessed via her blog, available online: https://badreputation.org.uk/2011/03/03/reproductive-justice-in-the-uk-part-2/ Date accessed: 15th August 2014.
10. In line with the normative feminist approach of this research, there is no reference to pro-life campaigning. Instead, opposition to pro-choice activism is framed as anti-abortion or anti-choice, which more accurately describes the dynamics of the two sides of the campaign.
11. Planned Parenthood promotes a 'common sense' approach to women's health and well-being. Its website is available online: www.plannedparenthood.org/about-us/ Date accessed: 2nd March 2014.
12. For information about NARAL visit its website, available online: http://action.prochoiceamerica.org/site/PageServer?pagename=sign_up Date accessed: 2nd March 2014.
13. No membership figures were listed on the website and the organisation is not registered with the Charity Commission.
14. The proposed Spanish law, subsequently dropped, would have meant that abortion would only be permitted in two circumstances: rape and risk to the mother. The risk must involve 'lasting harm' to the mother's health. My Belly is Mine raised awareness of the bill and campaigned against it in solidarity with Spanish women, holding several demonstrations outside of the Spanish Embassy in London, available online: http://mybellyismine.tumblr.com/url Date accessed: 28th August 2014.
15. The 2014 Planned Parenthood Congressional scorecard is available online: http://www.plannedparenthoodaction.org/elections-politics/congressional-scorecard/ It also shows that only three states (Connecticut, Delaware and Vermont) have a 100 per cent score, which means that all of the State's Congressmen and women have voted with Planned Parenthood's position. Date accessed: 4th September 2014.
16. The National Right to Life is the oldest anti-abortion organisation: established in 1968, it defends the right of an unborn baby's right to life with reference to the Declaration of Independence, which specifies 'Life' as an 'unalienable right': http://www.nrlc.org/about/mission/ Date accessed: 27th February 2014.
17. The group Feminists for Life focuses its anti-abortion activism on creating improved access to prenatal care for pregnant women from economically deprived backgrounds. Its website is available online: http://www.feministsforlife.org/ Date accessed: 28th February 2014.

18. The Bill was co-sponsored by the California ProLife Council, who argued that the ease with which women could access abortion in California meant that 'some Indian women get on a plane to have their abortions in our state, only to return home after killing their baby girl'. For coverage of the Bill, see the *LA Weekly* article, available online: http://www.laweekly.com/informer/2014/05/07/california-abortion-law-targeting-asian-immigrantsfails?utm_campaign=Choice&utm_medium=Argyle%2BSocial&utm_source=twitter&utm_term=2014-05-07-17-45-34 Date accessed: 2nd September 2014.
19. The Society for the Protection of the Unborn Child also has a disability rights awareness group, No Less Human, which campaigns for rights for disabled people from conception to natural death. Its website is available online: https://www.spuc.org.uk/about/aims-activities Date accessed: 1st September 2014.
20. As this *Guardian* article highlights, The UK Life League engaged in a number of controversies during the mid-2000s: http://www.theguardian.com/uk/2006/mar/27/faithschools.religion Date accessed: 1st March 2014.
21. The Center for Bio-Ethical Reform is based in California. Its website is available at www.abortionno.org, which contains graphic images of aborted foetuses. Date accessed: 25th September 2014.
22. 40 Days for Life claims that its vigils have led to eight abortion clinics closing, 13 abortion workers quitting, and that 728 lives have been saved: http://www.40daysforlife.com/location.html Date accessed: 1st March 2014.
23. See Pew's '5 Facts about Abortion', available online: http://www.pewresearch.org/fact-tank/2014/01/22/5-facts-about-abortion/ Date accessed: 3rd October 2014.
24. Republican Senate candidate for Missouri and House Representative Todd Akin discussed his abolitionist views on abortion with a local radio station, see available online: http://www.nytimes.com/2012/08/20/us/politics/todd-akin-provokes-ire-with-legitimate-rape-comment.html?_r=0. Date accessed: 1st September 2014. Indiana State Treasurer and Senate hopeful Richard Mourdock argued that pregnancy from rape was 'something God intended', available online: http://www.huffingtonpost.com/2012/10/23/richard-mourdock-abortion_n_2007482.html. Date accessed: 1st September 2014. Whilst Washington County Councilman and Representative hopeful John Koster claimed that the 'rape thing' was not cause for abortion, available online: http://www.oregonlive.com/pacific-northwest-news/index.ssf/2012/10/washington_congressional_candi.html Date accessed: 1st September 2014.
25. Personhood USA was founded in 2008 and is a Christian anti-abortion group that advocates a personhood constitutional amendment. Its website is available online: http://www.personhoodusa.com/ Date accessed: 27th February 2014.
26. David Cameron gave an interview to *The Catholic Herald* where he outlined his position on abortion, available online: http://www.telegraph.co.uk/news/election-2010/7565422/General-Election-2010-David-Cameron-says-abortion-limit-should-be-lowered.html Date accessed: 28th February 2014.

27. The ProLife Alliance Party focuses its attention on abortion, euthanasia, human cloning, and embryo abuse. Its website is available online: http://prolife.org.uk/about/ Date accessed: 1st March 2014.
28. The House of Lords used to be home to the highest court in the land; a supreme court was established in 2005 in order to properly separate the judiciary from Parliament.
29. The ProLife Alliance Manifesto is available online: http://www.politicsresources.net/area/uk/man/prolif97.htm Date accessed: 1st March 2014.
30. The Stop Patriarchy abortion rights freedom ride has an official report of the ride. Available online: http://www.stoppatriarchy.org/freedom-ride-report.html Date accessed: 1st September 2014.
31. For further information on the guidelines, see the bpas briefing. Available online: http://www.bpas.org/js/filemanager/files/bpas_press_briefing_nurses_and_midwives.pdf Date accessed: 10th July 2014.

Bibliography

Abramowitz, Alan I. 1995. 'It's Abortion, Stupid: Policy Voting in the 1992 Presidential Election', *The Journal of Politics* 57 (1): 176–186.

Ainsworth, Scott H. and Hall, Thad E. 2011. *Abortion Politics in Congress: Strategic Incrementalism and Policy Change*. New York: Cambridge University Press.

Allen, Jaffner (ed). 1990. *Lesbian Philosophies and Cultures*. New York: CUNY Press.

Amery, Fran. 2014. 'Abortion Politics in the UK: Feminism, Medicine and the State', University of Birmingham. Unpublished PhD thesis.

Arceneaux, Kevin. 2002. 'Direct Democracy and the Link between Public Opinion and State Abortion Policy', *State Politics and Policy Quarterly* 2 (4): 372–387.

Archer Mann, Susan and Huffman, Douglas J. 2005. 'The Decentering of Second Wave Feminism and the Rise of the Third Wave', *Science and Society* 69 (1): 56–91.

Arizpe, Lourdes. 1999. 'Preface: Freedom to Create Women's Agenda for Cyberspace' in Wendy Harcourt (ed). *Women@internet*. London: Zed Books. pp.xii–xi.

Armstrong, Jennifer and Wood Rudúlph, Heather. 2013. *Sexy Feminism*. New York: Houghton Mifflin Harcourt Publishing Company.

Ashe, Jeanette, Campbell, Rosie, Childs, Sarah and Evans, Elizabeth. 2010. ' "Stand By Your Man" Women's Political Recruitment at the 2010 General Election', *British Politics* 5 (4): 455–480.

Attwood, Feona. 2007. 'Sluts and Riot Grrrls; Female Identity and Sexual Agency', *Journal of Gender Studies* 16 (3): 233–247.

Bacchi, Carol. 2006. 'Arguing for and against Quotas: Theoretical Issues' in Drude Dahlerup (ed). *Women, Quotas and Politics*. Oxon: Routledge.

Bagguley, Paul. 2002. 'Contemporary British Feminism: A Social Movement in Abeyance?' *Social Movement Studies* 1 (2): 169–185.

Banjaree, Subhabrata Bobby. 2008. 'Corporate Social Responsibility: The Good, the Bad and the Ugly', *Critical Sociology* 34 (1): 51–79.

Banyard, Kat. 2010. *The Equality Illusion*. London: Faber and Faber.

Bartley, Paula. 2007. *Votes for Women*. London: Hodder.

Bashevkin, Sylvia. 1994. 'Confronting Neo-Conservatism: Anglo-American Women's Movements under Thatcher, Reagan and Mulroney' *International Political Science Review* 15 (3): 275–296.

Bashevkin, Sylvia. 1996. 'Tough Times in Review: The British Women's Movement during the Thatcher Years', *Comparative Political Studies* 28 (4): 525–552.

Bates, Laura. 2014. *Everyday Sexism*. New York: Simon and Schuster.

Baumgardner, Jennifer. 2008. *Abortion and Life*. New York: Akashic Books.

Baumgardner, Jennifer. 2012. *F'em! Goo Goo, Gaga, and Some Thoughts on Balls*. New York: Seal Press.

Baumgardner, Jennifer and Richards, Amy. 2000. *ManifestA: Young Women, Feminism and the Future*. New York: Farrar, Straus and Giroux.

Baumgardner, Jennifer and Richards, Amy. 2005. *Grassroots: A Field Guide for Feminist Activism*. New York: Farrar, Straus and Giroux.

BBC. 2006. *Woman's Hour: Celebrating Sixty Years of Women's Lives*. London: John Murray.

Begum, Nasa. 1992. 'Disabled Women and the Feminist Agenda', *Feminist Review* 40: 70–84.

Berkman, Michael B. and O'Connor, Robert E. 1993. 'Do Women Legislators Matter? Female Legislators and State Abortion Policy', *American Politics Research* 21 (1): 102–124.

Bligh, Michelle C., Schlehofer, Michele, Casaf, Bettina J. and Gaffney, Amber M. 2012. 'Competent Enough, but Would You Vote for Her? Gender Stereotypes and Media Influences on Perceptions of Women Politicians', *Journal of Applied Social Psychology* 42 (3): 560–597.

Bobel, Christine. 2010. *New Blood: Third Wave Feminism and the Politics of Menstruation*. New Brunswick: Rutgers University Press.

Boddy, Janice. 1998. 'Violence Embodied? Circumcision, Gender Politics, and Cultural Aesthetics' in Rebecca Emerson Dobash and Russell P. Dobash (eds). *Rethinking Violence against Women*. London: Sage. pp.77–109.

Braidotti, Rosi. 1996. 'Cyberfeminism with a Difference' in Michael A. Peters, Mark Olssen and Colin Lankshear (eds). *Futures of Critical Theory: Dreams of Difference*. London: Rowman and Litlefield. pp.239–260.

Brooks, Siobhan. 2002. 'Black Feminism in Everyday Life: Race, Mental Illness, Poverty and Motherhood' in Daisy Hernández and Bushra Rehman (eds). *Colonize This! Young Women of Color on Today's Feminism*. California: Seal Press. pp.99–118.

Brown, Wendy. 1997. 'The Impossibility of Women's Studies', *Differences: A Journal of Feminist Cultural Studies* 9 (3): 79–101.

Brown, Wendy. 2005. *Edgework: Critical Essays on Knowledge and Politics*. Princeton: Princeton University Press.

Bruce, Steve. 1988. *The Rise and Fall of the New Christian Right*. New York: Oxford University Press.

Bryson, Valerie and Heppell, Timothy. 2010. 'Conservatism and Feminism: The Case of the British Conservative Party', *Journal of Political Ideologies* 15 (1): 31–50.

Budgeon, Shelly. 2011. *Third Wave Feminism and the Politics of Gender in Late Modernity*. Basingstoke: Palgrave.

Butler, Judith. 1990. *Gender Trouble*. Oxon: Routledge.

Butler, Judith. 1993. *Bodies That Matter*. Oxon: Routledge.

Butler, Judith. 2004. *Undoing Gender*. New York: Routledge.

Calhoun, Cheshire. 1994. 'Separating Feminist Theory from Lesbian Practise', *Ethics* 104 (3): 558–581.

Campus, Donatella. 2013. *Women Political Leaders and the Media*. Basingstoke: Palgrave.

Celis, Karen. 2006. 'Substantive Representation of Women: The Representation of Women's Interests and the Impact of Descriptive Representation in the Belgian Parliament (1900–1979)', *Journal of Women, Politics and Policy* 28 (2): 85–114.

Celis, Karen and Childs, Sarah. 2012. 'The Substantive Representation of Women: What to Do with Conservative Claims?' *Political Studies* 60 (1): 213–225.

Celis, Karen, Childs, Sarah, Kantola, Johanna and Krook, Mona Lena. 2009. 'Rethinking Women's Substantive Representation', *Representation* 44 (2): 113–124.

Chappell, Louise and Hill, Lisa (eds). 2006. *The Politics of Women's Interests*. Abingdon: Routledge.

Chen, Eva. 2013. 'Neoliberalism and Popular Women's Culture: Rethinking Choice, Freedom and Agency', *European Journal of Cultural Studies* 16 (4): 440–452.

Childs, Sarah. 2004. *New Labour's Women MPs: Women Representing Women*. Oxon: Routledge.

Childs, Sarah. 2007. 'Representation' in Georgina Blakeley and Valerie Bryson (eds). *The Impact of Feminism on Political Concepts and Debates*. Manchester: Manchester University Press. pp.73–91.

Childs, Sarah and Evans, Elizabeth. 2012. 'Taking It out of the Hands of the Parties: Women's Descriptive Representation in the UK 2010–2015', *The Political Quarterly* 83 (4): 742–748.

Childs, Sarah, Evans, Elizabeth and Webb, Paul. 2013. 'Abortion and the Human Fertilization and Embryology Act 2008: "Quicker Than a Consultation at the Hairdressers" ', *New Genetics and Society* 32 (2): 110–134.

Childs, Sarah and Krook, Mona Lena. 2006. 'Should Feminists Give up on Critical Mass? A Contingent Yes', *Politics and Gender* 2: 522–530.

Childs, Sarah and Webb, Paul. 2011. *Sex, Gender and the Conservative Party*. Basingstoke: Palgrave.

Chodorow, Nancy. 1989. *Feminism and Psychoanalytic Theory*. London: Polity Press.

Chomsky, Noam. 1999. *Profit over People: Neoliberalism and Global Order*. New York: Seven Stories Press.

Cochrane, Kira. 2013. *All the Rebel Women*. London: Guardian Shorts.

Collins, Patricia Hill. 2000. *Black Feminist Thought*. New York: Routledge.

Connell, R.W. 1987. *Gender and Power*. Stanford: Stanford University Press.

Coppock, Vicki, Haydon, Deena and Richter, Ingrid. 1995. *The Illusions of 'Post Feminism': New Women, Old Myths*. London: Taylor and Francis.

Cott, Nancy F. 1984. 'Feminist Politics in the 1920s: The National Woman's Party', *The Journal of American History* 71 (1): 43–68.

Cowley, Philip (ed). 1998. *Conscience and Parliament*. London: Frank Cass.

Cowley, Philip. 2013. 'Why Not Ask the Audience? Understanding the Public's Representational Priorities', *British Politics* 8: 138–163.

Crenshaw, Kimberlé. 1989. 'Demarginalizing the Intersection of Race and Sex: A Black Feminist Critique of Antidiscrimination Doctrine, Feminist Theory and Antiracist Politics', *University of Chicago Legal Forum* 140: 138–167.

Crenshaw, Kimberlé. 1991. 'Mapping the Margins: Intersectionality, Identity Politics and Violence against Women of Color', *Stanford Law Review* 43 (6): 1241–1299.

Crow, Barbara. (ed). 2000. *Radical Feminism: A Documentary Reader*. New York: New York University Press.

Cudd, Ann. E and Holmstrom, Nancy. 2011. *Capitalism, for and against: A Feminist Debate*. New York: Cambridge University Press.

Dalton, Russell J. 2008. 'Citizenship Norms and the Expansion of Political Participation', *Political Studies* 56 (1): 76–98

Darcy, R., Welch, Susan and Clark, Janet. 1994. *Women, Elections and Representation*. Lincoln: University of Nebraska.

Davis, Angela. 1982. *Women, Race and Class*. London: The Women's Press.

Davis, Kathy. 2008. 'Intersectionality as Buzzword: A Sociology of Science Perspective on What Makes a Feminist Theory Successful', *Feminist Theory* 9 (1): 67–85.

Day, Christin L. and Hadley, Charles D. 2002. 'Similarities and Differences between Contributors to EMILY's List and WISH List', *Women & Politics* 24 (2): 53–67.

Dean, Jonathan. 2009. 'Who's Afraid of Third Wave Feminism?' *International Feminist Journal of Politics* 11 (3): 334–352.

Dean, Jonathan. 2010. *Rethinking Contemporary Feminist Politics*. Basingstoke: Palgrave.

Deckman, Melissa and McTague, John. 2014. 'Did the "War on Women" Work? Women, Men and the Birth Control Mandate in the 2012 Presidential Election', *American Politics Research* doi: 10.1177/1532673X14535240

DeLombard, Jeannine. 1995. 'Femmenism' in Rebecca Walker (ed). *To Be Real: Telling the Truth about the Changing Face of Feminism*. New York: Anchor Books. pp.21–34.

Denfeld, Rene. 1996. *The New Victorians: A Young Woman's Challenge to the Old Feminist Order*. New York: Time Warner.

Dhamoon, Rita Kaur. 2011. 'Considerations on Mainstreaming Intersectionality', *Political Research Quarterly* 64 (1): 230–243.

Dicker, Rory and Piepmeier, Alison. (eds). 2003. *Catching a Wave: Reclaiming Feminism for the 21st Century*. Boston: Northeastern University Press.

Digby, Tom. (ed). 1998. *Men Doing Feminism*. New York: Routledge.

Donath, Judith S. 1999. 'Identity and Deception in the Virtual Community' in Peter Kollock and Marc Smith (eds). *Communities in Cyberspace*. London: Routledge. pp.29–59.

Dovi, Suzanne. 2007. *The Good Representative*. Oxford: Blackwell Publishing.

Duménil, Gérard and Lévy, Dominique. 2005. 'The Neoliberal (counter-)Revolution' in Alfredo Saad-Filho and Deborah Johnston (eds). *Neoliberalism: A Critical Reader*. London: Pluto Press. pp.9–19.

Eisenstein, Zillah R. 1977. 'Constructing a Theory of Capitalist Patriarchy and Socialist Feminism', *Critical Sociology* 7 (3): 3–17.

Eisenstein, Zillah R. 1984. 'The Patriarchal Relations of the Reagan State', *Signs* 10 (2): 329–337.

Eschle, Catherine. 2005. 'Skeleton Woman: Feminism and the Anti-Globalisation Movement', *Signs* 30 (3): 1742–1769.

Evans, Elizabeth. 2011. *Gender and the Liberal Democrats*. Manchester: Manchester University Press.

Evans, Elizabeth. 2012. 'From Finance to Equality: The Substantive Representation of Women's Interests by Men and Women MPs in the House of Commons', *Representation* 48 (2): 183–196.

Evans, Elizabeth and Chamberlain, Prudence. 2014. 'Critical Waves: Exploring Identity, Discourse and Praxis in Western Feminism', *Social Movement Studies* doi:10.1080/14742837.2014.964199

Eveline, Joan and Bacchi, Carol. 2005. 'What Are We Mainstreaming When We Mainstream Gender?' *International Feminist Journal of Politics* 7 (4): 496–512.

Faludi, Susan. 1992. *Backlash: The Undeclared War against Women*. London: Vintage.

Farrell, Amy E. 1998. *Yours in Sisterhood: Ms Magazine and the Promise of Popular Feminism*. Carolina: University of North Carolina Press.

Ferguson, James. 2009. 'The Uses of Neoliberalism', *Antipode* 41: 166–184.

Findlen, Barbara. (ed). 1995. *Listen Up! Voices from the Next Feminist Generation*. California: Seal Press.

Finley, Laura and Reynolds, Stringer Emily. 2010. *Beyond Burning Bras*. California: Praeger.

Firestone, Shulamith. 1979. *The Dialectic of Sex: The Case for Feminist Revolution*. New York: Bantam.

Franceschet, Susan and Jennifer, Piscopo. 2008. 'Gender Quotas and Women's Substantive Representation: Lessons from Argentina', *Politics and Gender* 4 (3): 393–425.

Fraser, Nancy. 2007. 'Feminist Politics in the Age of Recognition: A Two-Dimensional Approach to Gender Justice', *Studies in Social Justice* 1 (1): 23–35.

Fraser, Nancy. 2013. *The Fortunes of Feminism: From Women's Liberation to Identity Politics to Anti-Capitalism*. New York: Verso Books.

Fry, Kimberly and Lousley, Cheryl. 2001. 'Green Grrrl Power', *Canadian Woman Studies* 21 (4): 148–151.

Frye, Marilyn. 1983. *Politics of Reality: Essays in Feminist Theory*. New York: Crossing Press.

Fuss, Diana. 1989. *Essentially Speaking: Feminism, Nature and Difference*. New York: Routledge.

Garland-Thomson, Rosemarie. 2005. 'Feminist Disability Studies', *Signs* 30 (2): 1557–1587.

Genovese, Michael A. 2013. 'Margaret Thatcher and the Politics of Conviction Leadership' in Michael A. Genovese and Jamie S. Steckenrider (eds). *Women as Political Leaders*. New York: Routledge. pp.270–305.

Gill, Rosalind. 2007a. *Gender and the Media*. Cambridge: Polity Press.

Gill, Rosalind. 2007b. 'Critical Respect: The Dilemma of "Choice" and "Agency" for Women's Studies', *European Journal of Women's Studies* 14 (1): 69–80.

Gillis, Stacey and Munford, Rebecca. 2004. 'Genealogies and Generations: The Politics and Praxis of Third Wave Feminism', *Women's History Review* 13 (2): 165–182.

Gillis, Stacey, Howie, Gillian and Munford, Rebecca. (eds). 2004. *Third Wave Feminism: A Critical Exploration*. Basingstoke: Palgrave.

Gimenez, Martha E. 2000. 'What's Material about Materialist Feminism? A Marxist Feminist Critique', *Radical Philosophy* 101: 18–19.

Ginsburg, Faye D. 1998. *Contested Lives: The Abortion Debate in an American Community*. California: University of California Press.

Goertz, Gary and Mazur, Amy. (eds). 2008. *Politics, Gender and Concepts: Theory and Methodology*. Cambridge: Cambridge University Press.

Gornick, Vivien. 2000. 'Consciousness' in Barbara Crow (ed). *Radical Feminism: A Documentary Reader*. New York: New York University Press. pp.287–300.

Graff, Agnieszka. 2003. 'Lost between the Waves? The Paradoxes of Feminist Chronology and Activism in Contemporary Poland', *Journal of International Women's Studies* 4 (2): 100–116.

Grant, Wyn. 2004. 'Pressure Politics: The Changing World of Pressure Groups', *Parliamentary Affairs* 57 (2): 408–419.

Green, Cheryl. 1995. 'One Resilient Baby' in Barbara Findlen (ed). *Listen Up! Voices from the Next Feminist Generation*. California: Seal Press. pp.138–148.

Grey, Sandra. 2006. 'Numbers and Beyond: The Relevance of Critical Mass in Gender Research', *Politics and Gender* 2 (4): 492–502.

Groeneveld, Elizabeth. 2009. 'Be a Feminist or Just Dress Like One: Bust, Fashion and Feminism as Lifestyle', *Journal of Gender Studies* 18 (2): 179–190.

Gunnarsson, Lena. 2011. 'A Defence of the Category "Women"', *Feminist Theory* 12 (1): 23–37.

Halberstam, Judith. 2005. *In a Queer Time and Place*. New York: New York University Press.

Hancock, Anne-Marie. 2007. 'Intersectionality as a Normative and Empirical Paradigm', *Politics and Gender* 3 (2): 248–254.

Haraway, Donna. 1985. 'A Manifesto for Cyborgs: Science, Technology, and Socialist Feminism in the 1980s', *Socialist Review* 15 (80): 65–107.

Haraway, Donna. 1991. *Simians, Cyborgs and Women: The Reinvention of Nature*. New York: Routledge.

Hardy-Fanta, Carol. (ed). 2011. *Intersectionality and Politics: Recent Research on Gender, Race and Political Representation in the United States*. New York: Routledge.

Harne, Lynne and Miller, Elaine. (eds). 1996. *All the Rage: Reasserting Radical Lesbian Feminism*. London: The Women's Press Ltd.

Hartmann, Heidi I. 1979. 'The Unhappy Marriage of Marxism and Feminism: Towards a More Progressive Union', *Capital and Class* 3 (2): 1–33.

Harvey, David. 2005. *A Brief History of Neoliberalism*. New York: Oxford University Press.

Hawthorne, Susan and Klein, Renate. (eds). 1999. *Cyberfeminism: Connectivity, Critique, Creativity*. North Melbourne: Spinifex Press Pty Ltd.

Henry, Astrid. 2004. *Not My Mother's Sister: Generational Conflict and Third Wave Feminism*. Indiana: Indiana University Press.

Hernández, Daisy and Rehman, Bushra B. (eds). 2002. *Colonize This! Young Women of Color on Today's Feminism*. California: Seal Press.

Herring, Susan, Job-Sluder, Kirk, Scheckler, Rebecca and Barab, Sasha. 2002. 'Searching for Safety Online: Managing "Trolling" in a Feminist Forum', *The Information Society* 18 (5): 371–384.

Herring, Susan, Johnson, Deborah A. and DiBenedetto, Tamra. 1995. '"This Discussion is Going too Far!": Male Resistance to Female Participation on the Internet' in Kira Hall and Mary Bucholtz (eds). *Gender Articulated: Language and the Socially Constructed Self*. New York: Routledge. pp.67–96.

Herrnstein, Richard J. and Murray, Charles. 2010. *The Bell Curve*. New York: Simon and Schuster.

Herzog, Dagmar. 2008. *Sex in Crisis: The New Sexual Revolution and the Future of American Politics*. New York: Basic Books.

Heywood, Leslie and Drake, Jennifer. (eds). 1997. *Third Wave Agenda: Being Feminist, Doing Feminism*. Minneapolis: University of Minnesota Press.

Hines, Sally. 2005. '"I am a feminist but..." Transgender Men and Women and Feminism' in Jo Reger (ed). *Different Wavelengths*. London: Routledge. pp.57–77.

Holland, Samantha and Attwood, Feona. 2010. 'Keeping Fit in Six Inch Heels: The Mainstreaming of Pole Dancing' in Feona Attwood (ed). *Mainstreaming Sex*. London: I.B. Taurus. pp.165–182.

Holm, Malin and Ojeda Castro, Jorge. 2014. 'Twitter – Only a Highway for the Already Privileged? Exploring the Gendered Consequences of Social Media for Claims Making in the New Public Spheres', Paper Presented at the 2014 ECPR General Conference, University of Glasgow.

hooks, bell. 1981. *Ain't I a Woman*. London: Pluto Press.

hooks, bell. 1991. 'Sisterhood' in Sneja Gunew (ed). *A Reader in Feminist Knowledge*. London: Routledge. pp.27–41.

hooks, bell. 1994. *Outlaw Culture*. London: Routledge.

Humm, Maggie. 1992. *Modern Feminisms: Political, Literary, Cultural*. New York: Columbia University Press.

Hurdis, Rebecca. 2002. 'Heartbroken: Women of Color Feminism and the Third Wave' in Daisy Hernández and Bushra Rehman (eds). *Colonize This! Young Women of Color on Today's Feminism*. California: Seal Press. pp.279–294.

Irving, Helen. 2008. *Gender and the Constitution: Equity and Agency in Comparative Constitutional Design*. Cambridge: Cambridge University Press.

Jackson, Stevi and Scott, Sue. (eds). 1996. *Feminism and Sexuality: A Reader*. New York: Columbia University Press.

Jeffreys, Sheila. 1994. 'The Queer Disappearance of Lesbians: Sexuality in the Academy', *Women's Studies International Forum* 17 (5): 459–472.

Jeffreys, Sheila. 2003. *Unpacking Queer Politics*. Cambridge: Polity.

Jeffreys, Sheila. 2014. *Gender Hurts*. London: Routledge.

Jervis, Lisa. 2006. 'Goodbye to Feminism's Generational Divide' in Melody Berger (ed). *We Don't Need Another Wave: Dispatches from the Next Generation of Feminists*. California: Seal Press. pp.13–18.

Joffe, Carol. 2005. 'It's Not Just Abortion, Stupid: Progressives and Abortion', *Dissent* 52 (1): 91–96.

Kantola, Johanna and Squires, Judith. 2012. 'From State Feminism to Market Feminism', *International Political Science Review* 33 (4): 382–400.

Kaplan, E. Ann. 2003. 'Feminist Futures: Trauma, the Post-9/11 World and a Fourth Feminism?' *Journal of International Women's Studies* 4 (2): 46–59.

Karamessini, Maria and Rubery, Jill. 2013. *Women and Austerity: The Economic Crisis and the Future for Gender Equality*. London: Routledge.

Karpf, David. 2010. 'Online Political Mobilization from the Advocacy Group's Perspective: Looking beyond Clicktivism', *Policy & Internet* 2: 7–41.

Kaufman, Michael. 2012. 'The Day the White Ribbon Campaign Changed the Game' in Christopher J. Grieg and Wayne J. Martino (eds). *Canadian Men and Masculinities*. Toronto: Canadian Scholars Press. pp.139–158.

Kaufman, Michael and Kimmel, Michael. 2011. *The Guy's Guide to Feminism*. California: Seal Press.

Kessler, Sanford and Reid, Traciel V. 2013. *American Debates on Sexual Equality*. London: Bloomsbury.

Kimmel, Michael. 1998. 'Who's Afraid of Men Doing Feminism?' in Tom Digby (ed). *Men Doing Feminism*. New York: Routledge. pp.57–68.

King, Deborah K. 1988. 'Multiple Jeopardy, Multiple Consciousness: The Context of a Black Feminist Ideology', *Signs* 14 (1): 42–72.

Kirkland, Anna. 2004. 'When Transgendered People Sue and Win: Feminist Reflections on Strategy, Activism and the Legal Process' in Vivien Labaton and Dawn Lundy Martin (eds). *The Fire This Time: Young Women Activists and the New Feminism*. New York: Anchor Books. pp.181–219.

Kleinman, Sherryl, Essell, Matthew and Frost, A. Corey. 2009. 'Reclaiming Critical Analysis: The Social Harms of "Bitch"', *Sociological Analysis* 3 (1): 47–68.

Koerber, Amy. 2001. 'Postmodernism, Resistance, and Cyberspace: Making Rhetorical Spaces for Feminist Mothers on the Web', *Women's Studies in Communication* 24 (2): 218–240.

Kollman, Ken. 1998. *Outside Lobbying: Public Opinion and Interest Group Strategies*. Princeton: Princeton University Press.

Kornbluh, Felicia. 1998. 'The Goals of the National Welfare Rights Movement: Why We Need Them Thirty Years Later', *Feminist Studies* 24 (1): 65–78.

Koyama, Emi. 2003. 'The Transfeminist Manifesto' in Rory Dicker and Alison Piepmeier (eds). *Catching a Wave: Reclaiming Feminism for the 21st Century*. Boston: Northeastern University Press. pp.244–259.

Kravetz, Diane. 1978. 'Consciousness-Raising Groups in the 1970's', *Psychology of Women Quarterly* 3 (2): 168–186.

Krizsan, Andrea, Skjeie, Hege and Squires, Judith. (eds). 2012. *Institutionalizing Intersectionality: The Changing Nature of European Equality Regimes*. Basingstoke: Palgrave.

Labaton, Vivien and Lundy Martin, Dawn. (eds). 2004. *The Fire This Time: Young Women Activists and the New Feminism*. New York: Anchor Books.

Lamp, Sharon and Cleigh, Carol W. 2011. 'The Heritage of Ableist Rhetoric in American Feminism from the Eugenics Period' in Kim Q Hall (ed). *Feminist Disability Studies*. Bloomington: Indiana University Press. pp.175–190.

Langbein, Laura I. and Lotwis, Mark A. 1990. 'The Political Efficacy of Lobbying and Money: Gun Control in the US House 1986', *Legislative Studies Quarterly* 15 (3): 413–440.

Law, Sylvia A. 1984. 'Rethinking Sex and the Constitution', *University of Pennsylvania Law Review* 132 (5): 955–1040.

Lawless, Jennifer and Fox, Richard. 2005. *It Takes a Candidate: Why Women Don't Run for Office*. New York: Cambridge University Press.

Leathwood, Carole. 2004. 'Doing Difference in Different Times: Theory, Politics and Women-Only Spaces in Education', *Women's Studies International Forum* 27 (5): 447–458.

Levy, Ariel. 2005. *Female Chauvinist Pigs: Women and the Rise of Raunch Culture*. New York: Free Press.

Loe, Meika. 1999. 'Feminism for Sale: Case Study of a Pro-Sex Feminist Business', *Gender & Society* 13: 705–732.

Lombardo, Emanuela, Meier, Petra and Verloo, Mieke. (eds). 2009. *The Discursive Politics of Gender Equality*. London: Routledge.

Long, Julia. 2012. *Anti-Porn*. London: Zed Books.

Lorber, Judith. 2010. *Gender Inequality: Feminist Theory and Politics*. Oxford: Oxford University Press.

Lorde, Audre. 1984. *Sister Outsider*. California: Crossing Press.

Lovenduski, Joni. 2005. *Feminizing Politics*. Cambridge: Polity Press.

Lovenduski, Joni and Randall, Vicky. 1993. *Contemporary Feminist Politics*. Oxford: Oxford University Press.

Lutz, Helma, Herrera Vivar, Maria Teresa and Supki, Linda. (eds). 2011. *Framing Intersectionality: Debates on a Multi-Faceted Concept in Gender Studies*. Farnham: Ashgate.

McBride Stetson, Dorothy. (ed). 2001. *Abortion Politics, Women's Movements, and the Democratic State*. Oxford: Oxford University Press.

McBride, Dorothy and Mazur, Amy G. 2008. 'Women's Movements' in Gary Goertz and Amy G. Mazur (eds). *Politics, Gender and Concepts*. Cambridge: Cambridge University Press. pp.219–243.

McCall, Leslie. 2005. 'The Complexity of Intersectionality', *Signs* 30 (3): 1771–1800.

McGerr, Michael. 1990. 'Political Style and Women's Power, 1830–1930', *Journal of American History* 77 (3): 864–885.

McLaren, Margaret A. 2002. *Feminism, Foucault, and Embodied Subjectivity*. New York: State University of New York.

McRobbie, Angela. 2009. *The Aftermath of Feminism*. London: Sage.

MacKinnon, Catherine A. 1989. *Towards a Feminist Theory of the State*. Boston: Harvard University Press.

MacKinnon, Catherine A. 1991. 'Reflections on Sex Equality under Law', *Yale Law Journal* 100: 1281–1328.

Mackay, Finn. 2015. *Radical Feminism Today*. Basingstoke: Palgrave.

Mansbridge, Jane. 1999. 'Should Blacks Represent Blacks and Women Represent Women? A Contingent "Yes" ', *The Journal of Politics* 61 (3): 628–657.

Marinucci, Mimi. 2010. *Feminism Is Queer*. London: Zed Books.

Martin, Courteney E. and Sullivan, J. Courtney. (eds). 2010. *Click: When We Knew We Were Feminists*. California: Seal Press.

Marx Ferree, Myra. 2009. 'Inequality, Intersectionality and the Politics of Discourse: Framing Feminist Alliances' in Emanuela Lombardo, Petra Meier and Mieke Verloo (eds). *The Discursive Politics of Gender Equality*. London: Routledge. pp.86–104.

Marx Ferree, Myra, Gamson, Anthony, Gerhards, Jűrgen and Rucht, Dieter. 2002. *Shaping Abortion Discourse: Democracy and the Public Sphere in Germany and the United States*. Cambridge: Cambridge University Press.

Marx Ferree, Myra and Yancey Martin, Patricia. (eds). 1995. *Feminist Organizations: Harvest of the New Women's Movement*. Philadelphia: Temple University Press.

Meyer, David S. and Staggenborg, Suzanne. 1996. 'Movements, Countermovements, and the Structure of Political Opportunity', *American Journal of Sociology* 101 (6): 1628–1660.

Millett, Kate. 1970. *Sexual Politics*. Illinois: University of Chicago Press.

Minta, Michael D. 2012. 'Gender, Race Ethnicity and Political Representation in the United States', *Politics and Gender* 8 (4): 541–547.

Mirowski, Philip. (ed). 2009. *The Road from Mont Pèlerin*. Boston: Harvard University Press.

Mooney, Christopher Z. (ed). 2001. *The Public Clash of Private Values: The Politics of Morality Policy*. New York: Chatham House.

Moraga, Cherrie and Anzaldúa, Gloria. (eds). 1984. *This Bridge Called My Back: Writings by Radical Women of Color*. New York: Kitchen Table Press.

Moran, Caitlin. 2011. *How to Be a Woman*. London: Ebury Press.

Morgan, Robin. (ed). 1970. *Sisterhood Is Powerful*. New York: Vintage Books.

Muaddi Darraj, Susan. 2002. 'It's not an Oxymoron: The Search for an Arab Feminism' in Daisy Hernández and Bushra Rehman (eds). *Colonize This! Young Women of Color on Today's Feminism*. California: Seal Press. pp.295–311.

Munford, Rebecca. 2010. 'Bust-ing the Third Wave: Barbies, Blowjobs and Girlie Feminism' in Feona Attwood (ed). *Mainstreaming Sex*. London: I.B. Taurus. pp.183–198.

Munro, Ealasaid. 2013. 'Feminism, a Fourth Wave?' Available online http://www.psa.ac.uk/insight-plus/feminism-fourth-wave, Accessed 26th November 2013.

Nadasen, Premilla. 2002. 'Expanding the Boundaries of the Women's Movement: Black Feminism and the Struggle for Welfare Rights', *Feminist Studies* 28 (2): 270–301.

Naples, Nancy A. 2011. 'Feminist Travels: A Historical and Textual Journey' in Kathy Davis and Mary Evans (eds). *Transatlantic Conversations: Feminism as Travelling Theory*. Farnham: Ashgate. pp.183–200.

Norris, Pippa. 2004. *Electoral Engineering*. Cambridge: Cambridge University Press.

Norris, Pippa and Lovenduski, Joni. 1995. *Political Recruitment*. Cambridge: Cambridge University Press.

Norris, Sian. (ed). 2011. *The Light Bulb Moment: The Stories of Why We Are Feminist*. Bristol: Crooked Rib Publishing.

Nussbaum, Martha. 1998. *Sex and Social Justice*. New York: Oxford University Press.

Oakley, Anne and Mitchell, Juliet. (eds). 1997. *Who's Afraid of Feminism?* London: Penguin.

Okin, Susan Moller. 1999. *Is Multiculturalism Bad for Women?* Princeton: Princeton University Press.

Ondercin, Heather L. and Welch, Susan. 2009. 'Comparing Predictors of Women's Congressional Election Success; Candidates, Primaries and the General Election', *American Politics Research* 37 (4): 593–613.

Orgad, Shani. 2002. 'The Transformative Potential of Online Communication: The Case of Breast Cancer Patients' Internet Spaces', *Feminist Media Studies* 5 (2): 141–161.

Orr, Catherine. 1997. 'Charting the Currents of the Third Wave', *Hypatia* 12 (3): 29–45.

Osborn, Tracy. 2012. *How Women Represent Women: Political Parties, Gender and Representation in the State Legislatures*. New York: Oxford University Press.

Oshana, Marina. 2011. 'Autonomy and the Partial-Birth Abortion Act', *Journal of Social Philosophy* 42 (1): 46–60.

Palley, Thomas L. 2005. 'From Keynsianism to Neoliberalism: Shifting Paradigms in Economics' in Alfredo Saad-Filho and Deborah Johnston (eds). *Neoliberalism: A Critical Reader*. London: Pluto Press. pp.20–29.

Paltrow, Lynn M. 2013. 'Roe v Wade and the New Jane Crow: Reproductive Rights in the Age of Mass Incarceration', *American Journal of Public Health* 103 (1): 17–21.

Pease, Bob. 2010. *Undoing Privilege: Unearned Advantage in a Divided World*. London: Zed Books.

Penny, Laurie. 2011. *Meat Market: Female Flesh under Capitalism*. Winchester: Zero Books.

Penny, Laurie. 2014. *Unspeakable Things: Sex, Lies and Revolution*. London: Bloomsbury.

Piepmeier, Alison, Cantrell, Amber and Maggio, Ashley. 2014. 'Disability Is a Feminist Issue: Bringing Together Women's and Gender Studies with Disability

Studies', *Disability Studies Quarterly* 34 (2): available online http://dsq-sds.org/article/view/4252

Phillips, Anne. 1995. *The Politics of Presence*. Oxford: Clarendon Press.

Phillips, Anne. 2010. *Gender and Culture*. Cambridge: Polity.

Phoenix, Ann. 2011. 'Re-narrating Feminist Stories: Black British Women and Transatlantic Feminisms' in Kathy Davis and Mary Evans (eds). *Transatlantic Conversations: Feminism as Travelling Theory*. Farnham: Ashgate. pp.55–68.

Pitkin, Hanna F. 1967. *The Concept of Representation*. California: University of California Press.

Plant, Sadie. 2000. 'On the Matrix: Cyberfeminist Simulations' in David Bell and Barbara M. Kennedy (eds). *The Cybercultures Reader*. London: Routledge. pp.325–336.

Pohli, Carol V. 1983. 'Church Closets and Back Doors: A Feminist View of Moral Majority Women', *Feminist Studies* 9 (3): 529–558.

Poo, Ai-Jen and Tang, Erica. 2004. 'Domestic Workers Organize in the Global City' in Vivien Labaton and Dawn Lundy Martin (eds). *The Fire This Time: Young Women Activists and the New Feminism*. New York: Anchor Books. pp.150–165.

Poirot, Kristan. 2009. 'Domesticating the Liberated Woman: Containment Rhetorics of Second Wave Radical/Lesbian Feminism', *Women's Studies in Communication* 32 (3): 263–292.

Power, Nina. 2009. *One Dimensional Woman*. London: Zero Books.

Preece, Jennifer. 2000. *Online Communities: Designing Usability: Supporting Sustainability*. Chichester: John Wiley.

Prins, Barbara. 2006. 'Narrative Accounts of Origins: A Blind Spot in the Intersectional Approach?' *European Journal of Women's Studies* 13 (3): 277–290.

Pugh, Martin. 2002. *The March of the Women*. Oxford: Oxford University Press.

Purdie-Vaughans, Valerie and Eibach, Richard P. 2008. 'Intersectional Invisibility: The Distinctive Advantages and Disadvantages of Multiple Subordinate-Group Identities', *Sex Roles* 59: 377–391.

Putnam, Robert. 2001. *Bowling Alone: The Collapse and Revival of American Community*. New York: Simon and Schuster.

Raymond, Janice. 1979. *The Transsexual Empire: The Making of the She-Male*. New York: Teachers College Press Columbia University.

Razack, Sherene. 1998. *Looking White People in the Eye: Gender, Race and Culture in Courtrooms and Classrooms*. Toronto: University of Toronto Press.

Read, Jen'nan Ghazal and Bartkowski, John P. 2000. 'To Veil or Not to Veil? A Case Study of Identity Negotiation amongst Muslim Women in Austin, Texas', *Gender & Society* 14 (3): 395–417.

Redfern, Catherine and Aune, Kristin. 2010. *Reclaiming the F Word*. London: Zed Books.

Reger, Jo. 2012. *Everywhere and Nowhere: Contemporary Feminism in the United States*. New York: Oxford University Press.

Reingold, Beth. 2000. *Representing Women*. Chapel Hill: University of North Carolina Press.

Renegar, Valerie R. and Sowards, Stacey K. 2003. 'Liberal Irony, Rhetoric, and Feminist Thought: A Unifying Third Wave Feminist Theory', *Philosophy and Rhetoric* 36 (4): 330–352.

Rendell, Jane. 1985. *The Origins of Modern Feminism: Women in Britain, France & USA 1780–1860*. Basingstoke: Palgrave.

Rich, Adrienne. 1980. 'Compulsory Heterosexuality and Lesbian Existence', *Signs* 5 (4): 631–660.

Ross, Karen, Evans, Elizabeth, Harrison, Lisa, Shears, Mary and Wadia, Khursheed. 2013. 'The Gender of News and News of Gender: A Study of Sex, Politics and Press Coverage of the 2010 British General Election', *The International Journal of Press/Politics* 18 (1): 3–20.

Ross, Loretta. 2006. 'Understanding Reproductive Justice: Transforming the Pro-Choice Movement', *Off Our Backs* 36 (4): 14–19.

Rowbotham, Sheila. 1997. *A Century of Women in Britain and the United States*. London: Viking.

Saad-Filho, Alfredo and Johnston, Deborah. (eds). 2005. *Neoliberalism: A Critical Reader*. London: Pluto Press.

Sanbonmatsu, Kira. 2008. 'Representation by Gender and Parties' in Christina Wolbrecht, Karen Beckwith and Lisa Baldez (eds). *Political Women and American Democracy*. New York: Cambridge University Press. pp.96–109.

Sapiro, Virginia. 1981. 'When Are Interests Interesting? The Problem of Political Representation of Women', *The American Political Science Review* 75 (3): 701–716.

Saward, Michael. 2006. 'The Representation Claim', *Contemporary Political Theory* 5: 297–318.

Schacht, Steven P. and Ewing, Doris W. 2004. *Feminism with Men: Bridging the Gender Gap*. Lanham: Rowman and Littlefield Publishers.

Scharff, Christina. 2012. *Repudiating Feminism: Young Women in a Neoliberal World*. Surrey: Ashgate.

Seltzer, Richard, Newman, Jody and Voorhees Leighton, Melissa. 1997. *Sex as a Variable: Women as Candidates and Voters in US Elections*. Colorado: Lynne Rienner Publishers.

Serano, Julia. 2007. *Whipping Girl*. California: Seal Press.

Settles, Isis. 2006. 'Use of an Intersectional Framework to Understand Black Women's Racial and Gendered Identities', *Sex Roles* 54: 589–601.

Shaw, F. 2013. 'Blogging and the Women's Movement' in Sarah Maddison and Marian Sawer (eds). *The Women's Movement in Protest, Institutions and the Internet*. Oxon: Routledge. pp.118–131.

Shugart, Helene. 2001. 'Isn't It Ironic?: The Intersection of Third Wave Feminism with Generation X', *Women's Studies in Communication* 24 (2): 131–168.

Sidler, Michelle. 1997. 'Living in McJobdom; Third Wave Feminism and Class Inequality' in Leslie Heywood and Jennifer Drake (eds). *Third Wave Agenda: Being Feminist Doing Feminism*. Minneapolis: University of Minnesota Press. pp.25–39.

Siegal, Deborah. 2007. *Sisterhood Interrupted: From Radical Women to Grrrls Gone Wild*. New York: Palgrave.

Smith, Allison G. 2008. 'The Implicit Motives of Terrorist Groups: How the Needs for Affiliation and Power Translate into Death and Destruction', *Political Psychology* 29 (1): 55–75.

Snyder, R. Claire. 2008. 'What Is Third Wave Feminism? A New Directions Essay', *Signs* 34 (11): 175–196.

Spender, Dale. 1995. *Nattering on the Net: Women. Power and Cyberspace*. Melbourne: Spinifex Press.

Spivak, Gayatri Chakravorty. 1996. *The Spivak Reader: Selected Works of Gayati Chakravorty Spivak*. New York: Routledge.
Springer, Kimberly. 2002. 'Third Wave Black Feminism?' *Signs* 27 (4): 1059–1082.
Springer, Simon. 2012. 'Neoliberalism as Discourse: Between Foucauldian Political Economy and Marxian Poststructuralism', *Critical Discourse Studies* 9 (2): 133–147.
Squires, Judith. 1999. *Gender in Political Theory*. Cambridge: Polity Press.
Squires, Judith. 2005. 'Is Mainstreaming Transformative? Theorizing Mainstreaming in the Context of Diversity and Deliberation', *Social Politics* 12 (3): 366–388.
Squires, Judith and Wickham-Jones, Mark. 2004. 'New Labour, Gender Main-Streaming and the Women and Equality Unit', *British Journal of Politics and International Relations* 6 (1): 81–98.
Staggenborg, Suzanne. 1987. 'Lifestyle Preferences and Social Movement Recruitment: Illustrations from the Abortion Conflict', *Social Science Quarterly* 68: 779–797.
Strid, Sofia, Walby, Sylvia and Armstrong, Jo. 2013. 'Intersectionality and Multiple Inequalities: Visibility in British Policy on Violence against Women', *Social Politics* 20 (4): 558–581.
Swers, Michele L. 2013. *Women in the Club: Gender and Policy Making in the Senate*. Chicago: University of Chicago Press.
Tasker, Yvonne and Negra, Diane. (eds). 2007. *Interrogating Postfeminism*. London: Duke University Press.
Taylor, Ula Y. 1998. 'Making Waves: The Theory and Practise of Black Feminism', *The Black Scholar* 28 (2): 18–28.
Thiele, L.P. 1999. *Environmentalism for a New Millennium: The Challenge of Coevolution*. Oxford: OUP.
Tilly, Charles and Tarrow, Sidney. 2007. *Contentious Politics*. London: Paradigm Publishers.
Tong, Rosemarie. 1989. *Feminist Thought*. London: Unwin Hyman.
Van Zoonen, Liesbet. 2001. 'Feminist Internet Studies', *Feminist Media Studies* 1 (1): 67–72.
Valenti, Jessica. 2002. *Full Frontal Feminism*. California: Seal Press.
Valenti, Jessica. 2007. *Full Frontal Feminism*. California: Seal Press.
Vanderford, Marsha L. 1989. 'Vilification and Social Movements: A Case Study of Pro-Life and Pro-Choice Rhetoric', *Quarterly Journal of Speech* 75 (2): 166–182.
Vickers, Jill. 2006. 'The Problem with Interests, Making Political Claims for "Women"' in Louise Chappell and Lisa Hill (eds). *The Politics of Women's Interests*. Abingdon: Routledge. pp.5–38.
Walby, Sylvia. 2011. *The Future of Feminism*. London: Polity Press.
Walker, Rebecca. (ed). 1995. *To Be Real: Telling the Truth about the Changing Face of Feminism*. New York: Anchor Books.
Walters, Suzanna Danuta. 1996. 'From Here to Queer: Radical Feminism, Postmodernism, and the Lesbian Menace (Or, Why Can't a Woman Be More Like a Fag?)', *Signs* 21 (4): 830–869.
Walter, Natasha. 1998. *The New Feminism*. London: Virago.
Walter, Natasha. 2011. *Living Dolls: The Return of Sexism*. London: Virago.
Weiner-Mahfouz, Lisa. 2002. 'Organizing 101: A Mixed-Race Feminist in Movements for Social Justice' in Daisy Hernández and Bushra Rehman (eds).

Colonize This! Young Women of Color on Today's Feminism. California: Seal Press. pp. 29–39.

Weir, Alison. 1996. *Sacrificial Logics*. London. Routledge.

Welch, Susan and Studlar, Donley T. 1996. 'The Opportunity Structure for Women's Candidacies and Electability in Britain and the United States', *Political Research Quarterly* 49 (4): 861–874.

Weldon, S. Laurel. 2002. 'Beyond Bodies: Institutional Sources of Representation for Women in Democratic Policymaking', *The Journal of Politics* 62: 1153–1174.

Weldon, S. Laurel. 2012. *When Protest Makes Policy*. Ann Arbor: University of Michigan Press.

Wendell, Susan. 1987. 'A (Qualified) Defence of Liberal Feminism', *Hypatia* 2 (2): 65–95.

Whelehan, Imelda. 1995. *Modern Feminist Thought*. Edinburgh: Edinburgh University Press.

Whittier, Nancy. 1995. *Feminist Generations*. Philadelphia: Temple University Press.

Williams, Daniel K. 2011. 'The GOP's Abortion Strategy: Why Pro-Choice Republicans Became Pro-Life in the 1970s', *Journal of Policy History* 23 (4): 513–539.

Wilson, Angelia R. (ed). 2012. *Situating Intersectionality: The Politics of Intersectionality*. New York: Palgrave.

Wlodarczyk, Justyna. 2010. *Ungrateful Daughters: Third Wave Feminist Writings*. Newcastle upon Tyne: Cambridge Scholars Publishing.

Wolf, Naomi. 1990. *The Beauty Myth*. London: Vintage.

Wolf, Naomi. 1994. *Fire with Fire*. London: Vintage.

Young, Iris Marion. 1990. *Justice and the Politics of Difference*. Princeton: Princeton University Press.

Young, Lisa. 2000. *Feminists and Party Politics*. Ann Arbor: University of Michigan Press.

Yuval-Davis, Nira. 2006. 'Intersectionality and Feminist Politics', *European Journal of Women's Studies* 13 (3): 193–209.

Zack, Naomi. 2005. *Inclusive Feminism: A Third Wave Theory of Women's Commonality*. New York: Rowman and Littlefield.

Zeilenger, Julie. 2012. *A Little F'd Up: Why Feminism Is Not a Dirty Word*. California: Seal Press.

Index

CPI Antony Rowe
Chippenham, UK
2016-12-22 13:41